The Life and Work of

Jalaluddin Rumi

The Life and Work of

Jalaluddin Rumi

Afzal Iqbal

Foreword by
A. J. Arberry

PAKISTAN NATIONAL COUNCIL OF THE ARTS
ISLAMABAD (PAKISTAN)

Karachi
Oxford University Press
Oxford New York Delhi

Oxford University Press, Great Clarendon Street, Oxford OX2 6DP
Oxford New York
Athens Auckland Bangkok Bogotá Buenos Aires Calcutta
Cape Town Chennai Dar es Salaam Delhi Florence Hong Kong Istanbul
Karachi Kuala Lumpur Madrid Melbourne Mexico City Mumbai
Nairobi Paris São Paulo Singapore Taipei Tokyo Toronto Warsaw
and associated companies in Berlin Ibadan

Oxford is a registered trade mark of Oxford University Press

This edition in paperback published by Oxford University Press by arrangement with Pakistan National Council of the Arts 1999
Reprinted by permission The Octagon Press Ltd., London

Not for sale in the United Kingdom and Europe

Second Impression 2000

ISBN 0 19 579067 7

Printed in Pakistan at
New Sketch Graphics, Karachi.

Published by
Pakistan National Council of the Arts,
Block 6-C, Markaz F-7, Islamabad
and
Ameena Saiyid, Oxford University Press
5-Bangalore Town, Sharae Faisal
P.O. Box 13033, Karachi-75350, Pakistan

To

Khalida

who is no more

Contents

Foreword, Professor A.J. Arberry xi
Preface xiii
Introduction xvii
A Portrait xxv

1. **The Age of Rumi (A.D. 1207–1273)** 1

The tottering fabric of Muslim society
The onslaught from Christian Europe
The Crusaders – their hopes and fears
Some contradictions analysed
A glimpse of the Christian mind in the thirteenth century
Shifting from Europe to Asia
Meeting the challenge of the Mongols
The sack of Baghdad (1258)
Defeat of the Mongols in Egypt (1260)
The origin and character of the Mongols
The social and economic conditions of Persia under the Mongols
A parallel between the roles of Ghazali and Rumi
Shifting to Konya – the centre of Rumi's activities
The rise of Saljuqs and the importance of Konya

2. **The Period of Preparation (A.D. 1207–1244)** 48

The story of Rumi's ancestors
The role of Baha-ud-din, Rumi's father
His hostility towards philosophy and conflict with Fakhr-ud-din Razi
Was Razi responsible for his exile from Balkh? The confusion about the dates of migration clarified
A royal invitation to settle in Konya
Rumi's education under his father – contemporary syllabus of studies analysed
The end of one phase of education at the death of Rumi's father and the beginning of another

An analysis of the intellectual horizon of Rumi at the age of thirty-four
Debt to Ghazali – a brief comparison
Debt to Sana'i and 'Attar – Rumi sees himself as a successor to both
Rumi's knowledge of Classical Islamic philosophy
Rumi heir to an impressive heritage of Sufism
Dhu'l-Nun al-Misri, hero of a story in the *Mathnawi*
Respect and admiration for Bayazid Bistami
Mathnawi replete with references to Ibrahim ibn Adham
Rumi's defence of Mansur Hallaj
Classical Manuals of Sufism in the tenth century
Kashf-ul-Mahjub quoted copiously in the *Mathnawi*
A brief comparison and contrast with Ibn 'Arabi's thought

3. The Romance of Revolution (A.D. 1244–1250) 105
An account of Shams-i-Tabriz
Four different versions of Rumi's meeting with Shams
The version of Rumi's son
The result of the meeting
Rumi's correspondence in verse with Shams
Reasons for Shams's unpopularity with Rumi's followers
Rumi's new mode of life
The role of Salah-ud-din Zarkob in this period
Rumi fails to find Shams but discovers himself

4. The Miracle of the Muse (A.D. 1245–1260) 128
Rumi becomes a poet at the age of thirty-seven
Consideration of his collection of odes called *Divan-i-Shams-i-Tabriz*
A critical estimate of his lyrics
Characteristics of his lyrics
His universal appeal

5. The Message of the *Mathnawi* (A.D. 1261–1273) 175
A general summary
Nature of existence
Nature of knowledge
Free-will and determinism
Nature of Love
Nature of Reality

6. The Poet as a Thinker (A.D. 1261–1273) 256

The difference between his method and the method of philosophers
The relation between Love and intellect
The nature of the self
His conception of evolution
Some difficulties in this conception
Determinism and responsibility
Knowledge of God
Revelation
The Ideal Man

7. Latin translation of the *Mathnawi* 284

Select Bibliography 315

Index 321

Foreword

Jalaluddin Rumi has been described by Professor E. G. Browne as 'without doubt the most eminent Sufi poet whom Persia has produced, while his mystical *Mathnawi* deserves to rank amongst the great poems of all time'. Professor R. A. Nicholson on completing his masterly edition and translation of that work remarked that 'familiarity does not always breed disillusion. Today the words I applied to the author of the *Mathnawi* thirty-five years ago, "the greatest mystical poet of any age", seem to me no more than just. Where else shall we find such a panorama of universal existence unrolling itself through Time into Eternity?' Sir Muhammad Iqbal, who many times acknowledged his indebtedness to the great Persian visionary, stated that 'the world of today needs a Rumi to create an attitude of hope, and to kindle the fire of enthusiasm for life'.

These are but three of the many tributes that have been paid to Rumi's greatness, which is acknowledged as much in the West as in the East. It is therefore all the more surprising, and regrettable, that until the publication of the present volume no attempt has been made to write for the general public a biography and aesthetic appreciation of the man who enriched humanity with such splendid and massive contributions to literature and thought. Indeed, until the appearance a few years ago of Professor Badi al-Zaman Farozan Far's Persian study of Rumi, no such work had been produced in any language.

Fortunately this lamentable neglect has now been repaired with the issue of Afzal Iqbal's *The Life and*

Thought [now *Work*] *of Maulana Jalal-ud-din Rumi*. The author of this excellent monograph describes it modestly as 'a critical introduction'; it is an introduction that does tardy justice to the great man whom it presents to the reader. Mr Iqbal has read deeply the extensive writings of Rumi, and what others have said on the subject in ancient and modern times. While his approach to the poet is sensitive, and his aesthetic analysis most delicate, he displays acute powers of scholarly criticism in discussing the difficult problems that surround Rumi's biography. I recommend this book warmly; it is a pleasure to read, and it holds the key to further delight for those many who will be encouraged by it to study further the immortal poetry of Rumi.

A. J. ARBERRY

Pembroke College
Cambridge

Preface

It was in the early fifties that I started writing this book. I was then in Tehran and had an opportunity of learning at the feet of Professor Farozan Far who was at that time considered the greatest authority on Maulana Jalaluddin Rumi. The work was by no means easy. There is ample material in Persian but it requires all the patience one can command to sift the grain from the chaff. The early chroniclers seem intent on clouding a man's personality by investing him with a halo of mystery.

In English one comes across numerous references to Rumi among works on Persian mystics. But even Professor R.A. Nicholson, who devoted a lifetime to completing his masterly edition and translation of Rumi's *Mathnawi*, has not had time to produce a critical study of the life and thought of Rumi whom he rightly considers 'the greatest mystical poet of any age'.

It was under these circumstances that I set myself the task of producing a biography of Rumi for a modern student of literature. The synopsis was simple. The study started with a description and an analysis of conditions obtaining in the thirteenth century, the period during which Rumi lived and worked in Persia. The idea was to create some kind of a perspective for Rumi's personality. The attempt at placing him properly in his milieu was original in that no other study of the poet offered this background. And yet without this basic information I found it hard to understand and appreciate the vital role that Rumi played in moulding the human material around him.

After providing a brief outline of the relevant currents in the thirteenth century, the study proceeds to analyse, in the second chapter, the formative period of Rumi's life. This phase, though devoid of the spectacular, is significant in that it provides a key to the coming events. In this chapter one sees glimpses of what Professor Arberry describes as 'acute powers of scholarly criticism in discussing the difficult problems that surround Rumi's biography'. His very date and year of birth is in doubt. but having questioned some old assumptions, we have refrained from fixing dates for a number of events in Rumi's life. The research continues and hasty conclusions are not called for.

The third chapter begins with the appearance of Shams-i-Tabriz and lasts, with all its attendant revolutionary results, until the death or disappearance of the man who completely transforms the life of Rumi. The period of intellectual activity during which the medium of expression was prose, is followed by a period of love and lyrical activity, during which the medium of expression changes into poetry. Rumi's is perhaps the only example in the history of literature where a man devoted to prose suddenly bursts forth into poetry in his middle-age and becomes the greatest mystical poet of any age.

The fourth chapter deals with the product of this revolutionary change, viz. the lyrical poetry that flows with such power, beauty and abundance over a period of sixteen years of intense spiritual turmoil. The disturbance settles down at last and disappears around A.D. 1261 when Rumi begins the monumental work of writing the *Mathnawi*. And now starts the period of poetry with a purpose, the phase which saw Rumi make his immortal contribution, which was later acclaimed as the Qur'an in Pahlavi. This period has been briefly dealt with in the fifth chapter which sums up the message of the *Mathnawi*.

From this summing-up emerges the next chapter which deals with Rumi's thought. The seventh and final chapter, which could well be an appendix to the main study, deals with portions of the *Mathnawi* whose translation has not hitherto been available to the English reader. Professor R. A. Nicholson, while translating the full text of the *Mathnawi* into English, rendered some hundred lines into Latin, for he thought they were 'scarcely fit to be translated' into English. Frankly, Professor Nicholson, a Victorian, was projecting his own prejudices in censoring verses which in his view were exceptionable. In the process he denied the reader an opportunity to judge for himself. The final chapter makes the expurgated portions of the *Mathnawi* available to the English reader for the first time.

The book has seen six editions. It is considered by far the most authentic work on the subject today. It is indeed very different from the first edition which came out from Lahore in 1956. The book has already been translated into Urdu in Pakistan, and is being rendered into Turkish in Turkey. In the Muslim world, we hope it will be read with some interest by those who are concerned with the spiritual predicament of the modern man, for 'the world of today needs a Rumi to create an attitude of hope, and to kindle the fire of enthusiasm for life'.

AFZAL IQBAL

Rawalpindi, Pakistan
1 March 1991

poetry with a romance, the phase which saw the triumphant launch of composition which was later acclaimed as the Qur'an in Pahlavi. This period has been dealt with at length in the fifth chapter which sums up the assessment of the Mathnavi.

From this assessment emerges the sixth chapter which deals with Rumi's thought. The seventh and final chapter, which could well be an appendix to the main study, deals with portions of the Mathnavi whose translation has not hitherto been available to the English reader. Professor R. A. Nicholson, while translating the full text of the Mathnavi into English, rendered some hundred lines into Latin, for he thought they were 'scarcely fit to be translated into English.' Professor Nicholson, a Victorian, was projecting his own prejudices in censoring verses which in his view were objectionable. In the process he denied the reader an opportunity to judge for himself. The final chapter makes the expurgated portions of the Mathnavi available to the English reader for the first time.

The book has seen six editions. It is considered by far the most authentic work on the subject today. It is indeed very different from the first edition which came out from Lahore in 1956. The book has already been translated into Urdu in Pakistan, and is being rendered into Turkish in Turkey. In the Muslim world, we hope it will be read with some interest by those who are concerned with the spiritual predicament of the modern man, for the world of today needs a Rumi to create an attitude of hope, and to kindle the fire of enthusiasm for life.

AFZAL IQBAL

Rawalpindi, Pakistan
1 March 198[illegible]

Introduction

Maulana Jalal-ud-din Rumi needs no introduction. For seven hundred years now his verse has inspired millions of men. Jami, the celebrated Persian poet, hailed him as a saint who was not a prophet but had a Book. The *Mathnawi* has been known for centuries as the Qur'an in Pahlavi. With the possible exception of Lucretius in the first century B.C., he is the only major thinker, throughout history, to express an entire system of thought in verse which has an aesthetic merit of its own.

The sublime humanism of Rumi fired the imagination of mankind long before the West discovered the dignity of man. Dante was a young boy at the time of Rumi's death. The great humanist of the West, Petrarch, came a full century after him; and Erasmus followed him two and a half centuries later.

Hegel considered Rumi as one of the greatest poets and thinkers in world history. The twentieth-century German poet Hans Meinke saw in Rumi 'the only hope for the dark times we are living in'. The French writer Maurice Barres once confessed, 'When I experienced Mevlana's poetry, which is vibrant with the tone of ecstasy and with melody, I realised the deficiencies of Shakespeare, Goethe and Hugo.

In Turkey, Iran, India, Pakistan and Afghanistan, Rumi is honoured as a saint, a sage and a seer. In contemporary England, Professor R. A. Nicholson translated the *Mathnawi* into English and characterised Rumi as 'the greatest mystic poet of any age'. And yet he charged him with obscenity. We are not unaware of some Western Orientalists who have levelled a similar charge against the Qur'an. Professor Nicholson denied the reader an opportunity to judge for himself because he translated the few verses from the *Mathnawi,* which he thought exceptionable, into Latin. So far as is known, this is the first attempt on the part of any student of Rumi to deal with this allegation at a level of scholarship. For the first time also, passages singled out for censorship by Nicholson are being made available to the discerning reader, who will judge for himself.

AFZAL IQBAL

Stockholm,
14 August 1975

(ii)

There is hardly a published work in English, Urdu or Persian which has escaped my notice in this field and I must say that Afzal Iqbal's is the first attempt of its kind which will be looked upon as a milestone in the literature on Rumi. No other work in my knowledge offers a study of the life and thought of Rumi with such critical detail and careful precision. The author who, I am surprised, has been able to find time despite his multifarious duties to undertake a work of such a monumental nature, is to be warmly congratulated on the labour of love, the chastity of taste, his scrupulous care in verifying of facts and his success in resisting the temptation to succumb to exaggerations. The Indo-Pakistan subcontinent has never lagged behind any country in its service to the Mathnawi and its distinguished author; but Afzal Iqbal has carved out for himself a path which is all his own. I hope he will continue to traverse his path with the same fervour and devotion.

(MAULANA) ABDUL MAJID DARYABADI

Daryabad, Barabanki
16th October, 1955

(iii)

Jalaluddin Rumi is admittedly one of the great poets of Persia: his *diwan* of lyrical poetry and his *Mathnawi* are equally immortal. When the great Sa'di was asked which was the best poem existing in the Persian language, he selected a lyric of Rumi's; and as for the *Mathnawi* the Persians call it the *Qur'an* in Persian. Western opinion is equally favourable. "The *Mathnawi,*" says Prof. R.A. Nicholson, "is a majestic river, calm and deep, meandering through many a rich and varied landscape to the immeasurable ocean; the *diwan* is a foaming torrent that leaps and plunges in the ethereal solitude of the hills." Now, as the chief contribution of Persia to world-culture is her poetry, if Rumi is one of the great poets of Persia, he becomes, *ipso facto,* one of the great poets of the world; nevertheless, neither the Persians among whom Rumi was born, nor the Turks among whom he lived and died, nor the Europeans among whom he has found many translators and interpreters, nor the Indians who have been assiduously cultivating the Persian language for a thousand years, ever attempted an exhaustive monograph on the thought of Rumi: Agha Faruzan Far's fine work deals only with the Life of Rumi; and before Prof. Nicholson could give to the world a critical exposition of Rumi's poetry and philosophy, death had stayed his hands! And so for various reasons, our knowledge of Rumi remained incomplete; and it redounds greatly to the credit of Mr. Afzal Iqbal that following in the footsteps of such masters as Whinfield, Browne, Nicholson and Faruzan Far, he should have produced a work of which it may be truly said: 'Age will not wither nor Time stale its infinite variety.'

Mr. Afzal Iqbal proceeds systematically. He first gives the historical background for "no study of Rumi so far had tried to put him in a proper perspective." This opening chapter makes delightful reading and several errors are decisively corrected. Bahau'd-Din did not leave Balkh on account of his enmity with Razi; he left Balkh in 1212 when his son Jalaluddin was 5 years of age; then returned to Balkh and finally abandoned it before the Mongol invasion of 1220 A.D. And so at the age of 13 Rumi started on that long march which took him to Konya "an island of peace in a vast sea of turbulence" in 1229. This firm grip on dates continues in the chapter on the Period of Preparation, for according to Aflaki, Rumi's grandmother was the daughter of 'Alau'd-Din Muhammad Khawarazmshah: if so, 'Alau'd-Din was born in the same year in which his daughter is supposed to have given birth to Rumi's father! It is obvious, therefore, that Jami and Aflaki have not differentiated between the homonymous 'Alau'd-Din Muhammads, one of whom was the Khawarazmshah and the other, Rumi's ancestor. Similarly Bahau'd-Din could not have stayed in the Mustansariyyah College at Baghdad for he was in Baghdad in 1220 and the College was completed in 1224.

Keeping this historical background before our eyes, Afzal Iqbal divides Rumi's life into a first phase which lasted from 1207 to 1244; a second phase which produced the *diwan* and began with the appearance of Shams-i-Tabriz in 1245 and lasted till the death of Zarkob in 1261; and a third phase which produced the *Mathnawi* and lasted from 1261 to 1273 A.D. In the first phase, Rumi was attached to Burhanu'd-Din; in the second to Shams-i-Tabriz and Zarkob and in the third to Husamu'd-Din Chalapi: Rumi was therefore never without a confidant in his life. And "if the friendship of a mortal man can contribute so much to the development of human personality," argues Iqbal, "how much influence for the good would the friendship of God exert on a man if he were sincerely to cultivate Him?"

Mr. Afzal Iqbal next proceeds to a critical analysis of Rumi's poetry; and all will agree with him and Coleridge that no man was ever yet a great poet without being at the same time a profound philosopher. But what was Rumi's philosophy of life? "It is," states Afzal Iqbal, "at once a description and explanation and a justification of his religious experience—where description, explanation and justification should be regarded as different notes combining and merging into a higher unity—Rumi's symphony of Love." "Passive life is of no use to Rumi," concludes Afzal Iqbal, "for struggling against destiny is the destiny of man."

Mr. Afzal Iqbal's task was difficult for he had to break new ground, but he knows how to pick and choose his words; he knows how to sift his material; he knows how to arrange his ideas; he knows how to argue with restraint and moderation. And the result is an extremely fine piece of work, interesting and instructive, and replete with much information that is new and original.

(PROF) HADI HASAN

Aligarh,
16th October, 1955

(iv)

Recently I had an opportunity to read, with great profit, a learned treatise on Maulana Jalaluddin Mohammed of Balkh, later of Konia, who is undoubtedly the greatest figure in the world of mysticism and literature. This book on Rumi, is indeed comprehensive and a brilliant study of the life and thought of a great thinker of the 7th century A.H. I wish a translator possessing as much insight in the works of the Maulana as the author of this treatise could translate it for the benefit of the reader.

The work under review comprises five chapters which deal with the age of Rumi, his period of preparation, the sudden revolution in his life, the spirit of his poetry and finally his thought. All these chapters abound in original matter. Much fresh ground has been broken and many new and subtle issues, which are the result of deep thought and strenuous research, have been raised. The reader does not get weary of reading the book over and over again; his thirst remains unquenched like that of the proverbial man by the Euphrates. "I am all the more thirsty," says the poet, "though the waters of the Euphrates have drowned me!" Among the atractive features of the work mention must be made of the beautiful quotations from the verse of the Maulana which embellish almost every one of its pages. These quotations have been translated in the chastest language.

It must be borne in mind that the art of writing a biography is recent in oriental literature. Biographers in the East have, therefore, to shoulder a great responsibility in as much as they have to collect and sift this material from a limited field of reliable data so often ingored by the ancient writers of Tazkaras. Besides, they have to delve deep into the essential spirit of their subject in order to collect "the royal pearls from the fathomless ocean of thought." It must the said to the credit of the author that he has successfully traversed both these difficult paths, and has done full justice to his subject according to modern methods of research. I for one consider Maulana Jalaluddin too great to be compared with any other famous thinker, reformer, saint or scholar. His equal has to be sought, if at all, among the divines possessed of the secrets of God or the great spiritual lovers who were free from material limitations. Nevertheless the author of this work has successfully drawn analogies between the Maulana and many other Islamic thinkers like Ghazali, Khawaja Toosi, and Iqbal of Lahore. He has discussed at length how the works of Maulana Jalaluddin have deeply influenced the four corners of the Muslim world and how Allama Mohammad Iqbal, in the recent past, derived his inspiration from this perennial spring of love. It is significant that the Maulana has enjoyed great popularity in India during the last three or four centuries during which many scholars and eminent literary figures of the sub-continent have written commentaries and appreciations of his work. Allama Shibli Naumani was one of them. It is now the turn of Mr. Afzal Iqbal, the young scholar from Pakistan, to keep the tradition alive by contributing this immortal treatise to the eminent list of great works already extant. May the holy soul of the Maulana bless his great labour of love!

ALI ASGHAR HEKMAT

New Delhi,
October, 17, 1955.

A Portrait

Have you ever seen a portrait of Rumi? I, for one, had longed to see one for years; and in my best appreciative moments I cursed the two Roman painters – Kaulman and Aynu Devala – who were his disciples – for having failed to leave a portrait of their Master. It almost became a lasting regret of my life. I was, however, greatly relieved when my friend, Aqai Ali Moatamadi, Iran's first Ambassador to India before partition, pointed out that he remembered having seen a portrait of Rumi in his own country. The point was too consequential to be dropped, and we both pursued it till we got a number of valuable pictures from the Ministry of Education in Tehran. Rumi's portrait and the other pictures printed here have been lent me by the kind courtesy of the Government of Iran. The portrait dating from the fifteenth-sixteenth century is preserved in the Topkapi Museum at Istanbul.

And now let us have a look at Rumi.

Pale and slim, his sunken eyes give me an impression of deep absorption. Even though he is squatting, it is easy to judge his size. He does not appear to be a tall man. In all probability he is wearing a professor's gown. His headgear suggests the dignity of a scholar. The one thing which strikes me, above the rest, is the keenness of his eyes – extremely sharp, deeply absorbing, small but severely critical, pale but penetrating. There is unmistakable lustre and brilliance about them. It must have been difficult to look straight into his eyes!

I have known this man for several years. He has helped me solve many a vexed problem of my life, but never before have I had an opportunity to look at him. It was a great joy to know him from his books, but to know him as a man is quite a different story. And as a man he is known but little.

Most of those who wrote on him devoted their time to a laborious analysis of his thought, a cumbersome interpretation of his simple, beautiful verses. Others raised him to the level of a superman, a saint, forgetting that a man commands a superior station to both.

Simple, sincere and selfless, Rumi was respected because he respected others. He was considerate even towards his enemies. He was no bigot. Petty differences of creed did not upset him. He always stood for tolerance and toleration. It was well-nigh impossible to provoke him. He always managed to keep his balance about him. Nothing could irritate him to anger. One day as he was in a deep mood of contemplation a drunkard walked in, shouting and stumbling. As he advanced towards Rumi, he fell on him. His intrusion was serious enough, but to have physically fallen on a saint in his contemplative moments was a crime for which no punishment was severe enough. Rumi's disciples rose as one man and were about to rush at the intruder when the Master waved his hand and rebuked them gently. 'I had thought,' said he, 'that the "intruder" was drunk, but now I see that it is not he but my own disciples who are drunk!' Wasn't it for this love and consideration even for the most unworthy members of society that he won their unflinching admiration and respect? Wasn't it because of this regard for the meanest of men that he became their unquestioned leader? It is quite easy to understand the devotion of Rumi's admirers who, while he lay on his bier and was washed by the hands of a loving and beloved disciple, did not allow a drop to fall on the ground and drank it as holy water! Nor is it difficult to understand the warmth of feeling with which men of every creed and colour – Muslims, Christians, Jews, Arabs and Persians, Turks and Romans – flocked to his funeral procession and smote their breasts and rent their garments.

But even such a man as Rumi had his critics in his own day. His uncharitable adversaries attempted to defame him. But never once in his whole life did he retaliate. There was a time when Sadr-ud-din Qonavi, who later became a great friend, was one of his outstanding adversaries. He came to know that Rumi as a Musalman had claimed to be at one with seventy-two sects. Such an unorthodox assertion was not to be easily swallowed by a great Muslim dignitary. He deputed one of his friends, an able scholar, to question Rumi in public. But Rumi found no reason to repudiate his statement, and that provided the scholar-friend of Qonavi with the pretext to rebuke him to his heart's content. In the public meeting, as Rumi listened to the long-winded abuses hurled at him, he was neither excited nor annoyed; he only laughed. Addressing the rebuker Rumi gently said, 'I also agree with what *you* are saying now.' He always drove home a point with a pleasant persuasive argument and maintained his poise and balance even in the midst of provocative criticism.

Far from being proud of his attainments he erred on the side of humility. Kings were his followers and disciples, but he never allowed vanity to get the better of him for a moment. He had a living, moving faith in his ideal and nothing could tempt or seduce him from it. He saw to it that his knowledge and wisdom did not become the monopoly of the moneyed men about the court; the largest number of his students consisted of what his critics called 'the tailors, the cloth-sellers and the petty shopkeepers'. The kings could meet him only when he had the time to spare for them, but these 'uncouth, uncultured ruffians' commanded his whole lifetime. It was for them that he lived, worked and thought.

It is this man — Jalaluddin Rumi — that we seek to know in the following pages.

Chapter 1

The Age of Rumi

Rumi was born on 30 September 1207 (6 Rabi' I 604) and died on 17 December 1273. His life, therefore, covers almost the entire span of the thirteenth century. If we are to have some idea of his contribution to life and thought, it is essential to start with a brief description and an analysis of the conditions prevailing at the time. No study of Rumi has so far taken this factor into consideration and it is, therefore, all the more necessary to have a clear idea of his milieu.

I

The thirteenth century of the Christian era was the seventh century of Islam. The Islamic commonwealth achieved its full political maturity within the first century and its entire geographical extent during the first seven hundred years of its existence. Rising from Mecca it flashed into Syria; it traversed the whole breadth of Northern Africa; and then leaping the Straits of Gibraltar, it hammered at the doors of Europe. Islam conquered Sicily and reached as far as the Campagna and Abruzzi in the south. Using Spain as a springboard it jumped into Provence, Northern Italy and even to Switzerland. From its stronghold in Spain and Sicily it transmitted its powerful cultural influence to the whole of Europe. In the thirteenth century, however, the social order of Islam no longer represented the best that it had to offer to the world. The passage of centuries had beclouded the vision which once inspired the whole world. Elements of decay, which had crept into the system, continued to work unnoticed, till it became clear that the grand structure represented by Islam in the thirteenth century was no longer a structure of steel. It was not yet a house of cards, either, but the edifice was certainly tottering, and if the rot was not checked in time the result could be disastrous.

The reasons leading to the decline of Islam can be understood best by a reference to the causes of its success. Islam owed its spectacular success entirely to the teachings of the Qur'an and the life-example of the Holy Prophet. The world of Islam flourished and progressed to an extent which was unparalleled in the annals of history. It produced a civilisation at once refined and progressive at a time when Europe was sunk in superstition, stagnation and reaction. It will be no exaggeration to say that the West owed its regeneration considerably to the intellectual energy released by the dynamo that was Islam. This period of regeneration is rightly referred to by the West as the Renaissance, which means re-birth, for so it was indeed for the stagnant civilisation of Europe.

These achievements were possible only because of the teachings of the Qur'an and the life-example of the Holy Prophet. They were possible as long as Muslims were ready and eager to surrender themselves to the commandments of their faith. They became difficult and impossible to a degree corresponding with the Muslims unreadiness to allow their lives to be conditioned and modelled on the tenets of the Qur'an and the *Sunnah*. While the pioneers of Islam found no sacrifice too great to observe and enforce the laws of the Qur'an, their successors, on whom fell the duty of preserving their legacy, proved unequal to the task, for they had learnt to place their own comfort before the demands of the fundamentals of their faith. They accepted what was convenient and rejected what appeared to be inconvenient. While paying lip-service to the Qur'an, they refused to pay it the homage of their actions without which Islam becomes a mockery. Instead of accepting the Qur'an as an unchallenged guide to life in all its manifold aspects, the Muslims relegated it to the status of a treatise on dogmas. No wonder, therefore, that the active vigour and utility of the system was neutralised. The *Sunnah* in the thirteenth century had become for the Sufi an ideogram of mere Platonic importance, for the theologian and the legist a mere system of laws, and for the Muslim masses nothing but a hollow shell without any living meaning. The intellectuals, slow to understand the limitations of their own intellect, had gone all out for Scholasticism, a subtle poison which had by this time eaten deep into the muscles and sinews of the Muslim body politic. It had sapped the courage of millions of men; it had gnawed at the roots of faith and had demonstrably weakened the fabric of Islam. We are not concerned with an analysis of the many and varied causes which led to this decay and degeneration. It is enough for our purpose to record that Islam in the thirteenth century was a tottering edifice. It had weathered many a storm during the seven centuries of its life, but it had now reached a stage when its inner vitality had been slowly sapped, and when one powerful blast might well have uprooted it from the soil on which it was leading a precarious existence.

It is a great paradox of history that while the light of Islam had spread over lands far away, the followers of Islam were deserting their own cause in the very heart of the Islamic commonwealth. The betrayal had indeed come, not from the mass of men, but from those whose duty it was to guide them to the right path by means of their knowledge and example. Such a force of character was, however, conspicuously lacking. The zeal for the faith was not unoften accompanied by a complete disregard for the law of Islam. There was a sharp cleavage between religious thought and activity. Comfort and convenience was the rule. The love of controversy had got the better of the love for truth. Islam had been split up into factions and the wood had been lost for the trees.

The Muslim society in the thirteenth century represented, therefore, a decadent social order incapable of dynamic growth and divested of a capacity for effective resistance. It is difficult for any society, under such circumstances, to survive a serious external danger. It was all the more difficult for Islamic society which was also threatened from within and had lost its inherent strength and capacity for healthy growth. And yet the Islamic commonwealth was confronted in this era with two of its most dangerous foes. One was the Crusader from the West; the other was the Mongol from the East.

The Crusader was a familiar character known to the world of Islam for nearly two centuries, for the Crusades started in 1096. It is one of the unfortunate facts of history that the first great clash between Europe and Islam came with the very beginning of European civilisation. The clash which started in the eleventh century continued till the end of the thirteenth. The proclaimed aim of these wars was to wrest the Holy Lands from the hands of the Muslims. This slogan had a tremendous psychological appeal for the mass of the Christians whose frenzy was roused to a pitch wholly unparalleled either before or since the Crusades. Little did the common man understand that the recovery of Palestine and the Holy Lands was but a pretext on the part of the Pope and the powerful regional kings of Europe to achieve their own personal ambitions. Little did he realise that he was being used as a mere pawn in the hands of religious and political intriguers whose own feelings were quickened only by political ambitions and economic rapacity. A movement which was based on such foundations and which lacked the cohesion and unity of purpose, so necessary for success, could not be expected to achieve any object, for it had no well-defined object in view. It was a mere expression of the new confidence which had grown in Europe with the dawn of civilisation. The different parties engaged in the Crusades sought to achieve different ends. The appearance of unity on the surface was deceptive indeed. In the thirteenth century, which was full of the Crusades, we find ample evidence of their inner contradictions. While the ostensible aim of these wars was the recovery of Palestine, they were waged, as has been well said, 'everywhere except in Palestine'.

In the period under discussion we clearly see the Crusaders completely uncertain of their goal. Quite oblivious of their real objective, they wandered uncertainly from Constantinople to Egypt and even to Tunis. They only succeeded in capturing the Christian city of Constantinople. And yet, Constantinople was the city which had originally invoked the Crusades. By the thirteenth century the French feudalism, which was the mainstay of the Crusades, was diverted to Greece. Palestine seems to have been left severely alone, for the centre of gravity shifted in this century to the debris of the Eastern Empire.

The simple fact that emerges from the history of the Crusades is that Christian Europe was determined to wipe out Islam from the face of the earth. It exterminated the Muslim element in Spain after the most ferocious and merciless persecution the world had ever known. When Islam came to Spain with Tariq in the eighth century, the aristocracy was absorbed in luxury,[1] the serfs were ill-treated[2] and reduced to the status of the slave,[3] the rich and opulent clergy

[1] S. Lane-Poole, *The Moors in Spain* (London, 1912), p. 7.
[2] McCabe, *Splendour of Moorish Spain* (London, 1935), pp. 15–16, 21, etc.
[3] Ibid., p. 7.

seemed supremely indifferent to their lot.[4] Poverty, corruption, ignorance and instability were the order of the day. And yet within the same century the Muslims established an enlightened and civilised rule which won the admiration of the whole of Europe. To the libraries and universities, set up by the Muslims in Spain, flocked students from France and Germany,[5] much in the same way as Muslim students go to Western universities today. So deep and universal was the satisfaction given to all classes of men that during the whole of the eighth century there was not a single revolt of the subject Christians.[6] These achievements sprang directly from the fact that those who had introduced Islam to Spain had landed there with a mission which made it impossible for them to be cruel, intolerant and greedy. The moment this lesson was lost on their successors, their unity of purpose was replaced by their clannish spirit which gave rise to many a domestic feud. At one time during the twelfth century, there were as many as twelve Muslim dynasties ruling over different parts of Spain. This, then, was a signal for collapse. In the thirteenth century, the Muslim rule over Spain was fast shrinking on account of the treachery of Muslim princes. By 1266 the Roman Church had reclaimed all Spain except Muslim Granada which finally fell in 1492. The Crusades, which failed in their original object of wresting Palestine from Muslim hands, succeeded in inflicting a crushing blow on the Muslims in Spain. The guiding spirit of the Crusades which wrought untold havoc in Spain is explained by a typical letter written to the Pope by the Crusaders after one of their victories in Palestine:

> God was appeased by our humility, and on the eighth day of our humiliation He delivered the city and its enemies to us. And if you desire to know what was done with the enemy who were found there,

[4] Ibid. [5] Lane-Poole, op. cit. [6] Ibid., p. 43.

know that in Solomon's porch and its temple our men rode in the blood of Saracens up to the knees of their horses.[7]

Such was the spirit of smouldering hatred which was let loose in Spain. All traces of Arab life and culture were ruthlessly destroyed. Even according to Christian historians, there was no greater tragedy in the history of Europe than the extinction of the Muslim civilisation in Spain which had contributed so much to the renaissance of Europe.[8]

St Dominic had founded the 'Order of Friar Preachers'[9] by 1215 when Rumi was still a lad of about eight years. The Order had taken a definite shape by 1220. The Friars wore a black mantle over a white habit and lived a very austere life. They had no property, no fixed income and were imbued with the spirit of preaching and missionising which soon led them to Greece, Palestine and then to Central Asia.

In the *Encyclopaedia Britannica*, Volume VII, p. 519, there is an interesting picture of St Thomas whose triumph over Averroes is depicted with pride. St Thomas is shown holding a Bible in his hand and four of his own works on his knee. He receives rays of wisdom from Christ on top of his head, while Moses, St Paul, Aristotle and Plato radiate rays of wisdom from left and right. At his feet is shown lying prostrate Averroes with a ray of refutation piercing his 'Commentary'. This is an eloquent commentary on the preoccupation of the Friars to refute Islam through all manner of means.

St Francis was already preaching to the poor in

[7] Grant, *History of Europe* (London, 1917), p. 33. Compare also Wells, *A Short History of the World* (London, Thinkers Library, 1945), p. 369.

[8] J. D. Conde, *History of the Domination of the Arabs in Spain* (1854), 3 vols., as quoted by Professor S. A. W. Bukhari, *History of Islam* (Bangalore, 1942), p. 189.

[9] For details about the Dominican Order, see *The Catholic Encyclopaedia* article 'Preacher'; P. Mandonnet, *St Dominic and His Work* (1944); A. Walz, *Compendium Historiae Ordinis Praedicatorum* (Rome, 1930); B. Jarret, *The English Dominicans* (London, 1921).

Assisi when Rumi was born. By the time Rumi became known as a leading scholar, St Francis was dead (3 October 1226). In his own life St Francis was respected as a great mystic. In 1219 he went to Egypt where the Crusaders were besieging Damietta, and on being taken prisoner was led before the Sultan. Earlier he went to Spain but returned without accomplishing his object.

The thirteenth century saw a widespread reaction in Europe against the rigid formalism of the Church and the scandalous lives of many of the clergy. In the beginning of the century, the foundation of the Dominican and Franciscan Orders furnished an outlet. Numerous convents sprang up throughout Germany. The German mind was a peculiarly fruitful soil for mysticism and a number of women saints appeared about this time. Mechthild of Magdeburg appears to have been the most influential. According to Mechthild, the reign of the spirit was to begin with the year 1260, when the abuses of the world and the Church were to be cured by the general adoption of the monastic life of contemplation. Very similar to this is the teaching of Amalric of Bena who died in the year that Rumi was born. The German mind had its most eminent exponent in the sphere of speculative mysticism in Meister Eckhart (1260–1327). His scholastic mysticism was largely practical and psychological in character, and so far as it was theoretical it was a theory of the faculties by which the union with God is attainable.[10]

In Spain, Ramon Lull, a Catalan author, mystic and missionary, launched a crusade against Islam. Local patriotism helped to magnify his merits and the circumstances of his death helped the people to hail him as a martyr. Born in Palma, the beautiful holiday resort of Spain, in 1232, Ramon Lull led a dissipated life till 1266 when he resolved to expose the 'errors' of

[10] *Encyclopaedia Britannica*, Volume XVI, pp. 52–53.

Islam. For this purpose he studied Arabic for nine years, acted for ten years as Professor of Arabic and Philosophy at a Franciscan monastery at Miramar and wrote many controversial treatises. His fantastic doctrines found many an enthusiastic follower in Catalonia and later throughout Spain where he was recognised as a saint, thinker and poet. He was, however, later repudiated by the Church.[11]

The thirteenth century which brought, with the invasion of the Mongols, the most tremendous shock to Asia and Europe was also the great period of mysticism, not only in Islam and in Christianity, but also in India where the Bhakti movement had made great strides. Ramanuja, a Southern Brahmin of the twelfth century, recognised Vishnu as identical with Brahma, the supreme spirit, animating the material world as well as the individual souls which have become estranged from God through unbelief, and can attain conscious union with Him again only through devotion or love, i.e. Bhakti. He strictly forbade his followers the eating of any food cooked or even seen by a stranger. It was an ascetic order, the followers of which soon split into two sects.[12]

A year before Rumi was born India had the first Muslim king of its own, Muhammad Ghauri, who ruled, not from an outside capital, but struck roots in the soil. The thirteenth century in India witnessed a galaxy of names. Shams-ud-din Altamsh, the founder of the Slave Dynasty, took the throne while Rumi was still a lad. He withstood the Mongol hordes who overran Persia. The Caliph of Baghdad sent an embassy in 1229 to invest Altamsh with the robe of office as the recognised sovereign of India. Altamsh was the first to introduce a purely Arabic coinage. Sultana Raziya, the daughter of Altamsh, a legendary figure in Muslim India, came to the throne in this period, and ruled briefly from 1236 to 1240.

[11] Ibid., Volume XIV, p. 478.

[12] Ibid., Volume XVIII, p. 963.

By a curious coincidence, three queens – the only three women who were ever elected to the throne in the Muslim world – reigned in the thirteenth century. Shajar-ud-Durr, the slave wife of Saladin's grand-nephew, the woman who defeated the Crusade of Louis IX, was queen of the Mamluks in Egypt in 1250; Abish, the last of the princely line of Salghar, patrons of the celebrated Persian poet Sa'di, ruled the province of Fars for nearly a quarter of a century during the troubled period of Mongol supremacy; and Raziya sat on the throne of Delhi for nearly three years and a half. Balban, a remarkable slave who rose to be the king of India, dominated the larger part of this century of India. He faced the terror inspired by the Mongols. It is interesting to see the writing of Amir Khusrau, a poet who lived at the court under the patronage of Balban's son Prince Muhammad. His picture of the Mongols riding on camels, with their bodies of steel and faces like fire, slits of eyes sharp as gimlets, short necks, leathery wrinkled cheeks, wide hairy nostrils and huge mouths, their coarse skins covered with vermin and their horrible smell, is the caricature of fear. 'They are descended from dogs, but their bones are bigger,' he says. 'The king marvelled at their bestial faces and said that God must have created them out of hell-fire. They looked like so many sallow devils, and the people fled from them everywhere in panic.'[13]

We have to contend with the important fact that while Islam in the thirteenth century was divided to the core and was split up into many factions, Christianity in this era was determined to make a supreme effort to sink all its differences with a view to overthrowing the Muslim power. All quarrels were composed, all schisms ended. Greek and Roman churches, always at variance, were now united into a joint force to launch an assault on the power of 'the

[13] S. Lane-Poole, *Medieval India under Mohammadan Rule*, p. 74.

infidels'.[14] This was clearly the crusading policy of Pope Innocent III. This policy was executed without any regard to scruples, for means did not seem to matter if the end could be somehow secured. Strange bedfellows came together, and a relentless war was waged against Islam from all scattered bases and all available platforms. By the middle of the thirteenth century a new vicissitude in the affairs of Islam was acclaimed in the West as the promise of better things to come. It was the founding of the Mongol Empire by Chingiz Khan, a man who professed neither Islam nor Christianity. The West which was frustrated in the battlefield in the East now turned to the field of diplomacy. Frantic efforts were made to convert the Mongols to Christianity and secure their help in sealing for ever the fate of Islam. But towards the end of the century all hope vanished; the prospect of a mass conversion of the Mongols dwindled and disappeared, the situation took an unexpected turn and the Mongols, instead of being converted to Christianity, embraced Islam in 1316. Taqudar (Ahmad) Khan (1282–1284)[15] and Ghazan Khan (1295–1304) were the first to embrace Islam in which religion the successors of the latter in Persia continued. Thus the Crusades which began with the Saljuq Turks encamped at Nicaea on the confines of Asia, ended with the Ottomon Turks encamped in Europe itself on the Danube!

A pertinent question arises at this stage: how is it that the Muslim commonwealth, weakened by dissensions and troubled by factions within its own ranks, succeeded at last in averting a catastrophe? We must look for an explanation to this miracle of history in more factors than one. We will take up the fundamental factor first. The Islamic world had clearly established, after two centuries of deadly struggle

[14] For details see H. A. L. Fisher, *History of Europe*, Chapter 23.
[15] E. G. Browne, *A Literary History of Persia*, Vol. II, p. 440.

with the Christian West, that its inner strength and social soundness were superior to anything mankind had till then experienced by way of social organisation. The resistance of the Islamic social organisation, despite its relative decay and decadence, was still invincible. There is only one explanation for this strength and that has to be sought in the religious teachings of the Qur'an and the life-example of Prophet Muhammad – the sources that sustained and served as a band of steel around the social structure of Islam. The Christian Empire had no such spiritual element to keep it together. While the world of Islam owed its progress and civilisation entirely to the teachings of its religion, the achievements of Europe emerged out of her age-long fight against the Christian Church and its outlook on life. 'It was not until the Western nations broke away from their religious law that they became more tolerant and it was only when the Muslims fell away from their religious law that they declined in tolerance and other evidences of highest culture.'[16] It is not relevant for our study to probe deep into the causes of the conflict of the European civilisation with the Christian Church. It is enough for our purpose to point out that one of the important causes of this conflict was the fact, often glossed over, that the civilisation of Europe was based essentially on the heritage of the Roman civilisation, with its utterly materialistic attitude as regards human life and its inherent values; another reason was the revolt of human nature against the Christian world contempt and the suppression of natural desires and legitimate endeavours of men. In the thirteenth century the influence of the Roman civilisation was still supreme as a fountain source of inspiration. The Byzantine Empire was an heir only in so far as it ruled over some of the territories which once formed part of the Roman Empire. The Roman ideas were still

[16] M. M. Pickthall, *Lectures on Islam* (Madras, Hoe & Co., 1932), p. 90.

cherished. They fired the imagination of Dante who was undoubtedly the greatest exponent of the Christian intellectual activity of the thirteenth century. We will presently have an opportunity of briefly acquainting ourselves with the ideas which inspired Dante, but meanwhile it is sufficient to record that the idea underlying the Roman Empire was the acquisition of power and exploitation of other nations for the benefit of Rome. The 'Roman Justice' was justice for the Romans alone. Such a conception of life was fundamentally at variance with the Islamic conception of life. It suffered, therefore, from all the disadvantages accruing from such a position. While the Muslim Empire could be sustained for a whole millennium by the ideals which were responsible for founding it, the Roman Empire which lacked the strength of similar ideals completely disappeared within one century. While the Islamic Empire grew to its fullness within less than a century, it took the Roman Empire nearly one thousand years to grow to its full political maturity. The contrast, both in the rise and fall of the two empires, is significant, and the only explanation for the glaring contrast between the long-drawn-out resistance of Islam and the sudden disappearance of the Roman Empire lies in the fact that, while the former sought its strength in the clear-cut universal laws laid down by the Qur'an, the latter had no such spiritual basis to fall back upon.

This, then, is the overriding consideration which the reader must constantly bear in mind. There were other factors, indeed numerous and complex, which contributed to the success of Islam's resistance to the Crusades in the thirteenth century, the most important of them being the failure of the crusading policy of Pope Innocent III. 'This is the Pope under whose rule the Western Church was imposed on Constantinople, who dared to place England and France under interdict, who launched the most successful of the

Spanish Crusades, who exacted from the rulers of England, Aragon and Portugal the surrender of their respective countries as fiefs to be held by the Holy See and did not scruple first to excommunicate King John and then, when the culprit had made an abject submission, to set aside the Magna Carta and to excommunicate the baron by whom he was supported.'[17] It was the view of the Pope that he was the Vicar of Christ, Prince and King in one, and that the whole empire should submit to him without demur. Fortunately for Islam his ambitious programme to forge unity for accomplishing the object that he had in view never succeeded. His interests were at variance with those of the European kings whom he wanted to use for his own ends. The result was that neither Richard I of England nor Philip Augustus of France nor the two contending Guelf and Ghibelline champions in Germany could be enticed to exchange their domestic interests for the distant adventure launched by the Pope. So perilous was the position that in 1209 Henry of Flanders, the second Latin Emperor of the East, allied himself with the Muslims of Rum against the Greeks of Nicaea. The trend of events was clearly towards the making of national States, not towards the acceptance of Papal supremacy. Although the Pope appeared to reign supreme, yet 'beneath this brilliant surface there was muttering, challenge, uncertainty. There were the Germans who asked what business the Pope had to interfere in their concerns. There were Englishmen who, despite the Pope's support of the versatile King John, were determined to defend their great Charter, and there were Frenchmen who were prepared to help them.' It will be seen, therefore, that while the settled purpose of the Papacy was to establish itself as the supreme power in the West, the national States, emerging for the first time in Europe, could not hope to live without

[17] H. A. L. Fisher, op. cit., p. 259.

frustrating this design. These inner contradictions weakened the fury of the Crusaders' attack which had lost a focal point and was being withered by diversions, which made the achievement of the proclaimed end – recovery of Palestine – a distant possibility. The diversion of the fourth Crusade to the conquest of Constantinople and the pillage of the most civilised of the European States is an instance which richly illustrates the lack of a central directive force. This incident has been dubbed as 'one of the most disgraceful acts in Medieval history'[18] and so it was, for it fully exposed the glaring contradictions and the inherent imbecility of the Crusades.

The eclipse of the hopes and aspirations associated with the age of the Papacy and with the launching of the Crusades will become more clear if we follow the careers of two kings of France – the country which was the most important recruiting ground for these wars. While we see St Louis, the King of France (1226–1270), ready to hearken to the voice of the Pope in complete disregard of the immediate interests of his own country, we see his grandson, Philip the Fair, lay hands upon the Pope himself. While St Louis was imbued with ideals of personal holiness and the happiness of his subjects, with King Philip of France the two great problems were always, no matter at what cost, power and wealth. And in this, King Philip represented the true basis of European civilisation. Nothing speaks more eloquently of the spirit of the times than the fact that Philip was able, without affronting his people, to have the Pope's person seized by violence. The fall in the Pope's prestige in Europe helped to bring out in bold relief the fundamental futility of the Crusades which were being launched to establish God's kingdom on earth. The enthusiasm for this cause could not be long sustained when the so-called Kingdom of God was falling apart in Europe

[18] Ibid., p. 224.

itself, due entirely to the avarice and greed for power displayed by the Vicar of Christ himself. This fall in prestige had its psychological reactions in the Muslim camp which was strengthened by the middle of the thirteenth century by the rise to power of the Mamluk Sultans of Egypt. The greatest of these Sultans defeated the attempts of the Mongols to establish themselves in Syria; he annexed Antioch, while his successors conquered Tripoli and then followed their successes with the capture of Acre, the last stronghold of the Latins on the Syrian Coast. Thus Christianity which threatened to strike at the very root of Islam in the opening of the thirteenth century found itself expelled from the mainland of Asia towards the end of the same century. The conversion of the Mongols to Islam was as sudden as it was unexpected, for they had been flirting with Christianity which tried hard to cast its net wide. With this development, which must again be attributed to the superiority of Islam over any other social order known to man, the Islamic commonwealth got another lease of life. It was now for the followers of this faith to prove worthy of the trust reposed in them – a great trial and a great opportunity.

The Crusaders launched a relentless attack on the forces of Islam. In 1218 they captured Damietta but could not withstand the co-ordinated attack of the Ayyubids; the next year Damietta was free again. Soon afterwards the complex machinations of European politics led to a renewed flare-up of the struggle for the possession of Jerusalem. The Hohenstaufen Frederick II, who had come to the throne as a ward of Pope Innocent III, had not only to approve the expansion of the ecclesiastical State consummated at the expense of the empire, and to waive the exercise of any influence on the episcopal elections in Germany, but had also to vow to crusade. The fulfilment of this vow, however, was very far from his intentions, since as heir of the Normans in Sicily he was thoroughly preoccupied with constructing a modern regime there which would enable him to win back Italy. Like the Normans, he also favoured Arabic culture and maintained Arab mercenaries. As he kept postponing the date for the beginning of the Crusade, Gregory IX excommunicated him in 1227. To absolve himself he had to set out for the Holy Land from Brindisi in 1228. Sultan Kamil had started negotiations with him even before this to secure his aid against Muʿazzam, the Sultan's brother, in Damascus. When Frederick II landed in Palestine, Muʿazzam had already died and Kamil had handed over Damascus to his brother in addition to his Mesopotamian holdings. Nevertheless, negotiations continued, and, in exchange for a promised guarantee of his Syrian possessions, Kamil surrendered Jerusalem together with Bethlehem and Nazareth and corridors to both Jaffa and Saida (Sidon) before any blows were exchanged. On 18 March 1229, Frederick was crowned as spouse of the ruler of the Holy Land, Isabelle of Brienne, in the Church of the Holy Sepulchre in Jerusalem. But this apparent diplomatic *coup* was approved by neither the Christians nor the Muslims. Indeed, the Pope had an interdiction laid on the city by the patriarch of Jerusalem as long as Frederick remained there.

But Kamil used the peace purchased in Palestine to expand his power in the north at the expense of the Seljuqs of Iconium. This aroused the jealousy of his brother Ashraf in Damascus. Kamil was relieved of this adversary by death, when he appeared before Damascus, but he himself died directly thereafter (1238). Only two years later his son was able, with a force of Khwarizmi Turks who had fled before Chingiz Khan, to reconquer Jerusalem. After the conquest of Jerusalem, Damascus also fell into Salih's hand in 1245, and thus almost the entire empire of Saladin as far as Aleppo and northern Mesopotamia was reunited. In 1248, while lingering in Damascus to arm for a campaign against Yusuf II of Aleppo, he was overtaken by the news of another incursion of the Franks in Egypt. Louis IX, the Saint of France, had landed in Damietta and secured possession of the city, since at the news of Salih's illness the discipline of his army had collapsed. When Salih died on 23 November 1249, his death was concealed by his wife, the former slave-girl Shajar-ad-Durr, until his son al-Malik al-Muʿazzam Turanshah arrived from Mesopotamia. He succeeded in reconquering Damietta, where Louis IX fell captive. To shut this port of entry, so often menaced from the sea, the city was razed and its inhabitants resettled.

The Ayyubid regime meant a period of prosperity for Egypt and Syria even after Saladin's death. The enmity with the Christians did not prevent it from concluding a series of trade agreements with European States. The relationship to the crusading knights, in constant altercation, animosity and peaceful intercourse, also led to many-sided cultural exchanges; together with other chivalric usages the heraldic system of the Ayyubids also seems to have been transplanted to the Occident.[19] At this time the Mongol tempest was overwhelming all the Near East and threatening Egypt with annihilation. In the Battle of ʿAyn Jalut in 1260, the Mongol tide came to a standstill for the first time, to recede slowly thereafter. In Egypt alone, among all the countries of Islam, the even course of cultural development was not interrupted by the Mongol invasion.

Baybars, an extremely able ruler, defended himself against his enemies with extraordinary valour. In Palestine he still had to deal with the Franks, but he managed to wrest one of the most powerful fortresses, Hisn al-Akrad, from the grasp of St John's Knights,

[19] See Yocoub Aetin Pasha, *Contribution à l'étude de blason en Orient* (London, 1902); L. A. Mayer, *Saracenic Heraldry* (Oxford, 1933).

and the city of Safed from the Templars. The Assassins had to cede Masyaf and a series of smaller castles, but he did not entirely dissolve the order. In the north he held the Armenian kings of Asia Minor in check by continually repeated incursions into their territory; in the south he attached Nubia to Egypt as a vassal State. Again and again the Mongols in Iraq were prevented by circumstances in the interior of their Asiatic empire from avenging the first defeat, even though Baybars frequently still had to ward off minor raids into his domain. He was protected against a repetition of the European Crusades by a treaty with the Byzantine Emperor Michael Paleologus, who had freed his empire from the rule of the Frankish knights.

The thirteenth century was one long challenge of Christianity to Islam. The challenge came from the West. We will do well, therefore, to pause for a while and conjure for ourselves a picture of the contemporary Catholic mind, for without this basic material we will not be able to appreciate Rumi's contribution to the Muslim mind in the same period. At the beginning of the thirteenth century the fabric of Christian belief in the West still retained the mould which it had received from the mind of St Augustine. The City of God stood out sharply against the City of man, eternity against time, perfection against sin. The priesthood alone, while performing the miracle of their priestly function, participated in the blessedness of the angels, but as the century advanced, new intellectual and spiritual movements, inspired primarily by the Muslim contact with the West, made themselves felt. Men of very different tempers and intellect began to feel that the sharp contrast of the great African father might not after all be so absolute, that even to fallen man it might be given to reach perfection on earth, that the spririt was more important than rituals and faith, and intellect more than the sacraments or formularies of the Church. Philosophers, travelling by a different route, were reaching conclusions equally perilous to the sacerdotal order. Aristotle, now for the first time fully known through the Arabic translations from Muslim Spain, came closely to be studied in the West, and became the serious concern of the University of Paris – Aristotle, who believed in everlasting time and uncreated mind; and this led to the appearance of eager Aristotelians like Siger of Brabant and his school maintaining such bold propositions as that the human intellect is eternal and the real source of such perfection as is permitted to man. These doctrines, the one of the self-sufficiency of individual faith, the other of the self-sufficiency of the individual intellect, struck hard at the heart of Papal authority and discipline.

One of the greatest exponents of the Catholic mind in the thirteenth century was Dante (1265–1321). He is not the first but certainly the most remarkable man in the long list of apocalyptic writers who attempted to depict the destiny of the soul through the allegory of an imaginary voyage or vision, if we may call it so. We are not concerned here with the literary aspect of the *Divine Comedy* which has it own beauty as it has its own violence, obscenity and grotesqueness; but our major interest lies in a study of Dante's ideas which give us an insight into the contemporary mind. Dante believed that the Roman Empire was the divinely appointed instrument of government on earth. In his opinion this was doubly true because Christ was born in the reign of Augustus. This was the period in which, according to Dante, the world enjoyed unusual peace for the first time. He believed that a universal monarchy is a God-ordained necessity for men and that the Roman Empire was providentially designed to exercise this monarchy, and finally that the Roman Emperor held his title directly from God and was not subject to the Pope. Dante was by temperament an aristocrat, by conviction an imperialist. He idealised the Roman Empire, not the Roman Republic; he idealised law, not liberty. It is significant that neither in the *Commedia* nor in any of his scattered writings is there any sign of sympathy for the poor as a class.

This, then, was the Catholic mind in outline as represented by its greatest exponent in the thirteenth century. We should be able to appreciate the contrast offered by the Muslim mind as we proceed to analyse the work of Rumi who was its greatest exponent in the same period.

II

We have some idea by now of the mind of Christian Europe as also of the manner in which it sought to express itself in the Muslim world of the thirteenth century. The Crusader was not the only foe that the Muslim world had to contend with. There was another one, far more formidable in the immediate effects of its destruction, and that was the Mongol. While the Crusades exercised an indirect, though an important, influence on the spiritual growth of Rumi, the Mongols have a direct bearing on his life. We now move nearer home and see Rumi – not as a distant spectator of the Crusades, but as a living actor in the bloody drama staged by the Mongols. In common with his compatriots, we now see him in the role of suffering humanity. Let us have a look at the stage – the Persian Empire.

At the beginning of the century 'Ala-ud-din Muhammad Khwarizm was the most important king of Persia. The founder of this dynasty, destined for over a hundred years to play the leading role in the history of the Middle East, 'Ala-ud-din was a slave from Ghaznah who served as a cup-bearer to the Saljuq Malikhshah and was appointed by him to the governorship of Khwarizm.[20] 'Ala-ud-din's empire extended from the Ural mountains to the Persian Gulf, from the Indus to the Euphrates, and included nearly the whole of Persia except a couple of provinces. By 1210, he reduced the greater part of Persia, subdued Bukhara and Samarkand. In 1210 he entered Afghanistan and took Ghaznah. He was preparing to end the Abbasid Caliphate when his career of conquest was suddenly cut short by the appearance on his northern borders of the Mongol hordes of Chingiz Khan.[21] Muhammad fled incontinently before this appalling swarm and died in despair on an island of the Caspian Sea in 1220 C.E. His three sons wandered for some time through the provinces of Persia, and one of them, Jalal-ud-din, visited India for two years; but after a decade of stirring adventures he was finally banished by the Mongols in 1231. At one time the rule of Khwarizmshah was almost coterminous with the Saljuq Empire, but this period of widest extent scarcely lasted a dozen years. In normal times this empire might have endured for a century or more but within a score of years we see it tottering. The Khwarizm king, in his eagerness to extend his dominions, annexed country after country. He was happy with the expansion of his empire, but unwittingly he brought about his own downfall. Within six years of his accession to the throne, an unknown Mongol called Temuchin had become so powerful that he was invested with the title of Chingiz Khan.[22]

The arrogation of this title was a challenge to the rulers of Central Asia. 'Ala-ud-din, always slow to understand and quick to act, failed to grasp the

[20] Al-Juwaini, *Ta'rikh-i-Jehan-Gusha*, ed. Mirza Mohammad (Leyden, 1916), Vol. II, p. 3; Ibn-ul-Athir, Vol. X, pp. 182–83.

[21] S. Lane-Poole, *The Mohammadan Dynasties*, p. 176.

[22] Spelt as Zingis, Tchimkis, Jenghis, Tchingnis, Chungaze, etc. *Zin* is said to mean great, and *gis* is the superlative termination.

significance of Temuchin's phenomenal rise. The danger from without did not create the usual unity within: it resulted in more dissensions. Most of the neighbouring Muslim States had been weakened and destroyed by 'Ala-ud-din; he was, therefore, clearly caught in a tightening ring of ill-will. He made no attempt to straighten the circumstances. On the contrary, he quarrelled with the Abbasid Caliph, who retaliated by intriguing against him with the Mongol upstarts.

Probably the Mongol invasion of Persia could not have been averted, but it was certainly facilitated and provoked by the greed, treachery and irresolution of 'Ala-ud-din – by his greed, because he had weakened and destroyed most of his neighbouring Muslim kingdoms, and no Muslim prince was willing to come to his rescue when the hour of danger came; by his treachery, because his alleged murder of Mongol envoys provided Chingiz Khan with a pretext to invade Persia; and by his irresolution, because at the first reverse he passed from arrogant and boastful defiance to extreme panic and indecision.[23]

It is interesting to know the beginning of the quarrel which so completely changed the course of history in Persia. Like Hitler in our own times, Chingiz seems to have planned it well in advance, and it reads like an account of a German 'peace mission' quietly proceeding about its business, when all of a sudden an 'incident' occurs on a frontier, and the Nazi armies move in to seek 'justice'! Chingiz sent to an important frontier town a company of merchants. They were murdered by the provincial governor of Khwarizmshah who pretended to believe they were Mongol spies. Chingiz acted promptly and despatched an embassy consisting of a Turk named Bughra and two Mongols to protest against the violation of the

[23] For a detailed study about the causes of the downfall of the dynasty, see *Tarikh-i-Mufassil Iran* by 'Abbas Iqbal (Tehran), Vol. I, pp. 93–100.

laws of hospitality. The mission demanded immediate recall of the governor concerned, and wanted him to be handed over to them. Khwarizmshah was equally prompt in his reply. He had Bughra killed and sent back the Mongol envoys with their beards completely shaved off. This was adding insult to injury. The Mongol chief was naturally furious. His armies moved to Utrar[24] – the town in which Bughra was killed. The siege lasted six months. The fighting was desperate. The Khwarizm governor, knowing that he was a doomed man, fought to the bitter end. But he fought against heavy odds, and there was no forgiveness when he gave up. Molten silver was poured into his eyes and ears, and the vengeance with which the Mongols fought was not satisfied with the brutal massacre of the guilty town. They continued their march and stormed Bukhara, a town of academies, of men of learning; a town of villas and gardens. After a few days defiance by a garrison, 20,000 strong, the gates of the city were flung open. The city was full of Mongol soldiers who made stables of libraries and litter of the leaves of the Qur'an. They feasted and held high revel. Musicians and singers were summoned, while the nobles of the city were made to groom the horses. The most precious containers of the Qur'an were used as mangers, while the sacred books were flung anywhere on the ground and trodden under foot.[25] According to Juwaini, one man escaped from Bukhara after its capture to Khurasan. Questioned about the fate of the city he replied, 'They came, they sapped, they burnt, they slew, they plundered and they departed.' Men of understanding who heard this description were all agreed that in the Persian language there could be nothing more concise than this speech.[26] The populace was inconsolable; the

[24] Now called Farab.
[25] Michael Prawdin, *The Mongol Empire: Its Rise and Legacy*, p. 168.
[26] J. A. Boyle, *The History of the World Conqueror*, Vol. I, p. 107.

wise men said it was necessary to suffer without murmuring, since it was the wind of God's anger blowing upon them. The great city, which in the morning was one of the most beautiful cities in all Asia, was, on that fatal evening, a heap of cinder and ruin. The seat of arts and science where Avicenna once studied philosophy presented a dreary picture of desolation. Chingiz is reported to have described himself in a speech as 'the scourge of God sent to men as a punishment for their sins.'[27] Ibn-ul-Athir, a contemporary authority, shudders at the narration of these horrors and wishes his mother had not borne him!

From Bukhara, Chingiz followed the fertile valley of Zarafshan to Samarkand which was strongly garrisoned. Here 30,000 artificers were distributed among the Mongols while the rest of the inhabitants were mostly massacred and the city was set on fire. 'Samarkand,' says Abul-Fida,[28] 'where the sky is perpetually clear, has fine stone buildings and public marketing places, and has considerable commerce with Great Tartary, India and Persia, whence all sorts of merchandise are brought; and this city furnishes Hindustan with the best fruit, green and dried. The silk paper made here is the finest in the world. There is a famous academy of sciences.'

All this prosperity vanished with the visit of the Mongols, never to return. But the Mongols desire for destruction was insatiable. They continued their march and next took the capital of the Khwarizmshahs. The Mongol armies, drunk with success, continued their victorious march. Balkh, Nishapur, Herat, Merv – conquest came after conquest; city fell after city. Some offered valiant resistance, others used the better part of valour. No wonder, the Mongols were universally feared as invincible supermen. No wonder, their heads turned and they massacred

[27] Juwaini, op. cit., Vol. I, p. 81. [28] Abul-Fida died in 1331 C.E.

with amazing disregard for human life. In Merv, the city of rose-gardens, half a million men were killed. The famous capital of Sanjar was laid to dust. In a letter written by Yaqut, the eminent contemporary author of the 'Geographical Dictionary', the *Mu'jam-ul-Buldan*, 'he describes in glowing language the rich libraries of Merv, which caused him to forget home, friends, and country, and on the contents of which he browsed "with the avidity of a glutton", and the wonderful prosperity of Khurasan, which, says he, "in a word, and without exaggeration, was a copy of Paradise."'[29] From the smouldering ruins of what was once a most prosperous city, the Mongol hordes passed to Nishapur. The city was carried by assault, the buildings were mercilessly demolished and the inhabitants were brutally massacred. Every town that fell met the same fate. And these cities flourished at a time when European towns north of the Alps were mostly in primitive infancy. The Khwarizm Empire which consisted of the countries now known as Afghanistan, Baluchistan, Persia (except some of the north-west) and Turkistan, was completely overrun. In ten years the Sultanate was levelled to the dust, and the countries composing it so completely devastated that never again have they been their former selves. Juwaini who is certainly not partial to the Khwarizm kings concedes that 'Khwarizm which was the centre of battling men and the venue of banqueting women, on whose threshold fate laid her hand and which the Phoenix of Fortune made its nest, became the abode of the jackal and the haunt of owl and kite.'[30] The illiterate nomad, who for the best part of his life could have no conception of the world, was now on his way to master it. And with his empire 'Ala-ud-din lost his life. Chingiz Khan followed him to the grave in 1227, but with the disappearance of these com-

[29] See E. G. Browne, op. cit., Vol. II, pp. 431, 439.
[30] Boyle, op. cit., Vol. I, p. 128.

batants from the stage, the terrible drama of blood did not come to an end. Jalal-ud-din, the brave son of a cowardly father, did not lose heart even though he had lost an empire. The fugitive prince fought against heavy odds. He fled from place to place for succour; even India could not offer him any help and Altamsh, the slave ruler, politely dismissed him with the remark that Delhi's climate would not suit His Majesty! The fate which was cruel now decided to become ironical, and the great soldier who could not be killed in the battlefield died by the treachery of a Kurdish tribesman. Thus, in 1231 C.E. ended the brilliant career of a most enterprising soldier. Despite his reverses and downfall he has left to fame a name which is honoured and respected. Sir Percy Sykes calls him 'one of the bravest and most enterprising soldiers who ever lived . . . a dazzling meteor, perhaps a prototype of Charles XII of Sweden.'[31]

The well-organised minority of Mongols had triumphed. Never before, neither during the struggle in Mongolia, nor during the campaign in China, had the Mongol army wrought such havoc. Vast cities lay in ruins and were depopulated. Terror prevailed from the sea of Aral to the Persian desert. Only in whispers did the survivors speak of 'the Accursed'. So widespread was the panic that an unsupported Mongolian horseman could come spurring into a village, cut down dozens of persons, and drive off the cattle without anyone daring to raise a hand against him. The populace had lost the capacity for resistance.

The chain of conquests did not stop with the death of the great Mongol. Apart from the ravages of Mesopotamia, Kurdistan, Adharbayjan, Armenia and Georgia, our main interest after his death shifts to the appointment as Governor in Persia, in 1251 C.E., of Hulagu Khan, one of the grandsons of Chingiz Khan.

[31] E. G. Browne, op. cit., *A History of Persia*, Vol. II, p. 90.

Of his character little that is good is known; he appears to have been strongly addicted to pleasure. Had he found a strong foe, it seems probable that his hordes, lacking a leader, would have been beaten. But he was fortunate in having to deal with weak and incapable men; and it is mainly owing to this accident that he became the founder of the Il Khan dynasty in Persia, and is known to posterity as a conqueror who profoundly affected the course of world history. The fact that such a general succeeded in overthrowing Baghdad, the traditional seat of Islamic learning, in a week's time, shows how greatly decadent must have been the Caliphs who ruled it. The dissolution of the Caliphate was due both to external and internal factors, but the latter were more important. The method of administration was not conducive to stability and continuity. Exploitation and over-taxation were recognised policies, not the exception but the rule.

Social and moral forces also contributed to a large degree to this disintegration. 'The blood of the conquering element became in course of centuries diluted with that of the conquered, with a subsequent loss of their dominating position and qualities. With the decay of the Arab national life, Arab stamina and morale broke down. . . . The large harems, made possible by the countless number of eunuchs; the girl and the boy slaves (*ghilman*), who contributed most to the degradation of womanhood and the degeneration of manhood; the unlimited concubines and the numberless half-brothers and half-sisters in the imperial household with their unavoidable jealousies and intrigues; the luxurious scale of high living with the emphasis on wine and song – all these and other similar forces sapped the vitality of family life.'[32]

It is not surprising then that the siege of Baghdad lasted only for a week. It raised a cry of horror

[32] P. K. Hitti, *History of the Arabs*, p. 485.

throughout prostrate Islam. One million of the inhabitants of Baghdad are said to have been massacred, and the loss to civilisation was terribly heavy. The Caliphate which had existed for more than six centuries became extinct at one blow. Muslim civilisation has never recovered from the devastation wrought by the Mongols. Not only were thousands of books utterly destroyed, but owing to the number of men of learning who perished, the very tradition of accurate scholarship and original research, so conspicuous in Arabic literature before this period, was almost liquidated. The Arabic language lost its proud position and gradually declined in importance. The awful nature of the cataclysm which set back progress among Muslim States is difficult to realise and certainly impossible to exaggerate.[33]

Sa'di's elegy on the sack of Baghdad has become a classic in Persian literature. The effect of the picture drawn by the poet is lost in translation but here is a couplet which gives an idea of the horror he has expressed at the terrible scenes he witnessed:

آسمان را حق بود گر خون ببارد بر زمین   بر زوال ملك مستعصم امیر المومنین
ای محمد گر قیامت سر برون آری ز خاك   سر برون آر و قیامت درمیان خلق بین

It is meet that Heaven should rain tears of blood on earth
At the destruction that has befallen
The Empire of Musta'sim, Commander of the Faithful.
O Muhammad! if on the Day of Judgment you will raise your head
above the earth,
Raise your head and see the tribulations of the people now.

With the sack of Baghdad, Hulagu reached the height of his glory. The Mongol kingdom of Persia founded by him extended from the Amu Darya to the borders of Syria and from the Caucasus to the Indian

[33] For details about the effect of the Mongol invasion on Persia, see Abbas Iqbal, op. cit., Vol. I, p. 108.

Ocean. He died in 1265, eight years before Rumi passed away.

The victorious career of the Mongols was checked by the Mamluk princes of Egypt. In September 1260, the Mongols were totally routed. 'The victory of the Egyptians was a turning-point in the world's history. It was the first time that the Mongols had been fairly and completely beaten, and although the defeat was largely due to the smallness of their numbers, it was none the less decisive. It stopped the tide of Mongol aggression, and in saving Egypt saved the last refuge where the arts of the Muslims should have taken shelter, where under the famous Mamluk dynasties, and under the new line of Caliphs, it blossomed over in wonderful luxuriance, and not only made Cairo the cynosure of Eastern cities, but was eventually the means of distributing culture to the Golden Horde, and very largely also to the empire of the Il Khans itself. Besides throwing back the Mongols in their conquering and devastating career, the successful stand of the Egyptians led to the centre of the Muslim life being transferred from Baghdad to Egypt.'[34]

Who were these Mongols that dominated the entire thirteenth century? The word itself, according to Schmidt, is derived from the root *Mong*, meaning brave, daring, bold. Ptolemy places their ancestors in the parallels of 50° and 60°, and longitudes 120° and 140°. They are described as shrewd and valiant people. Juwaini who died in 1284 C.E. says that Chingiz Khan's country was much to the east and north of the desert side of Tartary; that the Mongols were divided into tribes; and that Chingiz's tribe called Niron Caiat was the only one that was civilised. A favourite hero of their early traditions is Kutula Khan, and from his description we may easily learn what manner of men the Mongols deemed their beau ideal of a hero.

[34] H. Howorth, *History of the Mongols*, Vol. III, p. 169.

'Kutula Khan's voice is compared to the thunder in the mountains, his hands were strong like bear's paws and with them he could break a man in two as easily as an arrow may be broken. He would lie naked near an immense brazier in the winter, heedless of the cinders and sparks that fell on his body, and on awakening, would mistake the burns merely for the bites of insects. He ate a sheep a day, and drank immense quantities of kermis (fermented mare's milk). Of such men the type was Chingiz Khan – the Scourge of God.'[35] The character of Mongols as conquerors makes the reader shudder with horror; and it has been aptly said of them that vanquished, they asked for no favour; vanquishing, they showed no compassion![36] The accounts of their campaigns are perhaps the most revolting chapters in history. Absolute contempt for human life; absolute disregard for the most solemn promises – such were the ruling marks of the Mongol in his day of conquest.

The laws of Chingiz Khan were of the Draconian order. Death was the ordinary punishment; torture to extort confessions was common. In his code, I quote Howorth,[37] 'he preserved many curious superstitious notions that the popular creed had sanctified. Thus it was forbidden to make water in a stream or on ashes, to have a table or a chair, to wash the hands in running water. It was forbidden to wash clothes, which were to be used till worn out; cooking and domestic vessels were not to be washed and this custom still prevails! To break these rules was to bring misfortune. In killing an animal it must be laid on its back, an incision made in its belly, and the heart torn out or squeezed with the hand. Those who killed animals in the Muslim way must themselves be killed.'

35 Ibid., Vol. I, pp. 43–44.

36 Letter from Yvo de Narbonne to the Archbishop of Bordeaux, Hakluyt, Vol. I.

37 Howorth, op. cit., Vol. I, p. iii.

No wonder, Muslims were completely stupefied. The historian Ibn-ul-Athir gives some examples of the decrepitude to which they were reduced. A Mongol entered a populous village and proceeded to kill the inhabitants, one after the other, without anyone raising a hand. Another wished to kill a man and having no weapon with him told him to lie down while he went for a sword; with this he returned and killed the man, who in the meantime had not even dared to move! Another officer with twenty-seven men met a Mongol who was insolent, and he ordered them to kill him. They said they were too few for the task, and so he had to kill the man himself, after which all immediately fled. Ibn-ul-Athir, in his preface to his account of the Mongol invasion, of which he was a contemporary witness, remarks that for years he had shrunk from mentioning that event as being too horrible to record. It was, he protested, the greatest calamity that had ever befallen mankind.[38] Juwaini, who was actually in the Mongols' service, could hardly be expected to echo such sentiments. But even he refers at least twice to the condition of hopeless desolation to which Khurasan, his own homeland, had been reduced.[39] He also refers to the disastrous effects upon the pursuit of learning. He talks of Sharaf-ud-din, the son of a porter, as the only scribe being available to accompany Chin-Temur from Khwarizm to Khurasan because no 'reputable scribe' was willing to undertake the journey which was 'intended to lay waste a Muslim country.'[40]

That which appears barbarous and inhuman to us today was part and parcel of the Mongol conception of life. 'What is the greatest happiness in life?' Chingiz asked his generals. One answered for the rest, 'To go a-hunting on a spring morning, mounted on a beauti-

[38] For details see E. G. Browne, op. cit., Vol. II, pp. 427–28.
[39] Boyle, op. cit., Vol. I, p. 75; Vol. II, p. 269.
[40] Ibid., Vol. II, p. 268.

ful horse, carrying on your hand a good falcon and watching it seize its foes.' 'No,' said Chingiz, 'the greatest pleasure is to vanquish your enemies, to chase them before you, to rob them of their wealth, to see those dear to them bathed in tears, to ride their horses, to clasp to your bosom their wives and daughters.'[41] We know of Ogotai, a Mongol chief, directing all the girls of a tribe above seven to be ranged in a row to the number of 4000. He picked out the finest for himself and his officers and sent the rest to the public brothels where they were scrambled for by his soldiers, and this before their fathers, husbands and brothers, and it is said no one murmured.[42]

In Central Asia during the thirteenth century Chingiz established the framework of a militarist state. Every man was fully enrolled. Peace was nothing else than a preparation for war. War and chase were the only handicrafts worthy of a man, and the hunt was simply a training for war. Every man was liable to war service from the age of fifteen to the age of seventy, and he who was not called into the field had to do labour service. The woman's most important obligation was to see that her husband was ready at any moment to change his fur cap for a leather helmet and ride into the field.[43]

At the general diet of Caracorum, where he took the name of Chingiz Khan, he promulgated the Mongol laws. 'By the first Creator of heaven and earth, Who alone gives life and death, riches and poverty, Who grants and denies whatever He pleases, and Who has over all things an absolute power, the enemy is not to be pillaged, till the general has granted leave, under pain of death. The meanest soldier is to share as the officer. Whosoever steals an ox or the value of one is to suffer death; for lesser thefts, from seven to seven

[41] Howorth, op. cit., Vol. I, p. 110.
[42] Kennedy, *History of the Great Mogals*, p. 23.
[43] Michael Prawdin, op. cit., p. 94.

hundred blows, or to pay nine times the things stolen. Adulterers are to suffer death.'

Persia in the thirteenth century was in a completely desolate state – morally, socially and economically. The degenerate Persian who could not withstand the Mongol hordes was now completely in the clutches of servility. We read that whereas in China and Transoxiana, the poorest could pay a gold piece as tribute, in Persia the minimum had to be reduced to one dinar and the maximum to seven. By the end of the century, the economic position in the country was in an absolute confusion. One of the Mongol Il Khans of Persia, Gaykhatu Khan, in his effort to improve the situation, issued unlimited paper money. To keep the paper from being altered, death was threatened to the defacer, his wives and children, besides confiscation of goods. The result is best described in the words of Howorth:

> The first issue of Chao (paper money) took place at Tabriz and it was accompanied by an edict declaring that whoever refused to accept, whoever bought or sold other money than Chao and whoever did not take his coin to the mint to be exchanged for paper money, was to be punished by death. This was shouted in the streets by criers. The fear of punishment caused the order to be obeyed for eight days, but afterwards the shops and markets were deserted. Nothing was to be sought in the city and people began to leave. The famished citizens rushed to the neighbouring gardens to get fruit. The Khan one day traversed the bazaar and, noticing that the shops were empty, enquired the reason why. The Vizier said that a great magistrate was dead, and that it was customary to leave the bazaar on such occasions.[44]

I think it is sufficiently clear by now that Rumi's period was a period of extraordinary turmoil. Seven days of slavery are enough to blot out the best in a man and the slavery of the Mongol was certainly the worst calamity that could ever befall a nation. This period saw the decline of Islam. The sack of Baghdad

[44] Howorth, op. cit., Vol. III, p. 371.

as the metropolis 'struck a fatal blow at the semblance of unity which had hitherto subsisted amongst the Muhammadan nations.'[45] Men of learning fled from place to place seeking a safer corner to pursue their studies. In an era of consistent political stress there can be no personal safety and certainly no social security. Persia was in a desolate state. Her economic condition was deplorable. The whole nation was groaning under the weight of a calamity. It is one of the paradoxes of history that while Persia suffered, Persian literature flourished. Three of the greatest poets of Persian, viz. Sa'di, 'Attar and Rumi, were living at the time of the Mongol invasion.

One cannot help admiring the vitality with which Islam resisted this calamity. It had to contend not only against the Mongols, but also against Christendom. Both threatened its very existence. There was a third insidious enemy within its own bosom which was poisoning its life and that was the notorious Hasan b. Sabbah. 'His disciples, drugged by *hashish*, obtained on awakening a foretaste of the delights he promised them in after-life as the reward for their obedience and unfaltering execution of his orders. Beautiful maidens gathered from every quarter helped in fastening his chains on the neck of his votaries. His emissaries, actuated by varied motives, but all subject to an irresistible driving force, abounded in every city, township and village of Central and Western Asia. Every household contained a concealed member of the dreaded fraternity. . . . The best and noblest of Moslems were struck down by these enemies of society. . . . Both men and women, and even children, were seduced from their faith by alluring hopes of immediate reward from Heaven. To contend against these enemies of Islam it had become essential to galvanise the conservative

[45] Browne, op. cit., Vol. II, p. 443.

forces into fresh vitality.'[46] Ghazali had achieved a similar revitalisation of conservative forces after the Christian onslaught in the eleventh century, and what Ghazali had achieved in the eleventh, Rumi achieved in the thirteenth century.

Earlier we have described at some length the conditions prevailing in Rumi's day; those in Ghazali's time were equally bad, if not worse. People like al-Harrani wrote commentaries on the Holy Qur'an and yet did not scruple to indulge in private drinking and carousals. The place of wine, women and song, not only in popular literature and poetry, but even in the noble talk of theologians and philosophers was in evidence.[47] Al-Baihaqi, the chronicler of the court at Ghazni, tells us that the zeal for the faith was often accompanied by a reckless disregard for the law of Islam as regards the use of fermented liquor. Not only the soldiers and their officers had drunken brawls, but Sultan Mas'ud himself used to enjoy regular bouts in which he frequently saw his fellow topers 'under the table'.

The decrepitude to which Muslim society had fallen can be imagined by the fact that when Chingiz Khan approached the city of Rayy,[48] the Mongols found it divided between two factions – the one composed of Shafi'ites, the other of Hanafites. The former at once entered into secret negotiations undertaking to deliver up the city at night, on condition that the Mongols massacred the members of the other sect. The Mongols, never reluctant to shed blood, gladly accepted the offer and, being admitted into the city, slaughtered both the Hanafites and the Shafi'ites.

It will be seen, therefore, that there was a wide gulf between religious thought and religious activity. Those who took pains to preach Islam took little care

[46] Ameer Ali, *The Spirit of Islam* (Christophers, London, 1923) p. 462.
[47] Zwemmer, *A Moslem Seeker after God*, p. 30.
[48] Rayy is now a suburb of modern Tehran.

to practise it. Belief, which must express itself in corresponding action, found the easier channels of controversy and idle speculation. Thus, faith, wholly divorced from deed, produced the inevitable atmosphere of decay and decadence in which it could no longer breathe the air which was vital for its existence. The faith, which had shot like a meteor and had reached the summit of its glory in a short span of eighty years, was now struggling for survival. The Empire, which had achieved its full maturity in the first century of Islam, was now groaning under the weight of superstition, ignorance, intellectual debauchery and moral cowardice. And this because the Muslims, led by their love for comfort, had abandoned their own faith to the care of the clergy for whom there was no place in the original concept of Islam. Elements of decay were corroding into and destroying the vitals of Muslim society.

It was in this atmosphere of hatred and hypocrisy, feuds and bloodshed that Ghazali lived. He took years to prepare himself to strike at the root cause of this decadence, and when he attacked contemporary theologians, busy with questions of legality, he touched these Pharisees to the quick and they not only squirmed but screamed loudly.

According to Dozy, the Qady of Cordova, Ibn Hamdin, declared that any man who read al-Ghazali's book *The Revival of Religious Sciences* was an infidel ripe for damnation, and he drew up a *fatwa* condemning all copies of the book to the flames. Al-Ghazali's book was accordingly burnt in Cordova and other cities of the Empire, and possession of a copy was interdicted on pain of death and confiscation of property. And all this fury because Ghazali had dared to lead men back from scholastic dogma to a living contact with the Qur'an and the Traditions. He saved Islam from scholastic decrepitude, opened before the orthodox Muslim the possibility of a life hid in God, and yet he was persecuted by Muslims in his lifetime, though they now acknowledge him as the greatest doctor of Islamic religion.'[49]

The impetus which Ghazali gave to emotional Islam lost its force in the life-and-death struggle with the crusading hordes which lasted for nearly two centuries. 'It is not improbable that the force of his example and precept became barren in the cataclysm that overwhelmed Islam not long after his death.'[50] Now it fell to the lot of Rumi to revitalise the decadent Muslim society and the recovery was surprising. Hard pressed between the mounted archers of the wild Mongols in the East and the mailed knights of the crusaders in the West, Islam in the early part of the thirteenth century seemed for ever lost. How different was the picture in the last part of the same century! The last crusader had been driven into the sea. The seventh of the Il Khans, many of whom had been flirting with Christianity, had finally recognised Islam as the State religion – a dazzling victory for the faith of Muhammad.[51] Rumi's contribution to this victory was indeed great. We see him standing out in this period of gloom as a 'sublime mountain-peak; the many other poets before and after him are but foothills in comparison. The influence of his example, his thought and his language is powerfully felt through all the succeeding centuries; every Sufi after him capable of reading Persian has acknowledged his unchallenged leadership.'[52]

III

We have scanned the wide canvas that was Europe in the thirteenth century; we came nearer home and

[49] D. B. Macdonald, *Muslim Theology, Jurisprudence and Constitution-Theory*, 1903.
[50] Ameer Ali, op. cit., p. 468.
[51] Hitti, op. cit., p. 488.
[52] Nicholson, *Rumi: Poet and Mystic*, p. 26.

scanned the Muslim world; nearer still we saw the drama unfold itself on the stage which immediately concerns our subject. And having studied the scene at large let us now shift to the major centre of Rumi's activities for a fleeting glimpse of Konya – a focal point where all the significant developments take place in the life of Rumi. Rumi was a young man of about twenty-two when he came to Konya[53] for the first time and, except for his travels in the pursuit of knowledge, he lived here for the rest of his life. It is well worth pausing for a while, therefore, to have some idea of the town which had such an important role to play in the life of the man whom we seek to understand in this study.

It was this town which gave shelter to Rumi when shelter was not easy to find in a country which was in the grip of chaos. Konya welcomed him with open arms and then saw Rumi being ceremoniously installed as a worthy heir of his great father. It was here that he started delivering the sermons which won him

[53] This note on Konya is based almost entirely on the material so kindly supplied me by Professor Ali Genjeli, formerly of the Istanbul University. The following references have been used:

(*a*) Astrabadi, *Thamrat-ul-Akhbar*, edited by Osman Turam, Ankara (1946).
(*b*) Mukrimin Khalil, *Seljuk, Devri*, Istanbul.
(*c*) Ahmed Ibn Kemal Pasha, *Nigaristan* – Manuscript in the Library of Istanbul University.
(*d*) M. Zia, *Konya, Siyahat Hatiralari*, Istanbul.
(*e*) Auliya Chelebi, *Siyahatnama*, Istanbul.
(*f*) Zainul Abidin Shirwani, *Bustan-ul-Siyaha* – Manuscript with Ali Genjeli, Istanbul.
(*g*) Ali Genjeli, *Konya*.
(*h*) Yaqut Hamavi, *Mu'jam-ul-Buldan,* Vols. III and IV.
(*i*) *Encyclopédie de L'Islam*, Konya.
(*j*) Hamdullah Mustawfi, *Nuzhat-ul-Qulub* – translated by Le Strange.
(*k*) Archives of the Konya Municipality.
(*l*) Guide to the Konya Museum.
(*m*) Shams-ud-din Sami, *Qamus-ul-'Alam*, Konya.
(*n*) C. Huart, *Les Saints des Derwiches,* Tourneurs, Paris, 1918, Vols. I and II.
(*o*) Le Strange, *The Lands of the Eastern Caliphate*, 'Quniah'.

recognition as an eloquent interpreter of orthodox Islam. The king himself sat in the circle of his disciples who listened reverently to his lucid and succinct exposition of some of the most complicated and baffling problems of religion. This phase lasted for a while and then came a stage when Konya saw the Master cast away his mantle, throwing all conventional decorum to the winds. It was in the streets of this town that Rumi moved about, singing and dancing in complete defiance of contemporary morals, and to the complete bewilderment of the people who had learnt to look upon him as the greatest exponent of Islam that was known for ages. It was here that he found and lost Shams-i-Tabriz, and it was here again that he discovered himself. Konya was a venue not only of Rumi's meeting with Shams, but it also saw all that followed it. It saw Rumi writhing in turbulent travail. It anxiously watched him cry in an agony and an anguish that might have set it on fire. With a unique sympathy, Konya followed all the ups and downs, all the ebbs and flows, all the doubts and conflicts of a sublime soul that had so much to give to posterity. It was here that Rumi's personality found its proper contours, it was here that it underwent a sudden and unique metamorphosis and it was here that it started radiating the rays which were later to illuminate the whole Muslim world. Konya it was where the Maulvi wrote the Qur'an in Pahlavi, and it was Konya from where he preached it to the whole world. Though the town did not have the honour of giving birth to him, it had the infinitely greater honour of giving him the spiritual birth and today it claims the proud privilege of having within its bosom the mortal remains of a soul that was truly immortal.

Rumi's was indeed a dominating influence while he lived in Konya. It is no less so as he lies there in peace. It is over seven hundred years since Rumi first came to Konya. The passage of centuries has not diminished the love and affection that the people of this town ever had for him. The high beautiful minarets of his tomb as also those of the surrounding madrassas stand out pre-eminently and serve as a beaconlight in the vast sea of darkness which surrounds it today but has not been able to submerge it.

The town in which Rumi lived, worked and died is no mean habitation. Situated in the north of modern Turkey it was once the capital of the Eastern Empire and was identified as Iconium. The name changed its Greek connotation and became Konya after the Muslim conquest. Everybody in the city will tell you today that he lives in a town of angels, not because Rumi lies buried amidst them but because of the popular belief that in the good old days, when history was still wrapped in the mist of antiquity, two angels flew from the West to the East in search of a suitable habitation. Having cast a glance at the site which is now Konya they seemed to like the place and descended after a brief celestial consultation to found the town. The conversation of the two angels as recorded by popular belief served as a basis for the name which the town carries today. 'Shall we sit down?'[54] asked an angel. 'Do sit down,'[55] came the reply, and the matter was settled in the twinkling of an eye!

The fame of Konya, which was called Iconium in the Byzantine days, is linked indissolubly with the rise of the Saljuqs. One cannot be separated from the other, and it is difficult to have an idea of the city without some knowledge of the men who made it the capital of an empire. In the ninth and tenth centuries, Byzantium was the undisputed queen of European culture. But within the fifty-seven years of feeble government which followed the death of Basil II, the empire suffered serious reverses at the hands of the Saljuqs –

[54] Konya: the word literally means 'sit down'.
[55] Konayim, the word literally means 'sit down' and is used for birds.

a new force which challenged and defeated the Byzantine Empire. 'So swift was their onward march to power that Togrul Beg, their leader, having already conquered Khorasan and Persia, was proclaimed Sultan in Baghdad. . . . The course of Turkish victories so brilliantly inaugurated by Togrul was continued by Alp Arslan, his successor . . . the invaders threw themselves upon the one formidable power which was left in Asia and gained an overwhelming victory. On the field of Manzikert, north of Lak Van, in Armenia, the flower of Byzantine army was mown down by Alp Arslan's horse archers, the Emperor Romanus Diogenes was taken captive, and all Asia Minor was laid prostrate before the Saljuqs.'

'The Byzantines had suffered many defeats . . . but none so serious as the one at Manzikert, for the force of the Empire depended upon its control of those Asiatic provinces which a single battle had now delivered into the hands of the infidels.[56] It was from the Anatolian provinces of Asia Minor that the Emperor had obtained his stoutest soldiers and most brilliant generals, from the Asiatic littoral that he had derived the best part of his fighting marine. Nowhere was the spirit of adventure more lively than on the frontiers of the Asiatic themes, nor a prouder tradition of service than among the great barons of Asia Minor, whose well-armed retainers and large resources, when not employed in mutiny, had constituted a powerful element in imperial defence. All these sources of power were now summarily cut off by the Sultans of Rum, who established themselves first at Nicaea and then at Iconium.'[57]

There was no immediate reply to the tremendous challenge, but ten years later there sat on the Byzantine throne a man who had the 'zeal of the educational reformer, the energy of the general, and the craft of

[56] By 'the infidels' the writer means 'the Saljuqs'.

[57] Fisher, op. cit., Chapter 18, p. 220.

the diplomatist.' Alexius Comnenus, who belonged to one of the great soldier families of Asia Minor, was determined to address himself to the menace presented by the Saljuqs. The whole of Christian Europe united in launching a military enterprise against the 'infidel'. Large bodies of enthusiasts, recruited from North-eastern France, Lorraine and Germany rushed to Constantinople and suffered a terrible penalty for their violent marauding. Decimated during their passage through Bavaria and Hungary, they were annihilated by the Saljuqs soon after they had set foot upon the Asiatic shore. They succeeded, nevertheless, in actually meeting before Constantinople and were able with Greek assistance to capture the Saljuq capital of Nicaea; they accomplished the long and thirsty march through Iconium to Antioch, besieged and took that strongly fortified and famous city; and they ultimately succeeded in capturing Jerusalem itself.

With the capture of Nicaea, Iconium became the capital of the Saljuq Empire and retained this dignity throughout the reign of this dynasty. The first Crusade was indeed a spectacular success. It dispelled the haunting fear of a Saljuq conquest of European Thrace. 'But this advantage was not destined to endure. Three capable Muslim rulers, coming one after another, altered in the course of half a century all the weights and balances of the Near East. Zangi of Mosul conquered Aleppo and Edessa. His son Noureddin made himself master first of Damascus and later of Egypt, and finally, when Noureddin died, his place was taken by Saladin the Kurd, to whose brilliant gift of leadership the whole East between the Tigris and the Nile was in time made submissive.[58]

The Greek Empire had fallen once more, after enjoying a whole century of prestige. Its main army

[58] Ibid., p. 231.

had been defeated with huge losses by the Sultan of Iconium. What remained of the conquest of the first Crusade was a line of Syrian ports which were preserved for another century by the strong interests of Italian commerce. Iconium became once again a flourishing capital of a Saljuq king, who, despite his preoccupation with the third Crusade, found time to add to the beauty of the city which had already started attracting men of letters whose presence in the court of Qilij Arslan II gave a lustre to Konya and which elicited praise from no less a person than the celebrated poet Nizami Ganjavi. The most ancient remains of the Saljuqs to be found in Konya today belong to this period. The peace of Konya was, however, gravely disturbed with the end of Qilij Arslan's reign which was followed by an internecine war between his two sons. The empire was to remain in a sorry state of affairs till the reign of 'Izz-ud-din Kaika'us who not only consolidated it but extended its frontiers to the Black Sea. And then came the peak period of prosperity under 'Ala-ud-din Kaiqubad. According to Hamdullah Mustawfi Qazwini,[59] the annual revenue of Konya at this time was 3,300,000 gold dinars. This large sum fell fifty years later to 135,000 – an eloquent commentary on the havoc wrought by the Mongols.

Being situated on the main trade-route starting from Syria, Iraq and Iran and converging on Constantinople, the centre of the Eastern Empire, Konya enjoyed a variety of advantages over towns which were less fortunately situated. Besides economic affluence, its situation resulted in a rich fusion of cultures, for the caravans brought not only goods that gave material prosperity but also the leaven of new ideas in which Konya itself was later to excel the rich neighbouring civilisations of Syria, Iraq and Iran. Konya had, therefore, a marked economic and cul-

[59] *Nuzhat-ul-Qulub.*

tural status under the Greeks; but it came to assume an added importance with its passage from the hands of the Byzantine Empire to those of the Turks who gave it the status of a capital. Konya remained the centre of the Saljuq Empire throughout the reign of this dynasty, but it was at the height of its glory and prosperity during the lifetime of Rumi, for it was then not only a capital of an empire and an important centre of trade and commerce, but also a dynamic centre of cultural patronage at the hands of 'Ala-ud-din Kaikubad.

The period of 'Ala-ud-din Kaikubad was indeed the golden era of the Saljuq dynasty. But while talking of peace and prosperity in Konya at this time, it will not be amiss to recall that it witnessed, for a whole century, not only many a dynastic feud among the Saljuqs themselves but also the terrible Crusades in which its own kings participated so bravely. Although it had become the capital of the Saljuqs in 1097, Konya did not really experience anything like a continuous spell of peace and prosperity until 1219. This was the year when Bukhara fell to the Mongols, and other famous towns in the neighbouring empire of Persia were tottering before the onrush of the Mongol hordes. Konya's peak period of prosperity paradoxically coincides with the most tragic period in the history of Persia. Within a few years of 'Ala-ud-din's gaining the Saljuq throne, the great cities of Balkh, Bukhara, Samarqand, Nishapur, Herat and Merv were razed to dust by the barbarian hordes of Chingiz Khan who died while 'Ala-ud-din was still on his throne. Konya was, therefore, an island of peace in a vast sea of turbulence. Such a fortunate situation was enough in itself to make it the refuge of suffering humanity in its neighbourhood, but what made it all the more attractive for men of letters was the significant fact that on its throne sat a man who was a great patron of learning. It is no wonder, therefore, that we find the king himself extending a personal invitation to Rumi to settle down in Konya, where his own father lay buried in an estate which had been earlier given him by the Saljuqs. This is exactly the site where we have today not only the museum, but the tomb of Rumi along with the surrounding madrassas.

Rumi's entry into Konya under these circumstances was not the entry of a desperate refugee fleeing about to find shelter and security; it was the return of the son, not in the least prodigal, to the land of his own father, where the entire populace, including the ruler himself, was waiting in eager expectation to receive him back in their midst. His spirit of freedom was far too valuable to be bartered away for personal security, for life itself was of no avail if it could not be dedicated to the service of the *millat*. We know of Najm-ud-din Kubra, a famous contemporary savant, having refused the invitation of Chingiz Khan to move away in safety while he massacred six hundred thousand inhabitants of the Khwarizm metropolis in 1221. Kubra preferred the gallant death of a martyr to the security of a slave. Rumi had in all probability the inspiring example of this savant in mind when he wrote:

O! we are of the noble band who grasp the cup of wine,
Not of the wretched beggar-crew who for lean kids do pine,
Who, with one hand, the wine unmixed of fiery faith do drain,
While, in the other, we grasp the heathen's locks amain.

Rumi's return to Konya, therefore, was indeed the return of a son to his own soil. It was the return of a man who not only belonged to the soil but was also known to and sought after by his compatriots who held him in high esteem for his piety and erudite learning. He received a truly royal reception. The whole populace of Konya went out to accord him an enthusiastic welcome, the king himself being represented by a minister of the court. Fate had decreed that the effulgent lustre of an inspired personality should radiate for centuries from amidst the ruins and remains of the Saljuq Empire. And yet Rumi was not the only man who came to Konya in this period. There were many more, the most distinguished among them being Maulana Sadr-ud-din Qonvi. To such men of learning Konya offered a haven of peace. Prosperous and powerful, it kept the Mongols at an arm's length. The bride that was Konya was jealously guarded by 'Ala-ud-din who raised a high wall with 140 watch-towers and twelve gates round the town to protect it from avaricious eyes. A deep trench was dug further to cover the 4500 metres of this wall. Peace was, therefore, no mean attraction in times when insecurity was the order of the day. Add to it the love for learning and the respect for the learned displayed by 'Ala-ud-din and you have the key to the situation then obtaining in the world of letters. This then was the place where Rumi could address himself freely to the great task assigned to him by Destiny.

Chapter 2

The Period of Preparation

Jalal-ud-din was born in Balkh on 6 Rabi' al-Awwal 604. Some chroniclers call him Khudawandgar,[1] while others refer to him as Maulana Khudawandgar.[2] He is also known as Maulana-i-Rum, perhaps by reason of the country[3] in which he lived. The word *Maulvi* is not used for him by his early chroniclers. In *Walad Nama*, a work by his son Baha Walad, he is invariably referred to as Maulana. Jami and Daulat Shah also refer to him as such. The earliest reference to the word *Maulvi* for him is found in the verse of Shah Qasim Anwar.[4] In

[1] *Manaqib-ul-'Arifin*.

[2] Yusuf b. Ahmad, *Al-Munhij-ul-Qavi li-Tullab-ul-Mathnawi* (Egypt, 1289).

[3] From early times the Persians and other Asiatics applied the name of Rum to the Roman Empire, and, after its division, referred it especially to the Eastern and Byzantine Empire, which, as is known, included the whole of Asia, Armenia, Syria, etc. Rum and the Qaisars of Rum are frequently mentioned in the *Shahnamah*. The Arab geographers continue to use the same name for designating the territories of the Byzantine Empire in Asia and Europe.

When, towards the end of the thirteenth century, the Saljuq Turks established their power in Asia Minor, the Asiatic nations retained the name of Rum for the territories of this monarchy but continued to call the Byzantine Empire likewise Rum. Subsequently, when, towards the end of the thirteenth century, the Saljuq dynasty disappeared and the Ottomans succeeded them in these territories, the name of Rum was transferred to the Ottoman Empire. In the *Zafar-Namah*, Rum is identified with Anatolia. Sharif-ud-din calls Byazi, the Ottoman Emperor whom Timur made prisoner in 1402, Qaisar-i-Rum. See Dr E. Bretschneider, *Medieval Researches from Western Asiatic Sources*, Note 1156.

[4] جان معنیٔ قاسم ار خواهی بخوان مثنویٔ مولویٔ معنوی

these pages, however, we will refer to him simply as Rumi.

Rumi was no obscure person even as a child, for he was the son of a great father who had set up for himself a reputation rivalled by few in his own generation. Rumi's father lived for twenty-four years after his birth and we propose, therefore, to follow Rumi's career while he grew up under his father's care. The first twenty-four years of Rumi, as indeed of any young man, constitute the most formative period of his life, and we will do well, therefore, to begin with a narration and an analysis of the varied influences received and imbibed by him during this period.

Rumi belonged to a family which had settled in Balkh, in the northern Persian province of Khurasan for several generations, and had produced a notable number of jurists and divines. Most of the family's history, which traces its descent from Abu Bakr, the first Caliph of Islam, is to a large extent legendary. Rumi's own works contribute almost nothing by way of historical data, and the Persian chroniclers take more delight in dabbling in the narration of supernatural phenomena attributed to the divines, than in an analysis of historical events. Fortunately, however, we are in possession of some old and relatively reliable sources which enable us to study, in outline, the story of the family in the light of history. We will make no attempt, therefore, to entangle ourselves in the controversy that surrounds the early ancestors of Rumi but will content ourselves with beginning our account with his grandfather, who is definitely a historical personality.

Husain ibn Ahmad Khatibi, the grandfather of Rumi, was a great scholar. The measure of his scholarship can be gauged by the fact that persons like Radi-ud-din Nishapuri came to learn at his feet.[5]

[5] For details about him see *Lubb-ul-Albab* (London), Vol. I, pp. 219–28. Also see *Majma'-ul-Fusaha* (Iran), Vol. I, pp. 231–33.

He was acknowledged as a great spiritual leader not only by divines and men of learning but also by contemporary rulers with whom he is said to have had some intimate blood-relationship. According to Aflaki, 'Ala-ud-din Muhammad, the Khwarizm king, married his daughter, Malika-i-Jahan, to Rumi's grandfather. This relationship has been accepted by Shibli, Rumi's biographer,[6] but it does not seem to be entirely correct. In fact the contradictory evidence supplied by the chroniclers makes it necessary to pause and ponder over this point very carefully. According to Aflaki, Rumi's grandmother was the daughter of 'Ala-ud-din Muhammad, son of Khwarizmshah. Amin Ahmad Razi considers her to be the daughter of 'Ala-ud-din Muhammad, the uncle of Sultan Muhammad Khwarizmshah. Our primary concern is to find out whether it was 'Ala-ud-din Muhammad Khwarizmshah who married his daughter to Rumi's grandfather. Let us examine a few dates before we come to a conclusion. Rumi's father, on his own authority in *Kitab al-Ma'arif*,[7] was fifty-five in the month of Ramadan 600/May 1204. He must have been born, therefore, round about 1148 C.E. and, to infer further, Rumi's grandfather must have married round about 1147, but the father of the girl, i.e. 'Ala-ud-din Muhammad Khwarizmshah, was also born in the same year in which his daughter is supposed to have given birth to Rumi's father! This confusion, however, can be explained. 'Ala-ud-din Muhammad, during his father's lifetime, was known as Prince 'Ala-ud-din. There was another prince of the same name and it is possible that he may have given his daughter in marriage to Rumi's grandfather. Jami and Aflaki have perhaps mixed up the two names.[8] It is clear, nevertheless, that Rumi's

[6] See Shibli, *Swanih Maulana Rum* (India), p. 2.
[7] See *Fihi-ma-Fihi*, p. 247, edited by Farozan Far.
[8] Badi'-uz-Zaman Farozan Far, *Swanih Maulavi* (Tehran), p. 7.

grandfather enjoyed a high social status, coupled with an equally high regard, won as a man of great spiritual eminence.

Rumi's father, Baha-ud-din Muhammad ibn al-Husain al-Khatibi al-Baqri, inherited, in an ample measure, the traditions of his father in the realm of knowledge and spiritual eminence. He was heir both to his material and spiritual wealth. Baha-ud-din, in his own day, was acknowledged as a man of deep learning and bore the title of King of Scholars (*Sultan-ul-'Ulama*). At the time of Rumi's birth in 1207, when Baha-ud-din was fifty-nine years of age,[9] he was at the height of his power and popularity. He was to live another twenty-four years to see his son being brought up in the true traditions of the family. His influence on the development of Rumi's personality is so deep and pervasive that it is necessary to study, even though briefly, the main currents of thought which determined his attitude towards men and matters.

Baha-ud-din was born in or about 1148. Not long before his birth, Imam Ghazali had attacked the entire system of philosophy, which had been built in the East on Greek foundation. Muslims have often said that if there could have been a prophet after Muhammad, Ghazali would have been the man.[10] A detailed study of his career lies beyond the scope of this chapter, yet a mention must be made of him, for he had a tremendous influence on Rumi's father who, as we shall see, influenced to a great degree Rumi's own ideas about life. Our readers must be familiar with the course of Ghazali's life, at least in outline – how, for all his theological training, he was a born critic; how he sought to discover a real basis for

[9] For greater biographical details about Rumi's father see: *(i) Risalah Faridun Sipahsalar* (Tehran), pp. 10–21; *(ii) Manaqib-i-Aflaki*; *(iii) Nafhat-ul-Uns* by Jami; *(iv) Sharh-i-Maulana* by Badi'-uz-Zaman Farozan Far (Tehran), pp. 5–36.

[10] Nicholson, *The Idea of Personality in Sufism* (Cambridge, 1923), p. 38.

knowledge and, finding none, drifted into utter scepticism; how he passed through a crisis in which 'the light of God' entered his heart; how he, then, regained the power to think, and setting forth in search of the truth turned at last to the writings of the Sufis and saw that he was now on the right track; how though he held a professorship at Baghdad, he could not make up his mind to abandon the world until, under the strain of this moral conflict, his health broke down and in despair he took refuge with God, Who made the sacrifice easy to him; how he left Baghdad and lived in retirement for ten years during which time he learned Sufism, not from books, but from actual experience; and how after having resumed his public teaching for a short while he went back to his birth-place, Tus, in Khurasan, where he died on 14 Jumadi al-Thani 505/19 December 1111.

In his negation of metaphysics and the defence of Islam, Ghazali achieved remarkable success. So completely did he silence the metaphysicans that their books, according to De Boer,[11] were burnt by public authorities. This seems to be a colourful exaggeration, but the fact remains that, as a result of Ghazali's crusade against philosophy, public opinion turned against the philosophers; and Ghazali, himself a first-rate philosopher, became a public hero. He came to be known in later times as *Hujjat-ul-Islam* or the Argument of Islam.

Baha-ud-din grew up in this atmosphere of hostility to philosophy. He was the son of a great Sufi and the Sufis, at any rate, have never acknowledged allegiance to Greek philosophy. It is, therefore, not surprising that Baha-ud-din was attracted by Ghazali and to his creed he brought many adherents.[12] He soon became enthusiastic about his new faith and tried to preach it with the zeal of a

[11] *History of Philosophy in Islam* (London, 1903), p. 183.
[12] *Manaqib-ul-'Arifin.*

missionary. By 1208, when Rumi was a child of one, his father was publicly declaiming against the philosophers and rationalists and was pressing for a fresh study of the precepts of Islam. He did not spare even the powerful courtiers who 'maligned him with the king, calling him an intriguer who had designs on the throne. The King Muhammad, the greatest Shah of Khwarizm, sent him the keys of his treasury and made him an offer of sovereignty. Baha answered that he had no concern with earthly greatness . . . and that he would willingly leave the country so as to remove from the king's mind all misgivings on this score.' These misgivings were the result of a conflict between the philosophers and the Sufis at the court of the Khwarizm king. The case of the former was represented by the able philosopher, Fakhr-ud-din Razi, who was both the courtier and the teacher of the king; while the case of the Sufis was represented by Rumi's father who wielded a strong influence on his own generation. The king was an admirer of Razi, but he was no less devoted to the Sufis to whom he often resorted for spiritual peace and comfort. The conflict between the two principles soon assumed serious proportions and became, in fact, a conflict between two personalities. It strained Baha-ud-din's relations not only with Razi but also with the king; and all this happened because Baha-ud-din displayed a fanatical allegiance to Ghazali, who in his own day had inflicted a crushing defeat on philosophy. But where Ghazali succeeded, Baha-ud-din failed. In his failure, however, lay the germs of success that his own son was destined to achieve in a manner which did not fall even to the lot of Ghazali.

The conflict between Baha-ud-din and Fakhr Razi had become so acute and acrimonious that it has often been said that it resulted in Baha's exile from Balkh at the instance of Fakhr Razi. This theory does not, however, stand much scrutiny. While it is true that a systematic thinker would have no sympathy with the ecstatic flights of the Sufis, and Razi, in particular, was so hostile to them that he had Majd-ud-din Baghdadi drowned in the Oxus.[13] This shows how powerful he was in the Court. The king is said to have paid him a visit at his own house. His hatred of the Sufis is proved not only by his treatment of Majd-ud-din Baghdadi but there is another interesting account of the same sentiment in Wassaf's 'History'.[14] It is said that the king was favourably inclined towards the Sufis and used to invoke their help in times of difficulty. The philosopher played a practical joke on the king. He ordered two caretakers of the royal stable to be clad in the Sufi attire, and then surrounded by a host of people who posed as their students and disciples. The king was requested to meet them. He paid them a visit, sat like a humble devotee in their presence and solemnly invoked their help. Later he was acquainted with the real situation by Razi who drove home the point that appearances were deceptive and that even donkey boys went about posing as spiritual leaders!

While his opinion about the Sufis in general was not complimentary, Razi had good grounds to be hostile to Baha who openly ridiculed him and his system. There is a whole chapter in his book *al-Ma'arif* which is full of taunts against Razi.[15] It is true that Razi took strong exception to Baha's public taunts against his person and his system. It is also true that there was not much love lost between the Sufi and the philosopher, but there is little direct evidence to support the conclusion that Razi manipulated Baha's exile. According to Aflaki, the quarrel between the two started in 1208 and Razi was alive to see Baha

[13] *Raudat-ul-Jannat* (Iran), Vol. IV, p. 191.

[14] See *Tarikh-i-Wassaf*, Vol. II – Account of Atabak Sa'd b. Abu Bakr Zangi.

[15] See the quotations from *al-Ma'arif* in Farozan Far, *Sharh-i-Hal-i-Maulavi* (Tehran), p. 11.

quitting Balkh. Baha left Balkh when Rumi was stated to have been a lad of five, and Rumi, it is agreed, was born in 1207. Baha, therefore, must have left Balkh in 1212. According to most biographers he left in 1213. But Razi died in 1209, i.e. four years before the departure of Baha from Balkh. If we take Aflaki's account as correct, the quarrel started in 1208 and Razi died the next year. It is rather difficult to believe, therefore, that Razi succeeded in securing Baha's exile four years after his death. In fact, a critical student of Rumi will do well to look elsewhere for the causes of this migration.

Baha left Balkh in 1213 C.E. By 1206 C.E. Temuchin – an obscure adventurer – had become so powerful that he had assumed the title of Chingiz Khan. With the assumption of this title came that sudden devastating destruction called the Mongol invasion. Afraid of the onslaughts of the Mongol hordes, people looked about for security and shelter. It was not Baha alone; we know at least of one more famous personality who took refuge in Konya. Sa'di quit Shiraz in 1226 C.E.[16] So savage were the Mongols that, in the words of their admirable historian, they 'murdered in cold blood . . . men, women and children; burned down towns and villages, transformed flourishing lands into deserts.'[17]

Baha was, therefore, not very wrong in thinking of discretion as the better part of valour. In any case there is no authentic evidence to prove that he left Balkh on account of his enmity with Razi. Sultan Walad, his own grandson, does not even mention the name of Razi when he talks of Baha's migration in his *Mathnawi*. On the other hand, he attributed it to the bad attitude of the people of Balkh. This is what he says:

[16] See E. G. Browne, *A Literary History of Persia*, Vol. II, p. 526.
[17] D'Ohsson, *Histoire des Mongols*, Vol. I, p. 387.

چونکه از بلخیان بهائی ولد   گشت دلخسته آن شهٔ سرمد
ناگهش از خدا رسید خطاب   کای یگانه شهنشهٔ اقطاب
چون ترا این گروه آزردند   دل پاك ترا ز جا بردند
بدر آ از میان این اعدا   تا فرستمشان عذاب و بلا
کرد از بلخ عزم سوئی حجاز   زانکه شد کارگر درو آن راز
بود در رفتن و رسید خبر   که ازآن راز شد پدید اثر

Since Baha Walad, the Sovereign of the Saints, was grievously offended by the people of Balkh, he suddenly received a Divine message to leave the company of his enemies and to quit Balkh so that God may send His retribution to those who were responsible for annoying His unique saint. Baha Walad, thereupon, set for the Hejaz at this bidding and, as he was on the way, news was received that God's promise had come true (i.e. his retribution had descended on the people of Balkh).

An important point emerges from the last line When did Baha leave Balkh? Most of the chroniclers put the date at 1213. But if we accept this as the year of his migration, it will inevitably mean that he left Balkh seven years before its invasion. But if that were so, his grandson, who really ought to know, would not have made the assertion that he has in the last line quoted above. Moreover, the chroniclers obviously contradict themselves by saying that Baha left Balkh in 1213 and that soon after his departure the wrath of God descended on the city. The fact is that the wrath of God – the Mongol invasion of Balkh – came in 1220 C.E. Again, Rumi is said to have met the famous Sufi poet Farid-ud-din 'Attar in Nishapur. He is alleged to have been six years of age at that time. According to the evidence cited above, Rumi's father must have left Balkh in or about 1220 and Rumi was born in 1207. Therefore, he could not have been less than thirteen when he met 'Attar. It was perhaps because of his comparative ripe age at the time of the meeting that he did not readily forget 'Attar's influence and later quoted a number of stories from him. A later historian[18] suggests that after sitting at the feet of ʿAttar, Rumi became a pupil of Sana'i. The suggestion is evidently preposterous as Sana'i died fifty years before the birth of Rumi.

No historian of Rumi has been able to fix the date of his father's migration from Balkh with any confidence. We have fortunately come across a reference to Rumi's presence in Samarqand at the time of its siege by Khwarizmshah, in a collection of his own speeches *Fihi-ma-Fihi*,[19] where Rumi talks of a beautiful young girl in Samarqand who miraculously escaped the clutches of the enemy because of her implicit faith in God. This evidence is of supreme importance in fixing the date of Baha-ud-din's first migration from Balkh and helps in resolving for good the controversy and confusion which has come to be centred round this point.

The Khwarizm conquest of Samarqand took place in the neighbourhood of the year 1210, according to Ibn-ul-Athir, while Juwaini considers it as having taken place in 1212.[20] Rumi must have been a child of five at that time. Now that we have Rumi's own reference to his stay in Samarqand at the time of its conquest by the Khwarizms, it should be easy not only to fix the date of his father's migration from Balkh but also to fix, with a certain amount of confidence, the reasons leading to it. Fakhr-ud-din Razi, who is popularly known to be the cause of this exile, died on 1 Shawwal 606/29 March 1210, three years before Baha left Balkh. While there is little doubt about his jealousy and ill-will, it does not appear reasonable to consider him to be the immediate and direct cause of this exile

[18] *Raudat-ul-Jannat*, Vol. IV, p. 198. This authority belongs to the latter part of the thirteenth century and naturally carries little weight. It is no surprise, therefore, that he has made this preposterous statement. Other statements of this source about Rumi should be taken with a pinch of salt.

[19] *Fihi-ma-Fihi,* edited by Farozan Far, p. 173.

[20] *Tarikh-i-Jahangusha* (Leyden/London, 1912), Vol. II, p. 125.

which in all probability was due to Baha's loss of favour with the king. It also becomes clear, for the first time, that Baha left Balkh in 1212 and later returned to his native town which he finally abandoned a year before the Mongol invasion of Balkh in 1220. This was the occasion when he quit the town for good after delivering a public address in the presence of the king and the people in the great mosque, where he is said to have foretold the advent of the Mongols to overturn the kingdom, possess the country, destroy Balkh, and drive out the king.

It will be clear by now that Rumi's life was not the life of a normal boy living peacefully under the care of his parents in a settled family. He had to leave his home while he was still a child of five, and as a child he witnessed the terrible and gruesome massacre perpetrated by the Khwarizm king of the poor and innocent people of Samarqand. The memories of this event left an indelible impression on his young mind, for we see him vividly recall some of the events of this period in his later life.[21] As a child, again, he had to undertake a journey back home in circumstances which were by no means conducive to a peaceful development of a child's mind. He was hardly thirteen when he had to leave his home once again, and this time it was a case of long and wearied travels with his father.

Leaving Balkh, in an atmosphere surcharged with deep hatred and intrigues and threatened with a danger which was to prove fatal to the very existence of the town, the party left for Nishapur. One can imagine the anguish and agony which Rumi must have felt in being forced by circumstances to tear himself away from the town which had been the home of his family for many generations. It is not difficult to visualise the wealth of associations and affectionate sentiments which had to be forsaken and buried in the

[21] See *Fihi-ma-Fihi*, edited by Farozan Far, p. 173.

town which contained not only the house of his father but, what is more painful, the graves of his forefathers. The die had been cast and there was no turning back. Rumi moved with his father to Nishapur – the home of Omar Khayyam – where he is said to have met 'Attar, the celebrated Persian poet, who took kindly to the young boy and gave him a copy of his own works. Rumi, as history has recorded, proved himself worthy of this tribute and was not ungrateful to the great Master whose work he was destined later to complete so beautifully.

From Nishapur, Baha went to Baghdad. According to Jami, he was received there by Shaikh Shihab-ud-din Suhrawardy, the well-known Sufi dignitary, and stayed for a couple of days in Madrasa Mustansaria and then left for Mecca on the third day. Aflaki agrees with Jami about the place of his stay but differs in respect of its duration. According to him, in Baghdad, 'the Caliph sent him a present of 3000 sequins, but he declined the gift as being money unlawfully acquired. He also refused to visit the Caliph, but consented to preach in the great mosque after the noon service of worship on the following Friday, the Caliph being present. In his discourse he reproached the Caliph to his face for his evil course of life, and warned him of his approaching slaughter by the Mongols. . . . The Caliph again sent him rich presents in money, horses, and valuables but he refused to accept them. Before Baha-ud-din left Baghdad, intelligence was received there of the siege of Balkh, of its capture and of its entire destruction by the Mongol army.'[22]

Baha left Baghdad in 1220, the year in which Balkh was sacked. Shibli thinks that he stayed for a very long time (implying years) in Baghdad.[23] We have earlier fixed Baha's year of departure from Balkh and from Aflaki's account of his stay in Baghdad quoted

22 *Manaqib-ul-'Arifin* (Trubner series), pp. 4–6.
23 See Shibli, op. cit., p. 5.

above, it appears that he left Baghdad in the same year as he left Balkh. In *Walad Nama* – an account by his own grandson – and *Tadhkira-i-Daulat Shah*, Baha's journey to Baghdad is not mentioned at all. In the face of this evidence it is rather difficult to believe that he stayed there for years. It is quite possible, however, that he stayed there for a couple of days and then left for Mecca. But where did he stay in Baghdad? Both Jami and Aflaki put him in Madrasa Mustansaria. This Madrasa was founded by al-Mustansar Billa, the Abbasid Caliph, in 1212, and was completed in 1224. And Baha-ud-Din was in Baghdad round about the year 1220, four years before the Madrasa was completed.

From Baghdad, Rumi went to Syria with his father, but the details of this journey are not known. After having performed the pilgrimage at Mecca, he went to Arzinjan. The ruler of Arzinjan at that time was Fakhr-ud-din Bahram Shah who was a great patron of learning. It was to him that Nizami Ganjavi dedicated his famous book *Makhzan-ul-Asrar*. From Arzinjan, the party went to Larinda. Here it was that Rumi, having attained to man's estate, being then eighteen years old, was married to a young lady named Gohar Khatun, daughter of Khwaja Lalai Samarqandi. The next year a son was born to Rumi. This son later became the author of *Mathnawi Waladi* from which we have quoted earlier in this chapter. A period of nearly five years of constant travelling ended in Larinda with the marriage of Rumi, and here it was that the family settled down to a life of comparative peace. This peace was to be disturbed, not by any upheaval of a political nature, but by the kind patronage of a king who sat on the Saljuq throne in Konya. It was at the invitation of 'Ala-ud-din Kaiqubad that the family was to move now to settle permanently in the capital of the Saljuq Empire. According to Aflaki, Baha arrived in Konya in 1220, but the same chronicler talks about him in Larinda in 1225. It is known for certain that Baha died in 1231. According to the author of *Mathnawi Waladi*, he died in Konya after two years' stay in that city:

بعد دو سال از قضائی خدا   سر بیالین نهاد او رعنا

We can, therefore, safely conclude that Baha arrived in Konya round about 1229 C.E. Rumi was twenty-two years of age at this time. Two years later his father died, and Rumi succeeded Baha according to the will of his father[24] or according to the desire of Sultan 'Ala-ud-din,[25] or in deference to the wishes of his father's followers.[26] On a young man of twenty-four now fell the mantle of the King of Scholars – at once a great opportunity and a great challenge. It needed a strong hand to hold the torch, and it needed a sure head and a sound heart to keep it aloft and alive. And what, we may ask, were Rumi's credentials to discharge the heavy responsibilities which now fell on his young shoulders?

II

We have followed Rumi's career for the first twenty-four years. It was indeed more of his father's story, for Rumi's role in this period was essentially subservient to that of his father. And yet this was the most important period of his life, as it saw the foundations of his mental make-up being truly laid. It was then for Rumi to build on them as beautifully as he could, but

[24] E. G. Browne, *A Literary History of Persia*, Vol. II, p. 438.
[25] *Tadhkira Haft Iqleem*, see chapter on the poets of Balkh.
[26] Sultan Walad, Rumi's son, says this in his *Mathnawi, Walad Nama*:

تعزیه چون تمام شد پس ازآن   خلق جمع آمدند پیر و جوان
همه کردند رو به فرزندش   که توئی در جمال ما نندش
بعد ازین دست ما و دامن تو   همه بنهاده ایم سوئی تو رو

before we get into the imposing mansion we should acquaint ourselves with the elements of the foundations for, without this, the eye will not be able to appreciate the beauty and grandeur of the edifice.

Rumi was the son of a father renowned for his religious knowledge and respected for his spiritual eminence. He lived in a period which was a period of revolt against the philosophic influences of Greece. The age of Baha was indeed the age of Ghazali – a protagonist of an intensely personal and passionate religion designed to lead men back from mere scholastic dogma to a living contact with the Qur'an and the Traditions. Rumi was thus born in a family and a society which was clearly hostile to philosophy. The atmosphere in his own house was one of scholarship and spiritualism. His father was a mystic of no mean order and he was to suffer many a personal discomfort for the sake of the principles which he boldly espoused and sincerely followed. It was in this atmosphere that Rumi had his first lesson in defiance of authority and in defence of principles without which the divine status of man would sink to the level of an animal. It is in this atmosphere that he learnt to place a premium on his trust in God against all the heavy odds that the ingenuity of man could devise; it is in this atmosphere that he learnt the value of devotion to duty in the face of all obstacles erected by human tyranny and social persecution. Rumi's father was an old man of nearly sixty at the time of Rumi's birth. He was keenly devoted to his son and was sincerely anxious to impart to him the best education that he could.

As a child Rumi was quick, intelligent and full of curiosity. In fact, the Persian chronicles start attributing spiritual powers to him during his very childhood. We have a story told of him at the age of six when, in response to a request from his playmates to jump to a neighbouring terrace, Rumi is reported to have replied, 'My brethren, to jump from terrace to terrace is an act well adapted for cats, dogs and the like to perform; come now, if you feel disposed, let us spring up to the firmament, and visit the regions of God's realm.' These sentiments are, perhaps, far too sublime to be put in the mouth of a child; it may well be an exaggeration due to an overdeveloped sense of devotion, but the fact remains that Rumi was a sophisticated child of extraordinary promise. His education like that of all other children of his age, started at home. He had the added advantage, however, of an atmosphere of dynamic mysticism. Besides imperceptibly imbibing this influence, the boy devoted himself to a study of what was an established syllabus of that time. The study of the Qur'an, as we know from contemporary sources, was invariably followed by that of the Traditions, of which the standard collections were already in circulation. A youth in Rumi's day would begin with the study of *Fiqh* and his first lesson would be on ceremonial purity by the use of ablution, the bath, the tooth-pick and the various circumstances of legal defilement when complete ablution is prescribed; of ailments of women and the duration of pregnancy. Then came the second part of the book on prayers, its occasions, conditions and requirements. He would learn all about *Zakat*, about fasting and pilgrimage, about the law of barter and sale and debt, about inheritance and wills – a most difficult and complicated subject. Then the pupil would pass on to marriage and divorce, a very large chapter. Then would follow the laws in regard to crime and violence, *Jihad* and the ritual of sacrifice at the Great Feast. The last three chapters of books on Jurisprudence generally dealt with oaths, evidence and the treatment of slaves. The studies included not only religious sciences but also a thorough knowledge of Arabic and Persian. The philosophical sciences taught during this period included mathematics, logic, physics, metaphysics, politics and moral philosophy.

It is known that Rumi's father had appointed for his son his own trusted and able disciple, Burhan-ud-din Muhaqqiq Tirmidhi, as a tutor charged with the responsibility of Rumi's education. He had become a devoted disciple of Rumi's father in Balkh and was assigned this task before their migration from Balkh. His selection as Rumi's tutor is indicative of the high regard in which he was held by Baha-ud-din. Rumi learnt at his feet with the love and loyalty characteristic of the best traditions of his age. By the time he was twenty-four, he had not only successfully completed the curriculum of studies prescribed for a man of his age but had achieved much more in the sphere of learning, for he was fortunate in having exclusively to himself a tutor who was both competent and devoted.[27] Rumi freely acknowledged his debt to him. Not only that. He symbolised his gratitude by placing his own son under the care of Burhan-ud-din, who was thus a tutor not only to Rumi but also to his son who later became the author of the celebrated *Walad Nama*, and proudly declared that he owed his learning and style to Burhan-ud-din: 'this content and this unique style is but the gift of Burhan-ud-din.'[28]

At the time of Rumi's succession to his father at the age of twenty-four, Burhan-ud-din was not present in Konya. In fact, he arrived there a year after the death of Rumi's father, unaware of the fact that the Master

[27] Of his own works — *Ma'arif-i-Burhan Muhaqqiq* – a book in chaste Persian dealing with miscellaneous problems of mysticism and a commentary on the Qur'an, is available in manuscript in Kitabkhana-i-Salim Agha in Istanbul. A photographic copy of the manuscript is available with Prof. Farozan Far of Tehran. For biographical details about him, see: *(i) Walad Nama, a Mathnawi* by Rumi's son (Tehran), pp. 193–97; *(ii) Risala Faridun Sipahsalar* (Tehran), pp. 119–22; *(iii) Sharh-i-Hal-i-Maulavi* by Farozan Far (Tehran), pp. 38–41.

[28] این معانی واین غریب بیان   دان بـرهان دین محقق زان

had passed away. Rumi's son has beautifully portrayed the state of his mind when the sad news was broken to him:

مدتی چون بماند در هجران طالب شیخ خویش شد برهان
گشت بسیار و اندر آخر کار داد با وی خبر یکی مختار
گفت شیخت بدان که در روم است نیست پنهان به جمله معلوم است
این طرف عزم کرد آن طالب عشق شیخش چو شد بر او غالب
چونکه شادان بقونیه برسید شیخ خود را ز شهر بان پرسید
همه گفتند آنکه میجوئی هر طرف بهر او همی پوئی
هست سالی که رفت از دنیا رخت را برده باز در عقبی

Having suffered the pangs of separation for a long time, Burhan now longed for the company of his Shaikh.
He searched a good deal and, at last, news was given to him by an (accredited) friend:
That the Shaikh was in Rum, and (the fact) was known to everyone.
He, therefore, made for Rum. . . .
When he reached his destination (Konya) in all happiness, he inquired after his Shaikh from the guardian of the city.
He was told that the object of his quest had passed away from this world about a year ago.

Burhan-ud-din, having lost his teacher, now turned to his pupil who had by this time ascended the *gaddi* of his father and was already directing the spiritual life of thousands of his followers. On arrival in Konya the tutor found his ward thoroughly well-equipped with the material knowledge which was a hundred times better than his father's, as he put it. The teacher now proceeded to bequeath his pupil with the spiritual treasure which he had inherited from his Master who was none else than Rumi's own father. The pupil surrendered himself completely to the teacher who was to take nearly nine years in completing this process. It was a process of complete surrender and unqualified devotion; it was a process of painful and persistent pursuit of knowledge; it was a process which at once inflicted death and revived life, a paradox which is possible only in the field of mysticism. In the words of Rumi's own son:

> He sincerely became his devotee and surrendered himself completely.
> He fell down before him like a corpse.
> When he died he was eternally revived,
> His grief now laughed to scorn the pleasure of the two worlds.[29]

It is this period of intensive training lasting nearly nine years[30] which Rumi later recalls in terms glowing with a sincere tribute to his teacher.

پخته گرد و از تغیر دور شو　　رو چو برهان محقق نور شو
چون زخودرستی همه برهان شدی　　چونکه گفتی بنده ام سلطان شدی

> Be mature and transcend all change,
> And become the light incarnate like Burhan Muhaqqiq.
> When you escape from yourself you become Burhan,
> When you say, 'I am a slave,' you become a king.

It will be clear by now that though Rumi formally succeeded his father at the age of twenty-four, he did not really step into his shoes till he was thirty-four. A further study of nearly ten years was necessary before Rumi could claim the proud privilege of being a true successor to his father who had the undisputed distinction of being the King of Scholars in his own age. It was no mean task to live up to this reputation and Burhan-ud-din, the tutor of Rumi, was determined to ensure that the succession of this pupil to his Master took place both in form and in effect, and that Rumi did not live simply on the laurels of his father. It

[29] شد مریدش ز جان و سر بنهاد　　همچو مرده به پیش او افتاد
پیش او چون بمرد زندش کرد　　گریه اش بر دو کون خندش کرد

[30] *Nafhat-ul-Uns*, *Haft Iqleem* and *Manaqib-i-Aflaki* are all supported by this line from *Walad Nama*:

بود در خدمتش بهم نه سال　　تا که شد مثل او به قال و بحال

was this consideration which took Rumi to Halab where he joined Madrasa-i-Halivia for pursuing further studies.

Halab and Damascus were the most important centres of Islamic learning in the thirteenth century. Both these places managed to remain immune from the onslaughts of the Mongols and, therefore, became a welcome refuge for scholars who flocked there and made them richer. Madrasa-i-Halivia, which Rumi joined first, was a flourishing Hanafi institution. Like any other Madrasa of the period, the professors and students lived on the income from the property attached to the institution. The person who had dedicated it to the Madrasa had made a provision that 3000 dinars should be given to the teachers in the month of Ramadan so that they might entertain religious scholars to a feast of sweets (*halwa*). This peculiar condition precisely explains the name of the institution.[31] When Rumi joined it, Kamal-ud-din ibn-ul-ʿAdim was the principal of the Madrasa. He had a reputation as a great scholar and poet. Aflaki calls him the 'scholar of the age, the mystic with an illuminated conscience'. Rumi was a student of extraordinary ability and, no wonder, he became a favourite of Kamal-ud-din. Any teacher would pay attention to a brilliant student and Rumi had the added advantage of being the son of a father who was universally respected as the King of Scholars. We have mentioned earlier that Halivia was a Hanafi institution. Kamal-ud-din himself was a Hanafi and there is ample evidence to prove that Rumi learnt most of his jurisprudence and religion at his feet.

The duration of Rumi's stay in Halab is not known. Aflaki – our only source about this journey – himself does not seem to know his mind. He thinks that Rumi left Halab in order to avoid publicity which was thrust on him by the populace. Again he contradicts him-

[31] For details see Kamil b. Husain, *Tarikh-i-Halab*, Vol. II, pp. 216–37.

self by saying that the ruling prince of Rum – 'Izz-ud-din – sent for him through a special messenger. But this is evidently belying history, for by the time 'Izz-ud-din came to the throne (1247) Rumi had already established himself in Konya as a famous professor and jurist.

It appears that after completing his education in Halab, Rumi went to Damascus where he presumably stayed for four years. Some chroniclers suggest seven, but this is improbable because he left Konya in about 1233, and he was present there at the death-bed of his teacher, Burhan-ud-din Muhaqqiq Tirmidhi, in 1241. Thus, in all he spent seven years both in Damascus and Halab.

Rumi's debt to Halab was great, for it was there that he came into contact with a scholar like Kamal-ud-din. But his debt to Damascus was greater, for it was there that he is said to have met Shams-i-Tabriz for the first time. Damascus occupies an important place in Rumi's life – one comes across numerous verses and *ghazals* in praise of this place in his works, and it was here that he later sent his son for education.

After spending seven years of his life in Syria, Rumi returned to Konya. On his arrival there he was received by the nobility. With them he entered the town where his father had died. Shams-ud-din Isfahani, the minister of the ruling Kaika'us, offered him his palace, but he politely declined on the plea that it was against his father's tradition to stay in a place other than the Madrasa in which he had taught.

Rumi now entrusted himself completely to Burhan-ud-din Muhaqqiq who is said to have directed him to undertake a course of mortification and ascetic practices for 120 days. The course was successful and the Master was happy that his ward had attained purity. He offered his gratitude to God, embraced Rumi in happiness and kissed him on his face. Addressing him he said, 'You were unparalleled in the world in rational, traditional, spiritual and acquisitive knowledge, and now this moment you are unsurpassed in the knowledge of divine secrets.' He then directed Rumi to start his mission of assisting and leading those who had gone astray.[32] Thus, Rumi became a full-fledged successor to his father.

At thirty-four Rumi was an acknowledged leader of men. His life was the life of a learned orthodox professor addressing vast audiences on religion, philosophy, jurisprudence and morals. He lived simply, studied deeply and lectured eloquently. His circle of disciples was already becoming unwieldy. Says his biographer son:

ده هزارش مرید بیش شدند　　گرچه اول ز صدق دور بدند
وعظ گفتی ز جود بر منبر　　گرم و گیرا چو وعظ پیغمبر

The number of his disciples grew to more than ten thousands, although in the first instance they were far from sincere (and devoted). He addressed (them) from the pulpit selflessly with feeling and eloquence, and his sermon was like the sermon of the Prophet himself.

Rumi had already won a name for himself, but he had yet to be the poet who wrote 'the Qur'an in Pahlavi'.

III

Let us now scan the intellectual horizon of Rumi who, at thirty-four, was an acknowledged leader of thought. Let us follow some of the main currents which shaped the mind of a man who was to exert a powerful influence on the Muslim world for centuries to come.

The first and by far the most powerful influence

[32] Farozan Far, *Sharh-i-Hal-i-Maulavi*, p. 48.

imbibed by Rumi during this period came from his own father. That Rumi accepted, in outline, the philosophy of life preached by Baha-ud-din, is clear even to the most casual student of his works. What surprises one, however, is the overwhelming impression of similarity that one forms after a cursory comparative study of his father's work, *Kitab-ul-Ma'arif*, and the *Mathnawi*. It appears a case of appalling plagiarism! In fact, so deep was the influence of his father on him that he had to be expressly forbidden to read his works during the period of Rumi's communion with Shams-i-Tabriz who dissuaded him equally strongly from reading the works of the Arab poet al-Mutanabbi, to whom Rumi was much attached.[33] We give below a few quotations from *Kitab-ul-Ma'arif* and the *Mathnawi* to bring out Rumi's debt to his father.

Rumi	*Baha-ud-Din*
۱ـ هیچ عاشق خود نباشد وصل جو	۱ـ اکنون چون تو خود را رغبتی
که نه معشوقش بود جویای او	دیدی به الله و صفات الله می
لیك عشق عاشقان تن زه کند	دان که آن تقاضای الله است و
عشق معشوقان خوش و فربه کند	اگر میلت بهشت است و در طلب
چون در این دل برق نور دوست جست	بهشتی آن میل بهشت است که
اندر آن دل دوستی میدان که هست	ترا طلب میکند و اگر ترا میل
در دل تو مهر حق چون شد دو تو	بآدمیت آن آدمی نیز ترا طلب
هست حق را بی گمانی مهر تو	میکند که هر گز از یك دست
هیچ بانگ کف زدن آید بدر	بانگ نیاید۔
از یکی دست تو بی دست دگر	
۲ـ چون ستاره سیر بر گردون کنی	۲ـ اخر تو از عالم غیب و از
بلکه بی گردون سفر بی چون کنی	آنسوی پرده بدینسوی پرده

[33] See *Fihi-ma-Fihi*, edited by Farozan Far, pp. 245–46.

Rumi	*Baha-ud-Din*
آنچنان گر نیست در هست آمدی هین بگو چون آمدی مست آمدی راههائی آمدن یادت نماند لیك رمزی با تو می خواهیم خواند	آمدی و بدانستی که چگونه آمدی و باز چو از این پرده بدانسوی پرده روی چه دانی که چگونه روی -
۳-اگر تو یار نداری چرا طلب نکنی و گر بیار رسیدی چرا طرب نکنی بکاهلی بنشینی که این عجب کارست عجب توئی که هوائی چنین عجب نکنی	۳- اگر راهی ندیده‌ئی جد کن تا راهی بینی و اگر دیدی توقف چه میکنی و چه اندیشهٔ غم میخوری -
۴-اندك اندك آب را دزدد هوا و اینچنین دزدد هم احمق از شما	۴-اکنون ای خواجه یقین حاصل کن در راه دین و آن مایه خود را نگهدار از دزدان و همنشینان که هم راحت ترا بدزدند همچنانکه هوا آب را بدزدد -

It is through his father that Rumi inherited, to a large degree, his passionate hostility to philosophy. We have had an occasion to dwell at some length on the fanatical allegiance of Rumi's father to Imam Ghazali. The echoes of Ghazali in Rumi's works can be directly traced to the influence of his father. At several places in the *Mathnawi* we see him arguing with the Mu'tazila, the philosophers and the atheists with arguments that might have been employed by Ghazali or Baha-ud-din, his father himself. It appears that such topics were often discussed in the assemblies of the learned and Rumi's lectures are replete with such discussions.[34]

Even a casual student of the *Mathnawi* and *Ihya*

[34] See *Fihi-ma-Fihi*, edited by Abd-ul-Majid Daryabadi, pp. 50, 63, 65, 79, 114, 145, 201 and 204.

'Ulum will find a striking resemblance between Rumi and Ghazali. Both come to the same conclusion though their methods are essentially different. The resemblance in fact is too overwhelming to need a detailed comparison. Apart from their ideas, one finds a striking resemblance in their lives. Both were educated in an atmosphere of mysticism, and we know from the contents of works taught in schools and universities during their time that the syllabus of studies, both in the age of Ghazali and Rumi, was almost identical. Both must have studied, therefore, from almost identical sources, and it can be safely presumed that their lives as students were not very dissimilar. And, what is even more remarkable, both embarked on their independent careers as teachers. Both gave *fatwas*, or legal opinions, on matters of law; both preached in the mosque and both were makers of men and ideas. Then came in both of them a great change resulting in temporary retirement from active life, and, in both cases, the abandonment of the academic honour held by the great teachers was unintelligible to the theologians of the day who regarded it as a great loss and a calamity for Islam. Both, however, emerged from their seclusion as greater men – protagonists of an intensely personal and passionate religion destined to lead men back from mere scholastic dogma to a living contact with the Qur'an and the Traditions as the best source of Islam.

Both Ghazali and Rumi were essentially mystics, but their mysticism was always accompanied by an orthodox insistence on the five articles of faith and the five pillars of practice. Their mysticism led them to emphasise the spiritual side of worship. The mere form is nothing in itself. The author of the *Mathnawi* seems to have mastered Ghazali and captured his spirit when he wrote:

Fools laud and magnify the mosque,
While they strive to oppress holy men of heart;
But the former is mere form, the latter, spirit and truth.
The only true mosque is that in the heart of saints
Is the place of worship of all, for God dwells there.

What Rumi says about the imitation of God is not dissimilar from Ghazali's description of God's attributes:

God calls Himself 'Seeing' to the end that
His eye may every moment scare you from sinning.
God calls Himself 'Hearing' to the end that
You may close your lips against foul discourse.
God calls Himself 'Knowing' to the end that
You may be afraid to plot evil.
These names are not mere accidental names of God.
As a negro may be called *kafur* (camphor);
They are names derived from God's essential attributes,
Not mere vain titles of the First Cause.

Let us now turn over the first few pages of the *Mathnawi* for a casual comparison with Ghazali. We come across Rumi's views on music:

همچو نی زهری و تریاقی که دید　　همچو نی دمساز ومشتاقی که دید
نی حدیث راه پر خون می کند　　قصه هائی عشق مجنون می کند

The *sama'* has been explained philosophically as a representation of the planets which love-desire impels to circle round the First Mover. Rumi and Ghazali could not have been unaware of the well-known Pythagorean conception of 'the music of the spheres' which assumes that the courses of the heavenly bodies and the distances between them are determined according to the laws and relations of musical harmony. According to Pythagoras, sounds are accidents produced in substances by the movement and permeation of the soul. Since the celestial spheres revolve and the planets and stars are moved, it follows that they must have musical notes and expression with which God is glorified and magnified, delighting the souls of the angels, just as in the corporeal world our souls listen with delight to melodies and obtain relief from care and sorrow. Rumi is certainly aware of this theory, for he says:

بس حکیمان گفته اند این لحنها   از دوار چرخ بگرفتیم ما
بانگ گردشهای چرخست این که خلق   می سرایندش بطنبور و بحلق

* * *

پس غذای عاشقان آمد سماع   که درو باشد خیال اجتماع
قوتی گیرد خیالات ضمیر   بلك صورت گردد از بانگ و صفیر
آتش عشق از نواها گشت تیز   آنچنانك آتش آن جوزریز

Hence philosophers have said that we received these harmonies from the revolution of the (celestial) sphere,
(And that) this (melody) which people sing with pandore and throat is the sound of the revolutions of the sphere; . . .

* * *

Therefore *sama'* (music) is the food of lovers (of God), since therein is the phantasy of composure (tranquillity of mind).
From (hearing) sounds and pipings the mental phantasies gather a (great) strength; nay, they become forms (in the imagination).
The fire of love is made keen (inflamed) by melodies, just as the fire (ardour) of the man who dropped walnuts (into the water).[35]

About music, an important element in the life of a mystic, Rumi explains:

رقص و جولان بر سر میدان کنند   رقص اندرِ خون خود مردان کنند
چون رهند از دست خود دستی زنند   چون جهنداَز نقصِ خود رقصی کنند
مطر بانشان از درون دف می زنند   بحر ها در شورِ شان کف می زنند

(Holy) men dance and wheel on the (spiritual) battle-field: they dance in their own blood.

[35] Book IV, lines 733–34 and 742–44.

When they are freed from the hand (dominion) of self, they clap a hand; when they escape from their own imperfection, they make a dance.
From within them musicians strike the tambourine; at their ecstasy the seas burst into foam.[36]

Ihya 'Ulum is written in concise prose but much the same views are expressed there in great detail.[37] And look at this passage from *Alchemy of Happiness*: 'The heart of men has been so constituted by the Almighty that, like a flint, it contains a hidden fire which is evolved by music and harmony, and renders man beside himself with ecstasy. These harmonies are echoes of that higher world of beauty which we call the world of spirits; they remind man of his relationship to that world, and produce in him an emotion so deep and strange that he himself is powerless to explain it. The effect of music and dancing is deeper in proportion as the natures on which they act are simple and prone to emotion; they fan into a flame whatever love is already dormant in the heart, whether it be earthly and sensual, or divine and spiritual.'[38]

Again on page 9 of the *Mathnawi*,[39] we see this line:

آفتاب آمد دلیل آفتاب   گر دلیلت باید از وی رو متاب

Compare this with Ghazali:[40]

عرفت ربی بربی و لولا ربی لما عرفت ربی

Of love Rumi says:[41]

[36] Book III, verses 96–98.
[37] Vol. II (Egypt), pp. 183–210.
[38] Ghazali, *The Alchemy of Happiness*, tr. Claud Field (Lahore, n.d.), p. 73.
[39] Vol. I, line 116.
[40] *Ihya*, Vol. IV, p. 182.
[41] Vol. I, line 205.

عشق هائی کز پی رنگی بود   عشق نبود عاقبت ننگی بود

Ghazali endorses his view emphatically.[42]
Again Rumi talks of the meaning of this world:[43]

این جهان زندان و ما زندانیان   حضره کن زندان و خود را وا رهان
چیست دنیا از خدا غافل بدن   نی قماش و نقره و میزان و زن

Ghazali seems to have expressed similar views, though it is difficult to say that Rumi did not arrive at these conclusions after going through a personal ordeal like Ghazali.

Given the necessary leisure, the curious reader will find much scope for comparison between Rumi and Ghazali.[44]

In Book I of the *Mathnawi*, for example, Rumi narrates an interesting story of contention between the Greeks and the Chinese in the art of painting. This allegory, illustrating the difference between formal theology and mysticism, is related earlier by Ghazali in *Ihya 'Ulum.*[45] Considering how often parables used in this chapter of *Ihya* appear in Book I of the *Mathnawi*,[46] it is highly probable that Ghazali is the source. Nicholson pertinently points out 'that while in both the older versions of the Story it is the Chinese who polish a wall in order that the pictures painted by the artists of Rum may be reflected on the sheeny surface, Jalal-ud-din represents the painting as being done by the Chinese and the polishing by the Rumis. His reason for making the change is evident. Since the polishers typify Sufi saints and mystical adepts, a Rumi in a poem addressed to Rumis could not fail to reverse the traditional roles; and of course the reversal is artistically right. The first readers of

[42] *Ihya*, Vol. IV, p. 258.
[43] Vol. I, p. 8.
[44] Vol. III, p. 161, and also pp. 17, 76 and 227 of Vol. IV of the *Mathnawi*.
[45] Chapter III, on the wonders of the heart, pp. 18 *sqq*.
[46] See verses 308, 310, 2710, 2821, 3635, etc.

the *Mathnawi* must have enjoyed the triumph of Rum as much as they would have resented the tactlessness of the poet if he had told them the Story just as he had received it.'[47]

The analogy of light and colour is a favourite theme with Rumi:

> How wilt thou see red and green and russet, unless, before (seeing) these three (colours) thou see the light?
> But since thy mind was lost (absorbed) in (perception of) the colour, those colours became to thee a veil from (debarred thee from contemplating) the light.
> Inasmuch as at night those colours were hidden, thou sawest that thy vision of the colour was (derived) from the light.
> There is no vision of colour without the external light: even so it is with the colour of inward phantasy.[48]

And now read the following passage from *Mishkat-ul-Anwar* of Ghazali:

> They have asserted that light is a meaningless term, and that there is nothing but colour with the colours. Thus they denied the existence of light, although it was the most manifest of all things . . . for it is the thing that is itself visible and makes visible. . . . But when the sun sank . . . they confessed that light is a form that lies behind all colour and is apprehended with colour, insomuch that, so to speak, through its intense union with the colours it is not apprehended, and through its intense obviousness it it invisible. And it may be that this very intensity is the direct cause of its invisibility, for things that go beyond one extreme pass over to the opposite extreme.[49]

Rumi says that the 'light of the heart (*nur-i-dil*), which is reason, illumines the light of the eye, i.e. the sense of sight, and thereby enables it to discern the real quality of the objects which it perceives; hence it may be said that "the light of the eye is produced by the light of hearts". Since animals possess only the

[47] R. A. Nicholson, *The Mathnawi of Jalalu'ddin Rumi*, Books I and II, Commentary, pp. 202–03.

[48] Book I, lines 1121–24.

[49] Translated by Gairdner, p. 66; quoted by R. A. Nicholson, *Mathnawi of Jalalu'ddin Rumi*, Books I and II (Commentary), p. 90.

former, they lack the power of induction common to all rational men and blindly follow their instincts. Both these "lights" have their source in the transcendent Light of God, though neither physical sense nor carnal reason is in immediate contact with it. The heart of the mystic, however, receives illumination without any "veil", so that he sees by the light of Pure Reason itself.'[50] This passage should be compared with *Mishkat,*[51] and the similarity would be found striking.

Rumi argues that until we know what a thing is not we do not know what it is.[52] The appearance of evil is necessary for the manifestation of good. This argument recurs frequently in the *Mathnawi.*[53] Ghazali uses the same argument in *Mishkat.* He says that 'the most manifest way to the knowledge of things is by their contraries,' and that God is hidden because He has none.[54]

In Book II of the *Mathnawi,* we come across the story of a Police Inspector who summoned a man who had fallen dead-drunk on the ground to go to prison.[55] The dialogue between the two brings to mind a familiar passage in the *Munqidh* of Ghazali:[56]

It became clear to me that what is most peculiar to them (the Sufis) cannot be learned, but can only be reached by immediate experience and ecstasy and inward transformation. How great is the difference between knowing the definition, causes, and conditions of drunkenness and actually being drunk! The drunken man knows nothing about the definition and theory of drunkenness, but he is drunk; while the sober man, knowing the definition and the principles of drunkenness, is not drunk at all.

[50] Nicholson, *Mathnawi,* Books I and II (Commentary), p. 90.

[51] Translated by Gairdner, pp. 45–48 and 66–68.

[52] *Mathnawi,* Book I, line 1130.

[53] See, e.g., Book II, lines 2927 *sqq.*; Book V, lines 574 *sqq.*; Book VI, lines 1747 *sqq.*

[54] Translation, p. 67, quoted by Nicholson, *Mathnawi,* Books I and II (Commentary), p. 91.

[55] Lines 2387–2391 *sqq.*

[56] Cairo, 1309, p. 20; quoted by Nicholson, *Mathnawi,* Books I and II (Commentary), p. 325.

In Book III, Rumi gives a description about the disagreement among people about the shape of the elephant which they see in darkness. The one whose hand fell on its trunk thought it was like a water-pipe, the one who touched its ear compared it to a fan, another who handled its leg considered the shape to be like a pillar. Another laid his hand on its back and said the elephant was like a throne.

This apologue occurs earlier in the *Hadiqah* of Sana'i[57] and in the *Ihya* of Ghazali.[58] Both these versions are a good deal fuller than the one given by Rumi. The chief difference is that while Sana'i and Ghazali describe the people who handled the elephant as blind, Rumi says they could not see the elephant because of the darkness of the place in which it was exhibited. Ghazali tells the story in reply to the criticism of his view that there is no fundamental contradiction between the doctrines of *jabr* (necessity) and *kasb* (freewill).

I have cited a few examples to show that the views of the two thinkers were not dissimilar, although their manner of approach is essentially different. Comparisons are always odious and the one between Rumi and Ghazali is particularly more so because of the fundamental difference in the approach of the two minds. A comparative study of their thought content is outside the scope of our work and it is enough for our purpose to record that, although Rumi expresses no obligation whatever to Ghazali, he has not been able to escape his influence which indeed was an overriding factor in shaping the religious views of his father. I would refer the reader, who is interested in a comparative study of Rumi and Ghazali, to the illuminating comments by Badi'uz-Zaman Farozan Far in *Fihi-ma-Fihi.*[59]

57 Book I, ed. Stephenson, 8, 10 *sqq.* 58 IV, 7, 10 *sqq.* (*Kitabu'l-Tawbah*).

59 See pp. 236, 250, 297, 303, 304, 309, 317, 320 and 33 in *Fihi-ma-Fihi*, edited by Badi'-uz-Zaman Farozan Far.

Ghazali was born in Tus in Iran in the eleventh century of the Christian era; Rumi was born in the same country two centuries later. At the age of thirty-three Ghazali was a professor in the University of Baghdad where he devoted himself to a study of the Purpose of Philosophy.[60] At the same age Rumi was addressing himself, with the same intensity, to the same problem in Konya. At thirty-four he had won for himself a reputation for scholarship and erudite learning, and was acknowledged the greatest living authority on Islam in the contemporary world.

We see the *Maqasid-ul-Falasifah* ('Aims of the Philosophers'), a work by Ghazali, being followed by his famous book the *Tahafut-ul-Falasifah* ('Incoherences of the Philosophers').[61] It clearly showed Ghazali's failure to find an answer to the problems of life in philosophy. Having failed in this field he turned to pastures new. A severe attack of paralysis, while he was still a professor at Baghdad, precipitated his decision to give up the teaching of religion and philosophy. During the next ten years we see him travelling off and on between Damascus and Alexandria; we see the learned professor retire from the activity of the university life to the seclusion and peace of prayer and contemplation. There is an almost corresponding parallel in the life of Rumi. His period in intellectual turmoil lasts nearly thirteen years, during which we find him travelling off and on between Konya and Damascus. Much like Ghazali, Rumi left his professorship at a time when the whole Muslim world had learnt to respect him for his knowledge of religion and philosophy. While it was an attack of physical paralysis in the case of Ghazali, with Rumi it was a complete paralysis of philosophy itself, as symbolised by the emergence of Shams.

60 مقاصد الفلاسفة

61 تهافة الفلاسفة

Ghazali was more fortunate inasmuch as he discovered the solution within a brief period of ten years. He was forty-one years old when he wrote *Ihya 'Ulum-ud-Din* ('Revivification of Religious Sciences') and *al-Munqidh min al-Dalal* ('Deliverance from Error'). The pangs that Rumi had to suffer were not only far more painful in their intensity, but were also incomparably longer in their duration, for it was not before he was forty-six years of age that he started his monumental work of writing the *Mathnawi*. His was a method essentially different from Ghazali's, though both arrived at the same conclusions. Of both it has been said that their greatest contribution has been that they found for mysticism a place in Islam which has given it a niche and an existence of its own in the Muslim polity. Both, I suggest, would reject this compliment with equal force if they were living today, for their great contribution does not really lie in the refutation of Greek philosophy only. Both tried, in their own way, to re-create and re-discover for themselves the original purity of Islam; both worked and pleaded in their own way for bridging the gulf between religious thought and religious deed. Both fought against tendencies which were reducing Islam to the status of a dogma; and both worked for winning for it the unchallenged allegiance due to it as a code of life. While one spoke in cold prose, the other spoke in the animate language of poetry – a difference which partly explains the incomparably greater influence which Rumi continues to wield on the thought and life of Muslims up to this day.

Ghazali rose far above the crippling limitations imposed by scholastic logic and the religious and philosophical fanaticism of his age; Rumi transcended similar, if not greater and stronger, barriers in his own day; both showed a surprising capacity for assimilating the learning of their own age without allowing themselves to succumb to it. Ghazali points out the impossibility of obtaining for mysticism the type of proof which is available in the problems of chemistry and mathematics.[62] Proof in logic and mathematics is distinct from the proof in mystical experience. The former deals with quantity, the latter with quality. Intuitive perception which is the core of religion is wholly foreign to logic. Knowing the symptoms of drunkenness as a doctor, he says, is one thing, but to have the experience of drunkenness itself is quite another. It is well nigh impossible to explain to a blind person the difference between various colours; no amount of metaphors and similes will dispel the darkness. It is the destiny of man, therefore, either to take a leap into the darkness or to remain completely ignorant. Both Ghazali and Rumi took this leap in their own day, and neither was the loser for it. Both saw the light and showed it to the world. There was, however, one fundamental difference between their approach to the same problem. While Ghazali arrived at the solution through a tortuous process of conscious reasoning and laborious cogitation, involving years of philosophical activity of a high order, the truth dawned on Rumi as it dawns on the soul of a Prophet, after years of agony and anguish, years which shook Rumi to the core and changed him out of all recognition. The change, however, came suddenly and spontaneously and not through any logical process of a conscious effort. The one attacked philosophy with its own weapons and ended up by erecting an elaborate system of his own; the other started with intuition and ended up with revelation which still gives light, faith and courage to millions of men all over the world. While the greatest contribution of Ghazali is *Ihya 'Ulum-ud-Din* ('Revivification of Religious Sciences') and *al-Munqidh min al-Dalal* ('The Deliverance from Error'), Rumi has left to posterity a work which is known as

[62] *Al-Naqd.*

nothing less than a 'Qur'an in Pahlavi'. This is the only basic difference between the two minds to whom Islam owes so much of its strength and stability today. We crave the reader's indulgence to quote, somewhat extensively, from al-Ghazali's work *al-Munqidh min al-Dalal* ('The Deliverance from Error') which is the primary source material on his life and contains an illuminating analysis of his spiritual growth.[63] This will help in the appreciation and understanding of the many close parallels between the experience and thought of Ghazali and Rumi as the reader goes through the following chapters which seek to analyse the growth and development of Rumi's personality.

The schools of philosophers, and how the defect of unbelief affects them all. . . .

The Theists in general attacked the two previous groups, the Materialists and the Naturalists, and exposed their defects so effectively that others were relieved of the task. 'And God relieved the believers of fighting' (Q. 33, 25) through their mutual combat. Aristotle, moreover, attacked his predecessors among the Theistic philosophers, especially Plato and Socrates, and went so far in his criticism that he separated himself from them all. Yet he too retained a residue of their unbelief and heresy from which he did not manage to free himself. We must therefore reckon as unbelievers both these philosophers themselves and their followers among the Islamic philosophers, such as Ibn Sina, al-Farabi and others; in transmitting the philosophy of Aristotle, however, none of the Islamic philosophers has accomplished anything comparable to the achievements of the two men named. The translations of others are marked by disorder and confusion, which so perplex the understanding of the student that he fails to comprehend; and if a thing is not comprehended how can it be either refuted or accepted? . . .

Theology or Metaphysics. Here occur most of the errors of the philosophers. They are unable to satisfy the conditions of proof they lay down in logic, and consequently differ much from one another here. The views of Aristotle, as expounded by al-Farabi and Ibn Sina, are close to those of the Islamic writers. All their errors are comprised under twenty heads, on three of which they must be reckoned infidels and on seventeen heretics. It was to show the

[63] Translation by W. Montgomery Watt. See his *Faith and Practice of al-Ghazali* (London, 1953, G. Allen and Unwin, Ltd.), pp. 30–65.

falsity of their views on these twenty points that I composed *The Incoherence of the Philosophers*. . . .

It is customary with weaker intellects thus to take the men as criterion of the truth and not the truth as criterion of the men. The intelligent man follows 'Ali (may God be pleased with him) when he said, 'Do not know the truth by the men, but know the truth, and then you will know who are truthful.'. . . It is not the strong swimmer who is kept back from the shore, but the clumsy tiro; not the accomplished snake-charmer who is barred from touching the snake, but the ignorant boy. . . .

The lowest degree of education is to distinguish oneself from the ignorant ordinary man. The educated man does not loathe honey even if he finds it in the surgeon's cupping-glass; he realises that the cupping-glass does not essentially alter the honey. The natural aversion from it in such a case rests on popular ignorance, arising from the fact that the cupping-glass is made only for impure blood. Men imagine that the blood is impure because it is in the cupping-glass, and are not aware that the impurity is due to a property of the blood itself. Since this property is absent from the honey, the fact that the honey is in such a container does not produce this property in it. Impurity, therefore, should not be attributed to the honey. . . .

Yet this is the prevalent idea among the majority of men. Wherever one ascribes a statement to an author of whom they approve, they accept it, even although it is false; wherever one ascribes it to an author of whom they disapprove, they reject it even although it is true. They always make the man the criterion of truth and not truth the criterion of the man; and that is erroneous in the extreme. . . .

The Ways of Mysticism. . . . It became clear to me, however, that what is most distinctive of mysticism is something which cannot be apprehended by study, but only by immediate experience, . . . by ecstasy and by a moral change. What a difference there is between *knowing* the definition of health and satiety, together with their causes and presuppositions, and *being* healthy and satisfied! What a difference between being acquainted with the definition of drunkenness – namely, that it designates a state arising from the stomach – and being drunk! Indeed, the drunken man while in that condition does not know the definition of drunkenness nor the scientific account of it; he has not the very least scientific knowledge of it. The sober man, on the other hand, knows the definition of drunkenness and its basis, yet he is not drunk in the very least. Again the doctor, when he is himself ill, knows the definition and causes of health and the remedies which restore it, and yet is lacking in health. Similarly there is a difference between knowing the true nature and causes and conditions of the ascetic life and actually leading such a life and forsaking the world. . . .

For nearly six months beginning with Rajab 488 A.H. (=July 1095 A.D.), I was continuously tossed about between the attractions of worldly desires and the impulses towards eternal life. In that month the matter ceased to be one of choice and became one of compulsion. God caused my tongue to dry up so that I was prevented from lecturing. One particular day I would make an effort to lecture in order to gratify the hearts of my following, but my tongue would not utter a single word nor could I accomplish anything at all. . . . *[Ghazali abandoned his professorship at Baghdad, left for Damascus where he remained for nearly two years in retirement and solitude. From Damascus he went to Jerusalem and then to the Hijaz for pilgrimage. This is what he says of this period of his life:]*

I continued at this stage for the space of ten years, and during these periods of solitude there were revealed to me things innumerable and unfathomable. This much I shall say about that in order that others may be helped: I learnt with certainty that it is above all the mystics who walk on the road of God; their life is the best life, their method the soundest method, their character the purest character; indeed, were the intellect of the intellectuals and the learning of the learned and the scholarship of the scholars, who are versed in the profundities of revealed truth, brought together in the attempt to improve the life and character of the mystics, they would find no way of doing so; for to the mystics all movement and all rest, whether external or internal, brings illumination from the light of the lamp of prophetic revelation; and behind the light of prophetic revelation there is no other light on the face of the earth from which illumination may be received. . . .

Of the things I do not remember, what was, was;
Think it good; do not ask an account of it. (Ibn al-Mu'tazz).

The True Nature of Prophecy. . . . Beyond intellect there is yet another stage. In this another eye is opened, by which he beholds the unseen, what is to be in the future, and other things which are beyond the ken of intellect in the same way as the objects of intellect are beyond the ken of the faculty of discernment and the objects of discernment are beyond the ken of sense. Moreover, just as the man at the stage of discernment would reject and disregard the objects of intellect were these to be presented to him, so some intellectuals reject and disregard the objects of prophetic revelation. That is sheer ignorance. They have no ground for their view except that this is a stage which they have not reached and which for them does not exist; yet they suppose that it is non-existent in itself. When a man blind from birth, who has not learnt about colours and shapes listening to people's talk, is told about these things for the first time, he does not understand them nor admit their existence.

. . . Just as intellect is one of the stages of human development in which there is an 'eye' which sees the various types of intelligible objects, which are beyond the ken of the senses, so prophecy also is the description of a stage in which there is an eye endowed with light such that in that light the unseen and other supra-intellectual objects become visible.

In general, the prophets are the physicians of the diseases of hearts. The only advantage of the intellect is that it informed us of that, bearing witness to prophetic revelation by believing (i.e. the trustworthiness of the prophets) and to itself by being unable to apprehend what is apprehended by the eye of prophecy; then it took us by the hand and entrusted us to prophetic revelation, as the blind are entrusted to their guides and anxious patients to sympathetic doctors. Thus far may the intellect proceed. In what lies beyond it has no part, save in the understanding of what the physician communicates to it.

Next only to the influence of his father and through him of Ghazali comes the influence of Rumi's tutor, Burhan-ud-din. He was a devoted disciple of Rumi's father, and it is not unreasonable to suppose that the influences which Rumi imbibed from his father were imbibed in an equal measure by his tutor who received his training at the feet of Rumi's father. Rumi's interest in Sana'i, however, could be traced to the almost fanatical allegiance that Burhan-ud-din owed to him. Rumi held Sana'i in great regard. We know of an occasion when Baha-ud-din Tusi, the poet, who wrote the history of Saljuqs in verse, expressed the opinion that Sana'i was not a Muslim because he frequently quoted the Qur'an in his poetry. Rumi took strong exception to this remark and is stated to have addressed the following reply to Tusi.[64] 'Could a

[64] Tusi fled during the Mongol onslaught and took refuge in Rum in the reign of Sultan 'Ala-ud-din Kaiqubad. He received great favours at the hand of the Saljuq kings. He wrote of 'Ala-ud-din Kaiqubad, Ghayath-ud-din Kaikhusraw and 'Izz-ud-din Kaika'us. As the poet laureate, he wrote the history of Saljuqs in verse.

Muslim perceive the grandeur of that poet,' he said, 'his hair would stand on end, and his turban would fall from his head. That Muslim, and thousands such as he – such as thee – would become real Muslims. His poetry which is an exposition of the mysteries of the Qur'an, is so beautifully embellished that one may apply to it the adage we have drawn from the ocean, and we have poured again into the ocean. Thou hast not understood his philosophy; thou hast not studied it. . . . The vicars of God have a technology, of which the rhetoricians have no knowledge. Hence these truths appear to be imperfect, because men of crude minds are prevented from comprehending them. Though thou hast no part in the lot of the recondite mysteries of the saints, it does not thence follow that thou fixest thy faith upon them and actest with true sincerity, thou shalt find on the Day of Judgment no heavy burden on thy shoulders.'[65]

Rumi's tutor was almost notorious for his habit of profusely quoting Sana'i in his speeches.[66] In his work *Ma'arif-i-Burhan Muhaqqiq* the original manuscript of which is preserved in Kutabkhana Salim Agha in Istanbul, we see a large number of quotations from Sana'i. It would be safe to infer, therefore, that Rumi's interest in Sana'i was aroused by his teacher. We read a tribute to Sana'i in *Fihi-ma-Fihi*, a work by Rumi. He has also devoted a whole ode to Sana'i in his *Divan*.[67]

گفت کسی خواجه سنائی بمرد   مرگ چنین خواجه نه کاریست خرد
کاه نبود او که ببادی پرید   آب نبود او که بسرما فسرد
شانه نبود او که بموئی شکست   دانه نبود او که زمینش فشرد
گنج زری بود درین خاکدان   کو دو جهان را بجوی می شمرد
قالب خاکی سوئی خاکی فگند   جان و خرد سوئی سموات برد
صاف بر آمیخته با درد می   بر سر خم رفت و جدا گشت درد

[65] Whinfield, Introduction to the Translation of the *Mathnawi*, p. 64.
[66] See *Fihi-ma-Fihi*, edited by Farozan Far, p. 207.
[67] Nicholson, *Selected Poems from the Divani Shamsi Tabriz* (Cambridge, 1952), p. 86.

Quoth some one, 'Master Sana'i is dead.'
The death of such a master is no little thing.
He was not chaff which flew on the wind,
He was not water which froze in winter.
He was not a comb which was broken with a hair,
He was not a seed which the earth crushed.
He was a treasure of gold in this dust-pit,
For he valued the two worlds at a barley-corn.
The earthly frame he flung to the earth,
Soul and intellect he bore to heaven.
The pure elixir mingled with the wine-dregs
Came to the jar's surface, and the dross settled apart.

While Rumi owed his interest in Sana'i to his own teacher, he owed his interest in 'Attar to a set of circumstances which took him to Nishapur after his father's migration from Balkh. We know of Rumi's meeting as a child with the celebrated poet in Nishapur where he received at the hands of 'Attar a copy of his *Asrar Namah*. While Rumi was not attracted towards Omar Khayyam in whose home town he met 'Attar, he found himself in full accord with both 'Attar and Sana'i. 'We may conjecture that the first impulse in his mind towards Sufism arose from the perusal of their celebrated poems, *the Mantiq-ut-Tair* and *Hadiqa*.'[68] Nicholson has accepted 'Attar and Sana'i as precursors of Rumi who himself declares that 'we have come after Sana'i and 'Attar' and who calls the latter as the spirit and the former as his two eyes.

عطار روح بود و سنائی دو چشم او　　ما از پی سنائی و عطار آمدیم

As you read the *Mathnawi* you come across several stories and individual verses which can be easily traced to *Hadiqa* and *Mantiq-ut-Tair*. Shibli has attempted a brief comparison between the *Mathnawi* and *Hadiqa*.[69] Farozan Far, in his notes on the *Mathnawi*, has pointed out several instances where Rumi has borrowed the outlines of his stories from

[68] Ibid., Introduction, p. xxxviii.
[69] Shibli, op. cit., pp. 63–65.

'Attar.[70] Aflaki quotes Rumi as having remarked that whosoever studied 'Attar carefully would understand the secrets of Sana'i, and whosoever studied Sana'i with faith and care would understand his work and benefit by it.[71]

Rumi sees himself as a successor to Sana'i and 'Attar. He by far excels the Masters, however, in that their *Mathnawis* have not been able to achieve the fame and acceptance that was destined for a disciple who became the author of the 'Qur'an in Pahlavi', a distinction which might have evoked the envy of both Sana'i and 'Attar.

Hadiqa, the title by which Sana'i's poem is generally known, does not occur in the *Mathnawi* where it is referred to as *Ilahi Namah.*

In Book I Rumi quotes verbatim from the *Divan* of Sana'i:[72]

بشنو این پند از حکیم غزنوی   تا بیابی در تن کهنه نوی
ناز را روئی بباید همچو ورد   چون نداری گرد بدخوئی مگرد
زشت باشد روئی نازیبا و ناز   سخت باشد چشم نابینا و درد

Hearken to this counsel from the Sage of Ghazna,
That thou mayst feel freshness in thy old body:
'Disdain needs a face like a rose;
When thou hast not (such a face), do not indulge in ill-temper.
Ugly is disdain in an uncomely face,
Grievous is eye-ache in an unseeing eye.'

Rumi again quotes a hemistich from the *Hadiqa* of Sana'i with alterations rendered necessary by the metre in verse 3426 of the *Mathnawi*, Book I:

بشنو الفاظ حکیم پردهٔ   سر همانجا نه که باده خوردهٔ

Hearken to the words of the Sage who lived in seclusion,
'Lay thy head in the same place where thou hast drunk the wine.'

[70] See خلاصه· مثنوی, pp. 87, 89, 112, 150, 215, 237.
[71] *Manaqib-ul-'Arifin* (Agra), p. 278.
[72] Lines 1905–1907.

Sana'i says:[73]

> When thou drinkest a cup of wine in this ruined house (the world), I counsel thee, raise not thy foot from the place of thy intoxication and lay thy head where thou hast drunk it; and when thou hast drunk it, rub a clod of earth on thy lips (i.e. keep silence). The God-intoxicated Sufi is a laughing-stock to the children of this world. It behoves him to confide in his Shaykh from whom he has quaffed the wine of Love, and consort with none but the initiated.

Rumi takes as a text for his discourse on Divine jealousy a verse in a *qasidah* by Sana'i beginning:

مکن در جسم و جان منزل که این دونست آن والا
قدم زین هر دو برون نه ، نه این جا باش نه آن جا

The verse Rumi picks up for his discourse in Book I of the *Mathnawi* is as follows:[74]

بهرچ ز راه وا مانی چه کفر آن حرف و چه ایمان
بهرچ از دوست دور افتی چه زشت آن نقش و چه زیبا

> Any thing that causes thee to be left behind on the Way, what matter whether it be infidelity or faith?
> Any form that causes thee to fall far from the Beloved, what matter whether it be ugly or beautiful?

Rumi's debt to 'Attar is equally great. In Book I of the *Mathnawi* a story is related how a parrot escapes from its cage by feigning death. Rumi has borrowed, adapted and expanded 'Attar's tale of the Hindu sage and the King of Turkistan.[75] On p. 99 of Book I, Rumi quotes a verse from a *ghazal* in the *Divan* of 'Attar and proceeds to expand on the theme:

تو صاحب نفسی ای غافل میانِ خاك خون میخور
که صاحب دل اگر زهری خورد آن انگبین باشد

[73] See *Hadiqa*, tr. Stephenson, p. 47.
[74] P. 108, Heading.
[75] *Asrar Namah*, 90, 6 *sqq*.

Thou art a sensualist: O heedless one, drink blood (mortify thyself) amidst the dust (of thy bodily existence),
For if the spiritualist drink a poison, it will be (to him as) an antidote.

In Book IV, Rumi tells the story of a tanner who fainted and sickened on smelling otto and musk in the bazaar of the perfumers.[76] There is a close and not accidental resemblance between this Story and the 'Tale of the Scavenger and his passing by the shop of the Perfumer', which 'Attar relates in his *Asrar Namah.*[77] Again, the account given by Rumi of Ibrahim ibn Adham's conversion to Sufism and abandonment of his kingdom is derived from 'Attar.[78]

Among the sayings of Rumi we read that after 150 years the Light of Mansur (Hallaj) revealed itself to 'Attar.

In Book V of the *Mathnawi*, Rumi speaks of a parrot which is trained to talk by means of a mirror, behind which is a man concealed in a curtain, so that when the parrot facing the mirror hears his voice it thinks the words are uttered by another bird like itself and tries to imitate them.[79] There is close resemblance between this story and a passage in 'Attar's *Asrar Namah* entitled 'The story of a parrot and the placing of the mirror before it'.[80]

In Book VI, Rumi refers to 'Attar by name.[81] Nowhere else in the *Mathnawi* does he acknowledge his numerous debts of this kind to the druggist of Nishapur.

In an attempt to catalogue the external influences on Rumi, Nicholson mentions the following:

[76] See p. 286, verses 257 *sqq*.
[77] 61, 4 quoted by R. A. Nicholson at p. 131 of his Commentary on Book IV, Vol. VIII.
[78] Ibid, p. 143.
[79] Book V, pp. 91 *sqq*.
[80] *Asrar Namah*, 97, 6 *sqq*.
[81] Line 1382.

(*a*) On his way to Balkh he met 'Attar at Nishapur and received a copy of *Asrar Namah* from him.
(*b*) He was well acquainted with the poems of Sana'i to whom he pays a tribute in one of his odes (XXII in Nicholson's *Selected Poems from the Divani Shamsi Tabriz*).
(*c*) His meeting with Sa'di.
(*d*) His reference to Nizami.
(*e*) Echoes of Omar Khayyam in his poetry.

We have dealt briefly with the first two. We will be quite safe in asserting that none of the last three made a deep impression on Rumi. He could not have been attracted by the extant compositions of Nizami, except, perhaps, the *Makhzan-i-Asrar*, while Omar Khayyam's philosophy was even less capable of laying any hold on him. Sa'di with his practical morality, his heart-felt piety, and half-hearted mysticism, could never have appealed to a sensitive God-intoxicated nature like Jalal's. The distinction comes out plainly enough in their writings. 'The ghazals of Sa'di,' says the Tabriz editor, 'are extremely elegant and exceedingly beautiful, but the thoughts will prove to be mostly profane and the diction full of amatory conceits: no revelation of the Truth or explanation of the mystic Path will be found there; the discerning critic and intelligent reader knows that in the utterance of Janabi Maulavi Ma'navi 'tis another story.'[82]

IV

Rumi was well equipped with classical Islamic philosophy. Al-Kindi, who is often identified in the West as the founder of Islamic philosophy was certainly not known to Rumi, because few of his treatises in Arabic were available until forty years ago. Abu Nasr al-

[82] Nicholson, *Selected Poems from the Divani Shamsi Tabriz*, Intro., p. xxxvii.

Farabi (870–950) was the real successor of al-Kindi. In logic especially, al-Farabi's works were significant because in them Aristotelian logic was expressed in exact and appropriate terminology which henceforth became a heritage of nearly all branches of Islamic learning. He calls Plato the *Imam* of the Philosophers. Rumi was certainly familiar with his works, though he neither followed him nor had much admiration for his method. This is also true of Abu Ali Sina (Avicenna) who sought to harmonise reason and revelation along lines already begun by al-Kindi, al-Farabi and others. Avicenna came under severe criticism by Ghazali and Fakhr-ud-din al-Razi, as well as by the Andalusian philosophers, especially Ibn Rushd or Averroes.

By no means an admirer of Avicenna, Rumi could not possibly escape such a leading influence in Islamic philosophy. The story of the King's falling in love with a handmaiden, told so beautifully in Book I,[83] reminds one of a passage in the *Qanun* of Ibn Sina. While most of the details seem to be due to the poet's imagination, one feature – the diagnosis of love-sickness by feeling the pulse – is traceable to Ibn Sina. E. G. Browne[84] mentions three sources whence the poet might have derived the episode:

(1) *Qanun* of Ibn Sina, 316, Section on Love.[85]
(2) Sayyid Isma'il Jurjani, *Dhakhirah-i-Khwarizmshahi*, Book VI, Guftar I, Juzz Ch. 3 translated in *Chahar Maqalah*, Eng. 89, note 1.
(3) *Chahar Maqalah*, 78 penult and *sqq*=88, 9 *sqq* in Browne's translation.

While the *Qanun* and the *Dhakhirah* explain the method of psychotherapy in general terms, the author

[83] See p. 6.
[84] *Arabian Medicine*, pp. 84-88.
[85] Translated by Browne, ibid., p. 86. R. A. Nicholson, *The Mathnawi of Jalalu'ddin Rumi,* Vol. VII, p. 23.

of the *Chahar Maqalah* gives full account of a case in which his method was successfully applied by Ibn Sina himself to a young kinsman of Qabus ibn Washmgir who had fallen in love with a girl in Gurgan. Ibn Sina does not converse with his patient – he only observes the movements of his pulse – the naming of streets, houses, etc., is done by a third person; but otherwise the details correspond closely with the *Mathnawi* story. Rumi takes care to eliminate every circumstance that would be derogatory to the character of a saintly physician of souls.

Rumi was heir to an impressive heritage of Sufism. Apart from his immediate environment, of which we have spoken earlier in some detail, the leading mystics of early Islam had no doubt their own influence on succeeding generations.

Among the well-known figures in Sufism in the eighth century were the Egyptian Dhu'l-Nun, the saint of Baghdad, al-Muhasibi, the prince Ibrahim ibn Adham and Bayazid al-Bistami, the Sage from Khurasan. There is no evidence of any reference to the Saint of Baghdad, but the other three appear prominently in the *Mathnawi*.

The famous Sufi Thawban ibn Ibrahim, generally known as Dhu'l-Nun al-Misri, appears as the hero of a story in Book II of the *Mathnawi*.[86] It is not known on what authority Rumi makes him the hero of a story which is related of Abu Bakr al-Shibli in *Kashf al-Mahjub*. According to *Tadhkirat-ul-Auliya'* by Farid-ud-din 'Attar,[87] Shibli fell into such an ecstasy that, after he had several times tried in vain to kill himself, he was put in chains and carried to a mad-house. 'In your opinion,' he said, 'I am mad and you are sane: may God increase my madness and your sanity, so that I may become nearer and nearer to God, and you farther and farther from Him.' When they were about

[86] See pp. 322-26.
[87] Ed. R. A Nicholson, London and Leyden, 1905–1907.

to force medicine down his throat, he exclaimed: 'Don't trouble yourselves, for this is not a malady that any medicine can cure.' Some persons came to see him. 'Who are you?' he asked. 'Your friends,' they answered. He began to throw stones at them, and they all ran away. 'O, you liars,' he cried, 'do friends run away from their friend because of a few stones? I see that you are friends to yourselves but not to me.'

One comes across references to Dhu'l-Nun in the first and the second volumes of the *Mathnawi*, which does not appear to refer to him again in the rest of the four volumes.[88]

Bayazid Bistami is an immense figure in Islamic Sufism and Rumi entertains feelings of the highest respect and admiration for him. The *Mathnawi* is replete with references to his insight, vision and integrity and there is ample internal evidence to indicate that Rumi not only knew all about him but that he tried in his own way to prove worthy of the lofty example set by Bayazid Bistami.[89]

Prince Ibrahim ibn Adham is a romantic figure in Islamic mysticism. A ruling prince who renounced a kingdom in search of truth inspires much curiosity and interest on the part of a reader and Rumi refers to him and his life on more than one occasion. A miracle is attributed to him. One day whilst he was seated on the bank of the Tigris, stitching his tattered cloak, the needle fell into the river. Someone said to him, 'You gave up such a splendid kingdom; what have you gained?' Ibrahim signified to the river that his needle should be given back. Immediately a thousand fishes rose from the water, each carrying in its mouth a needle of gold. He said to them, 'I want my needle,' whereupon a poor little fish came to the surface with

[88] See Vol. I, 1529, and Vol. II, 142, 1384, 1386, 1500–01, 1716, 3134, 3191.

[89] For Rumi's treatment of Bayazid see: Pref., p. 2, 1. V: 428, 1743, 2652, 3464. Vol. II, 926-27, 1916, 717, 1351–52, 1765, 1916, 2218, 3764. Vol. III, 1343–44, 1699–1701, 4745. Vol. IV, 1802, 1807–08, 1926, 2401, 1549, 2102, 2103, 2125, 2401. Vol. V, 872, 1683, 2020, 1428, 1743, 2652, 2799, 3356, 3464

the needle in its mouth. 'This,' said Ibrahim, 'is the least thing I have gained by giving up the kingdom of Balkh; the other things you cannot know.'[90]

At the end of the ninth century the sober school of Sufism of Baghdad was headed by Junaid. Around him assembled such eminent figures as Nuri, Shibli and Hallaj. Junaid, a major figure in Islamic mysticism, finds an appropriate place in the *Mathnawi*.[91]

Nuri is not referred to at all while Shibli's anecdotes appear in all but the last volume of the *Mathnawi*.[92]

Mansur Hallaj, the famous Sufi executed in 309 A.H. is referred to in line 1809 of Book I.[93]

تافت نُورِ صبح و ما از نُورِ تو   در صبوحی با میِ منصُورِ تو

'The wine of thy Mansur' in Rumi's verse refers to the phrase *Ana'l-Haqq* in which Hallaj declared his mystical union with God.[94]

> Thy Spirit is mingled in my spirit even as wine is mingled with pure water;
> When anything touches Thee, it touches me.
> Lo, in every case Thou art I.

Rumi comes to the defence of Hallaj and gives a highly original explanation of the slogan which led to his execution at the hands of the theologians who merely applied the letter of the law and failed com-

[90] R. A. Nicholson, Commentary on Book II, p. 351, Gibb Memorial New Series. Vol. IV. Also see reference to Ibrahim ibn Adham in *The Mathnawi*. Vol. II, 532, 929, 930, 3210. Vol. IV, 668, 726, 731, 3078. Vol. V, 1271, 2428. Vol. VI, 3986.

[91] Vol. I, 19, 133, 1529, 1546. Vol. II, 1386. Vol. III, 3261. Vol. IV, 1549. Vol. V, 2019, 2694–95.

[92] See Vol. I, Pref., p. 2, 1. V; 517, 1529, 1546, 2205, 2652, 3338. Vol. II, 299, 517, 532, 762, 1500–01, 1574. Vol. III, 1960, Pref. p. 1, I; I, 4621. Vol. IV, 2102. Vol. V, 2694–95.

[93] For a full account of his life and doctrine, see Massignon's *La passion d'al-Hallaj* (Paris, 1922).

[94] See *Kitab-ul-Tawasin*, 134, ed. Louis Massignon (Paris, 1913).

pletely to grasp the spirit. In *Fihi-ma-Fihi* Rumi offers the following explanation:[95]

When a fly is plunged in honey, all the members of its body are reduced to the same condition, and it does not move. Similarly, the term *istighraq* (absorption in God) is applied to one who has no conscious existence or initiative or movement. Any action that proceeds from him is not his own. If he is still struggling in the water, or if he cries out, 'Oh, I am drowning,' he is not said to be in the state of 'absorption'. This is what is signified by the words *Ana'l-Haqq*, 'I am God'. People imagine that it is a presumptuous claim, whereas it is really a presumptuous claim to say *Ana'l-'abd*, 'I am the servant of God'; and *Ana'l-Haqq*, 'I am God,' is an expression of great humility. The man who says *Ana'l-abd*, 'I am the servant of God,' affirms two existences, his own and God's, but he that says *Ana'l-Haqq*, 'I am God,' has made himself non-existent and has given himself up and says 'I am God,' i.e. 'I am naught, He is all: there is no being but God's.' This is the extreme of humility and self-abasement.

On the contrary, Pharaoh's claim to Divinity was an impious act of self-assertion and overweening arrogance. Nevertheless, some Muslim mystics, including Hallaj himself,[96] have attempted to justify it.

Hallaj indeed fires the imagination of Rumi who looks upon him as an inspiring example.[97]

Rumi quotes with approval from Hallaj and pays him the great compliment of imitating some of his verses.[98]

In the tenth century appeared such classical manuals of Sufism as the:

(1) *Kitab al-Luma'* of Abu Nasr al-Sarraj.
(2) *Kitab al-Ta'arruf* of Kalabadhi.
(3) *Kashf al-Mahjub* of Hujwiri.

95 *Fihi-ma-Fihi*, pp. 49, 2 *sqq*., quoted by R. A. Nicholson, Commentary on Book II, p. 248.

96 *Tawasin*, 51; cf. 93 *sqq*.

97 For details of references to Hallaj in *The Mathnawi* see: Vol. I, 1809, 3056. Vol. II, 59, 305, 1398, 1790, 2523, 2674–75, 2642–44. Vol. III, 1086, 3845, 4000. Vol. IV, 1926, 2102. Vol. V, 2038. Vol. VI, 2095, 2242, 3405.

98 See *The Mathnawi*: Vol. I, 3934, 3935. Vol. II, 1437. Vol. III, 3839, 4186–87. Vol. V, 2675. Vol. VI, 3840, 4062.

(4) *Qut al-Qulub* of Abu Talib al-Makki.
(5) *Risalat al-Qushayriyah* of Qushayri.

Rumi certainly had read them all though no reference is to be found in his writings to the first book. The second is referred to only once.[99]

Kashf al-Mahjub is quoted quite copiously in the *Mathnawi*.[100]

Hujwiri, like Rumi, holds that there is no 'seeking' without 'finding',[101] i.e. immediate perception by the 'inner light' and that ultimately the former depends on the latter, just as man's love of God depends on Divine love and favour. Rumi says in the *Mathnawi*:[102] The *muqallid* only becomes a real seeker (*muhaqqiq*) when by Divine grace his eyes are opened to the Truth. Does the seeker find or the finder seek? he asks. Is *mujahadah* the cause of *mushahadah*?

On this question Hujwiri writes: 'One says, "He who seeks shall find," and another says, "He who finds shall seek." Seeking is the cause of finding, but it is no less true that finding is the cause of seeking. The one party practises mortification [*mujahadah*] for the purpose of attaining contemplation [*mushahadah*], and the other party practises contemplation for the purpose of attaining mortification. The fact is that mortification stands in the same relation to contemplation as Divine blessing (*tawfiq*), which is a gift from God, to obedience (*ta'at*): as it is absurd to seek obedience without Divine blessing, so it is absurd to seek Divine blessing without obedience, and as there can be no mortification without contemplation, so

[99] See *Mathnawi*, Vol. VI, 1111.

[100] See Vol. I, 132, 231, 1111, 2113, 2353, 2696–97, 2711, 2773, 3338. Vol. II, 31–32, 931–32, 1465–68, 1707, 1935, 3006–07, 3235, 3370–74, Vol. III, 1132–34, 1985. Vol. IV, 392–94. Vol. VI, 662, 3091, 3133, 3405, 3578, 3998, 4415–17.

[101] *Kashf al-Mahjub*. Abridged translation by R. A. Nicholson, Gibb Memorial Series, XVII (London, 1911, re-issued 1936).

[102] Verses 2996–97, Book II.

there can be no contemplation without mortification.'[103]

Qut al-Qulub of Abu Talib al-Makki is quoted at five places in the *Mathnawi*[104] while the *Risalah* of Qushayri finds a more frequent mention.[105]

The most important philosopher who was more or less a contemporary of Rumi was Ibn 'Arabi, born in Murcia, the south of Spain in 1165. He went to Seville where he grew up. At Cordova he met Averroes, the master interpreter of Aristotle, who died in al-Marrakush in A.D. 1198. In 1207, the year in which Rumi was born, Ibn 'Arabi was threatened with mortal danger in Cairo by the Jurists and took refuge in Mecca. After spending some time there he set out for Anatolia, where in Konya he met Sadr-ud-din al-Qonawi, his most celebrated disciple. He died in Damascus in 1240. Rumi was thirty-three years at this time. Ibn 'Arabi followed most of all the earlier Sufis, especially Hallaj, Bayazid al-Bistami, and al-Ghazali.

It is essentially through Sadr-ud-din al-Qonawi, that several lines of influence of Ibn 'Arabi's doctrines in the East can be traced. Qonawi was a close associate of Rumi and in fact served as his *imam* during the daily prayers. It is through him that one must trace the link between Ibn 'Arabi and Rumi who stands as the other great mountain of Islamic spirituality, dominating the landscape of Sufism.

The doctrine that all things, as modes of Divine being, are endowed with life and know and worship God according to the necessity of the original nature of each, is stated by Ibn 'Arabi,[106] in a characteristically paradoxical way. Minerals are the brightest form of creation; after them come plants, and then animals.

[103] *Kashf al-Mahjub*, tr, Nicholson, p. 203.

[104] See Vol. I, 927. Vol. III, 1285, 4591. Vol. IV, 1314–18. Vol. VI, 2653.

[105] See Vol. I, 19, 133, 856, 1790, 2847. Vol. II, 336 566–68. Vol. III, 1285, 1699–1701. Vol. IV, 369, 3072. Vol. V, Pref., p. 1, 1, 2. Vol. VI, 2653.

[106] *Fusus*, 82 penult, and *sqq*.

All these know their Creator through mystical revelation (*Kashf*). Man, on the other hand, is in bondage to intellect, thought and religion. This paradox can be deduced from the first principles of Ibn ʿArabi's philosophy. If God is the essence of all that exists, and if His attributes are identical with His essence, it follows that where existence is, there is life, perception, knowledge, reason, etc. But though God pervades with His Oneness every particle of the universe, these attributes are not *manifested* everywhere. The fact that they are *latent*, i.e. existent *potentially*, in minerals and plants is known only to mystics. Man, having sensation and consciousness, possesses a 'self' (*nafs*) and consequently is veiled from God by his egoism and the exercise of his faculties, whereas the mineral and in a lesser degree the plant, in virtue of their external insensibility and unconsciousness, *implicitly* acknowledge the Divine omnipotence and glorify the Creator with the tongue of their 'inward state'.

Rumi draws the same contrast in the story of the moaning pillar when they make a pulpit for the Prophet and the pillar complains of its separation from the Prophet who buried that pillar in the earth, that it may be raised from the dead, like mankind, on the Day of Resurrection.[107]

Take the following passage from the story: 'The Jewish King and the Christians' in Book I,[108] where the disciples raise objections against the vizier's secluding himself:

Thou didst show the delightfulness of Being unto not-being,
After thou hadst caused not-being to fall in love with thee.
Take not away the delightfulness of thy bounty;
Take not away thy dessert and wine and wine-cup!
And if thou take it away, who is there that will make inquiry?

[107] See *Mathnawi*, Vol. I, p. 116. Also see lines 2370 *sqq*. Vol. II; lines 1020 *sqq*. Vol. III; lines 2819 *sqq*. Vol. IV.
[108] P. 35.

How should the picture strive with the painter?
Do not look on us, do not fix thy gaze on us:
Look on thine own kindness and generosity.
We were not, and there was no demand on our part,
(Yet) thy grace was hearkening to our unspoken prayer (and calling us into existence).[109]

The leading ideas in this passage come from Ibn ʿArabi though their provenance is disguised as usual by the poetical form in which they are represented. Ibn ʿArabi's system postulates a universal Being which may either be regarded as the Essence of phenomena (*al-Haqq*, the Real, God, the One) or as the phenomena manifested by that Essence (*al-Khalq*, Appearance, the World, the Many). This Being is all that exists; there is nothing else. The term 'not-being' should, therefore, be applied only to what is absolutely non-existent and cannot possibly exist; but Ibn ʿArabi and Rumi frequently make use of the same term to denote things which, though non-existent in one sense, are existent in another, e.g. the external world which exists as a form but not as an essence, or the intelligible world which exists as a concept but not as a form.[110]

Ibn ʿArabi believes that correlative terms, such as Being and not-being, the One and the many, Creator and creature, Lord and slave, are merely names for different aspects of the same Reality, each aspect logically necessitating the other and being interchangeable with it. Thus is may be said that a king is the slave of his subjects, inasmuch as the existence of subjects is a necessary condition for kingship; and that a beloved person is devoted to the lovers on whom his 'belovedness' depends. Hence every lover is a beloved, and every beloved a lover. If Love needs and desires Beauty, no less does Beauty need and desire Love. God, Who is Absolute Beauty and Love, loves

[109] Vol. I, lines 606–10.
[110] See A. J. Wensinck, *Muslim Creed* (Cambridge, 1932), p. 212.

those who love Him, and since He loves them He leaves nothing of themselves in them: they are one with Him, and in reality He is the only beloved and the only lover.[111]

Rumi gives a poetical form to the familiar doctrine of Ibn 'Arabi in the following verses:

All kings are enslaved to their slaves,
All people are dead (ready to die) for one who dies for them.
All kings are prostrate before one who is prostrate before them,
All people are intoxicated with (love for) one who is intoxicated with them.
The fowler becomes a prey to the birds
In order that of a sudden he may make them his prey.
The hearts of heart-ravishers are captivated by those
Who have lost their hearts (to them):
All loved ones are the prey of (their) lovers.[112]

It should be interesting to illustrate briefly the difference between Ibn 'Arabi and Rumi as exponents of mystical ideas. This is best done by summing up Rumi's views on the beauty of Eve and her place in the scheme of Divine creation and comparing them with those expressed by Ibn 'Arabi.

According to Rumi, 'Woman is the highest type of earthly beauty, but earthly beauty is nothing except in so far as it is a manifestation and reflexion of Divine attributes.'[113] 'That which is the object of love is not the form;'[114] ''tis the draught of Divine beauty, mingled in the lovely earth, that thou art kissing with a hundred hearts day and night.'[115] When Iblis desired God to give him a means of temptation that should be irresistible, he was shown the beauty of woman and was amazed by the revelation of Divine glory: ''twas as though God shone forth through a thin veil.'[116] Sweeping aside the veil of form, the poet beholds in woman the eternal Beauty which is the

[111] See *Lawa'ih* by Jami, XXI, ed. and tr. Whinfield and Mirza. Muhammad Kazvini (London, 1906).
[112] Book I, lines 1736–39.
[113] Book III, 554 *sqq*., V, 985 *sqq*.
[114] Book II, 703
[115] Book V, 374.
[116] Book V, 954 *sqq*.

inspirer and object of all love, and regards her, in her essential nature, as the medium *par excellence* through which that uncreated Beauty reveals itself and exercises creative activity. From this point of view she is a focus for the Divine *tajalli* and may be identified with the life-giving power of its rays.

'You must know that God cannot be seen apart from matter (*shuhud-i Haqq subhanahu mujarrad az mawadd mumkin nist*), and that He is seen more perfectly in the human matter (*maddah*) than in any other, and more perfectly in woman than in man. For He is seen either in the aspect of *agens* (*fa'illyyah*) or in that of *patiens* (*munfa'iliyyah*) or as both simultaneously. Therefore when a man contemplating God in his own person (*dhat*) has regard to the fact that woman is produced from man (*zuhur-i-zan az mard*), he contemplated God in the aspect of *agens*; and when he pays no regard to the production of woman from himself, he contemplates God in the aspect of *patiens*, because as God's creature he is absolutely *patiens*, in relation to God; but when he contemplates God in woman he contemplates Him both as *agens* and *patiens*. God, manifested in the form of woman, is *agens* in virtue of exercising complete sway over the man's soul (*nafs*) and causing the man to become submissive and devoted to Himself (as manifested in her); and He is also *patiens* because, inasmuch as He appears in the form of woman, He is under the man's control and subject to his orders: hence to see God in woman is to see Him in both these aspects, and such vision is more perfect than seeing Him in all the forms in which He manifests Himself. This is what the Mawlawi means in the hemistich,

> She is creative, you might say she is not created,

for both the attributes, *agens* and *patiens*, belong to the Essence of the Creator, and both are manifested in woman: therefore she is creative and not created.'[117]

Ibn 'Arabi, according to a commentator, is reported to hold the following views:[118] He argues that woman alone combines these two aspects of creation, whereas man has only one of them: he is *fa'il* (in the act of begetting), while she is both *munfa'il* (in conceiving) and *fa'il* (in the formation and development of the embryo). She is the *mazhar* in which the Divine Names are displayed.[119] The ascription of creative powers to human beings is justified by the Qur'an, xxiii. 14 (*Allahu ahsanu'l-khaliqin*). But what Rumi has in view is not the physical functions of women but the spiritual and essentially Divine qualities in her which 'create' love in man and cause him to seek union with the true Beloved. 'Whether love be from this (earthly) side or from that (heavenly) side, in the end it leads us Yonder.'

These, then, were some of the salient features of Rumi's intellect. The intellectual activity covering a period of thirty-four years of his life was, however, a means to an end – an end of which Rumi himself was not sufficiently aware and towards which he was only groping with the aid of an unreliable prop. He was destined to wait for another four years before he could lay his hands on something surer than mere intellect.

[117] R. A. Nicholson, Commentary on Book I, pp. 155–56.
[118] Wali Mohammad, *Sharh-i-Mathnawi*, quoted by R. A. Nicholson, Commentary on Book I, pp. 155–56.
[119] The Qur'an, lxxx. 19; lxxxii. 7, etc.

Chapter 3

The Romance of Revolution

At thirty-four Rumi was an acknowledged leader of men. He had attained a reputation for profound knowledge and had won for himself recognition as an authority on religion – a subject on which he spoke with passionate eloquence and penetrating sincerity. The circle of his adherents had already become unwieldy; his fame had crossed the frontiers of his country; and he himself appeared fully satisfied with his mission, which he was pursuing with a singleness of purpose and a zeal so devout that everybody who came into contact with him found himself under the spell of a compelling personality whose spontaneous sincerity was enough to disarm even his most uncharitable adversaries. So great was the prestige of the teacher that the ruling king and his courtiers considered it an honour to be admitted into his circle. And yet this circle was nothing exclusive to which admission had to be sought through influential intermediaries. It was an open assembly which anybody, who had the inclination to do so, could join without seeking any formal permission. And to this assembly flocked the meanest of men who heard the Master explain the simple faith that was Islam. Accessible both to kings and commoners, Rumi really felt at home with what his learned contemporaries called 'the ruffians, the tailors and the shopkeepers'. It was truly for them that he lived and worked. His contemporaries, full of contempt for the common man, and proud of their own intellectual superiority stood scornfully aloof and watched with growing disdain the activities of a member of their own tribe who appeared so painfully to demolish, in one blow, all the exclusive prestige and prerogative which the order of the Ulema had accumulated for themselves over the course of centuries. Not infrequently he was taunted for so freely associating with the mass of wicked men. 'Were my disciples good men of eminence,' he would reply with a smile, 'I would have been their disciple! Since they are bad men, they accept my leadership so that I may change them.'

Rumi embarked on this mission of reform at the age of thirty-four in 1241. For four years he strove to show the light as he had seen it himself. These years were devoted to an explanation, in simple prose, of the Reality which Rumi felt had been obscured beyond recognition by the scholastic ingenuity of those who, in an effort to evade the operative clauses of Islam, had made a virtue of it by colourfully concealing their attempt in the garb of philosophic activity. Rumi, therefore, set to himself the task, in this period of confusion, of trying to separate the grain from the chaff. In doing so he was clearly conscious of the difficulties which had to be surmounted before Islam, which had been reduced by then to the imbecility of a mere dogma, could be restored to its original simplicity and attendant success. He preached with the fervour of a man who had made the unique discovery for himself that the theory of Islam alone could not carry the nation very far. He spoke with an accent on simplicity and practicability and set out to give an example of a man who not only preached but practised every word of what he commended to others. His faith in the Qur'an as a permanent guide to all mankind was as unfailing as his belief that the mere knowledge of the Book would be of no avail to suffering humanity, if it could not find a way of applying the panacea. He set out, therefore, to show ways and means of bringing about a healthy change, but before he could change the life of many a man, his own life was to undergo a sudden and a revolutionary change.

At thirty-seven Rumi appeared to all intents and purposes to be wholly satisfied with the success he was achieving as a teacher of Islam; he had reasons to be proud of his popularity; his influence for the good was growing more rapidly than he had himself anticipated; but the career which had begun so well was destined to come to an abrupt end – an end which proved indeed to be the real beginning of his mission. While Rumi was fully occupied with his work of reform, there appeared suddenly on the scene a 'weird figure, wrapped in coarse black felt'.[1] He had an 'exceedingly aggressive and domineering manner'.[2] So sudden and pervasive was his influence that the cool, self-possessed professor of theology left his lectures only to become an humble devotee of the sage. With his appearance in Rumi's life, there came a complete change which can only be explained by considering the man who brought it about, i.e. Shams-i-Tabriz.

Curiously enough, Shams-i-Tabriz belonged to the Assassin tribe of Hasan b. Sabbah. His grandfather, Nur-ud-din Muhammad, a lieutenant of Hasan b. Sabbah, succeeded his chief in A.D. 1166. He it was who converted the great philosopher Fakhr-ud-din Razi by 'weighty and trenchant arguments', i.e. by gold and dagger. He died in 1210 and was succeeded by his son Jalaluddin, who utterly reversed the policy of his father and grandfather, abolished all antinomianism and declared himself an orthodox Muslim whence he was known as 'Nau Musalman'.[3] Shams-i-Tabriz is said to be his son, according to

[1] R. A. Nicholson, *Selected Poems from the Diwani Shamsi Tabriz*, Introduction, p. xviii.

[2] Redhouse, Tr., *Masnawi*, Book I. P. 10 of Translator's Preface.

[3] E. G. Browne, *A Literary History of Persia*, Vol. II, pp. 455–56.

Daulat Shah.[4] But Jalal-ud-din Nau Musalman had no other son except 'Ala-ud-din Muhammad.[5] Besides, according to some statements,[6] Shams was an old man of sixty when he arrived in Konya in 1244. He must have been born, therefore, in the year 1185. Daulat Shah's statement about Shams's heredity cannot, therefore, be easily accepted. However, here we are concerned with his meeting with Rumi. He arrived in Konya on 12 Jumada II 642 (30 November 1244).[7] The exact date of the meeting is not known. There are four different versions about the meeting itself. The first is by Aflaki.[8]

This great man, after acquiring a reputation for superior sanctity at Tabriz, as the disciple of a certain holy man, a basket-maker by trade, had travelled about much in various lands, in search of the best spiritual teachers, thus gaining the nickname of *Parindah* (the flier). He prayed to God that it might be revealed to him who the most occult of the favourites of the Divine will was, so that he might go to him and learn still more of the mysteries of the Divine love. The son of Baha-ud-din Walad, of Balkh, was designated to him as the man most in favour with God. Shams went, accordingly, to Konya, arriving there on Saturday, the 12th Jamada II, 642. He engaged a lodging at an inn and pretended to be a great merchant. In his room, however, there was nothing but a broken water pot, an old mat and a bolster of unbaked clay. He broke his fast once in every ten or twelve days, with a damper soaked in the broth of sheep's trotters. One day, as he was seated at the gate of the inn, Rumi passed by, riding on a mule, in the midst of a crowd of students and disciples following him on foot. Shams arose, advanced and took hold of the mule's bridle addressing Rumi in these words: 'Exchanger of the current coins of recondite significations, who knowest the names of the Lord! Tell me, was Muhammad the greater servant of God, or Bayazid of Bistam?' Rumi answered: 'Muhammad was incomparably the greater – the

[4] *Tadhkirah Daulat Shah* (London), p. 195.
[5] *Tarikh-i-Jahangusha* (Tehran), Vol. III, p. 134.
[6] *Maqalat-i-Walad Chalpi* quoted by Farozan Far, خلاصهٔ مثنوی, p. 542. Also note Rumi's own verse:

بازم ز تو خوش جوان خرم ای شمس الدین سالخورده

[7] *Maqalat-i-Shams-ud-Din*, photographic edition published by the Ministry of Education, Tehran, and quoted by Farozan Far, op. cit., p. 90.
[8] *Manaqib-ul-'Arifin*.

greatest of all Prophets and Saints.' 'Then,' rejoined Shams, 'how is it that Muhammad said: "We have not known Thee, O God, as Thou rightly shouldst be known,"[9] whereas Bayazid said: "Glory unto me! How very great is my Glory".[10] On hearing this question Rumi fainted away. On coming to, he took the questioner home where both were closeted for forty days in holy communion.[11]

Jami[12] has endorsed Aflaki's account with the difference that he does not finish the meeting with a question by Shams but quotes Rumi as replying to him in an impressive and convincing manner. He then closets them together for three months as against the forty days of Aflaki. Both are, however, equally emphatic about the secret nature of the meetings during this period.

Muhyid-Din 'Abdul Qadir, who was the contemporary of Sultan Walad, the son of Rumi, has the following account to offer:[13]

Rumi was addressing his students as usual in his house. Before him was lying a heap of books. During the lecture, a man entered and politely took his seat in a corner after formal greetings. Pointing towards the books the visitor said: 'What is this?' Rumi who was busy with his lecture must have been annoyed with such a silly interruption for the books were there for anybody to see, and on the face of it the question was both preposterous and irrelevant. It was, moreover, a breach of good manners for a student to interrupt the Master so insolently during the course of his lecture. It must have both surprised and annoyed Rumi for he was at that time the most eminent religious scholar of the age and had never experienced anything but unfailing respect and unfettered attention at the hands of his students. Rumi, therefore, brushed the question aside by simply saying, 'You don't know,' and tried to continue his lecture. But no sooner had he uttered the words than the books caught fire. Bewildered and aghast Rumi looked about for an explanation of this phenomenon. 'What is this?' he asked, turning his face towards the

[9] ما عرفناك حق معرفتك

[10] سبحانی ما اعظم شانی Rumi himself has narrated Bayazid's story in Book IV of the *Mathnawi*, p. 381.

[11] E. H. Whinfield, *Rumi* (London, Trubner's Oriental Series, 1887) pp. 23–25.

[12] *Nafhat-ul-Uns*.

[13] *Al-Kawakib al-Muziyyah* (Hyderabad), Vol. II, pp. 124–25.

new-comer who simply repeated Rumi's own words, 'You don't know!' and quietly walked away. Rumi left his lecture, and, according to 'Abdul Qadir, went in search of Shams but could not trace him.

Jami and a few others[14] offer a slightly different version of the same incident. In their account, the books are not set on fire but are thrown in a tank of water around which the students were sitting. On Rumi's protest at the waste of such a treasure, Shams is credited with having brought out the books intact from the tank without the least sign of any damage.[15]

Let us now listen to Daulat Shah's version:[16]

Shams-i-Tabriz was in search of a man – a man who could share his spiritual confidence, a man who could bear the brunt of his dynamic personality, a man who was capable of receiving and imbibing his emotional experience, a man whom he could shake, destroy, build, regenerate and elevate. It was in search of such a man that he flit from land to land like a bird. His master, Rukn-ud-din Sanjabi, put him at last on the right track and bade him go to Konya. There he went and stayed in the Caravanserai of Sugar Sellers. One day Rumi, followed by his students and disciples, passed by the Serai. Shams stopped him and shot forth a question. 'What is the purpose of wisdom and knowledge?' he asked. 'To follow and reach the Prophet,' replied Rumi with an air of confidence about him. 'This is commonplace,' retorted Shams. 'What, then, is the purpose of knowledge?' asked Rumi. 'Knowledge is that which takes you to its source,' replied Shams and quoted this verse from Sana'i:

علم کزتو ترا نه بستاند جهل زان علم به بود بسیار

Ignorance is far better than the knowledge which does not take you away from yourself.

Rumi is said to have been so much impressed by this answer that he decided to become the disciple of Shams on the spot.

Before we examine the different versions, let us hear the one by the celebrated traveller Ibn

[14] For example, Amin Ahmad Razi, the editor of *Tadhkirah Hatf Iqlim*.
[15] Shibli, op. cit., p. 9.
[16] *Tadhkirah-i-Daulat Shah*, pp. 126–98. The same account appears in *Tadhkirah Atish-Kadah*.

Battutah who visited Rumi's tomb in the first half of the eighth century Hijrah. His account makes interesting reading. This is what he says:

Rumi was addressing his students. A sweetmeat vendor who sold a piece a penny passed by. Rumi sent for him and asked for a piece. The vendor gave him one and refused to accept payment. He then went away and refused to sell sweetmeats to others. Rumi abandoned his lecture and went in search of the vendor. Failing to find him he continued his search in the course of which he began uttering some ambiguous Persian verses which were later collected by his disciples in the form of the celebrated *Mathnawi*.

The account is too fantastic to deserve serious consideration. We will, therefore, pass on to the examination of other statements given above.

It will be seen that both Daulat Shah and Aflaki agree about the immediate cause of Rumi's conversion. There also seems to be general agreement about the fact that the meeting was sudden and unexpected.[17] The difference exists only in respect of the questions asked by Shams-i-Tabriz. The question quoted by Aflaki seems to be more intelligent than that quoted by Daulat Shah. It is really difficult to believe that a person, who was admitted to be an erudite scholar and was heir to a great Sufi, did not know the mystic meaning of knowledge. It becomes all the more difficult to believe it when we are told that at the age of six, the same person, in response to a request from his playmates to jump on to a neighbouring terrace, remarked: 'My brethren, to jump from terrace to terrace is an act well adapted for cats, dogs and the like to perform; come now, if you feel disposed, let us spring up to the firmament, and visit the regions of God's realm.' This statement ascribed to him as a child seems to be as incredible as the statement about his conversion to Tabriz. Aflaki's

[17] Refer to Rumi's line:

منم آن نا گهان ترا دیده گشته سر تا بپا همه دیده

account, however, appears to be more sensible. Besides, it finds corroboration in Sipahsalar, a pupil who spent forty years with Rumi. But if corroboration is the only criterion, ʻAbdul Qadir's account is borne out by Jami with minor differences of detail. Shibli has more or less accepted Sipahsalar's version but that is really not enough for our purpose. We should examine the most important source, i.e. *Mathnawi Waladi*. This is what Rumi's own son has to say in this matter:

آنکه اندر علوم فائق بود   به سری شیوخ لائق بود
مفتیان گزیده شا گردش   ....
بر مریدش ز با یزید افزون   بر یکی در و له دو صد ذوالنون
با چنین عز و قدر و فضل و کمال   دائماً بود طالب ابدال
خضرش بود شمس تبریزی   آن که باو اگر در آمیزی
هیچکس را بیك جوی نخری   پرده هائی ظلام را بدری
آن که از مخفیان نهان بود او   خسرو جمله و اصلان بود او
اولیا گر ز خلق پنهانند   خلق جسمند و اولیا جانند
این چنین اولیا که بینا اند   از ازل عالمند و والا اند
شمس تبریز را نمی دیدند   در طلب گرچه بس بگر دیدند
غیرتِ حق ورا نهان می داشت   دور از وهم و از گمان می داشت
نزد یزدان چو بود مولانا   از همه خاصتر بصدق و وفا
گشت راضی که روی بنماید   خاص با او بران بیفزاید
طمع اندر کسی دگر نکند   مهر باقی ز دل برون فگند
بعد بس انتظار رویش دید   گشت سرها برو چو روز پدید
دید آن را که هیچ نتوان دید   هم شنید آنچه کس ز کس نشنید
شد برو عاشق و برفت از دست   گشت پیشش یکی بلندی و پست
دعوتش کرد سوئی خانهٔ خویش   گفت بشنو شها ازین درویش

خانه ام گرچه نیست لائق تو   نیك هستم بصدق عـاشق تو
بنده را برچه هست و هرچه شود   بی گمان جمله آن خواجه بود

He who excelled in all branches of knowledge deserved to be leader of the Shaikhs. He counted great muftis among his disciples every one of whom was better than Bayazid. Two hundred Dhunnuns did not compare favourably with a single disciple of his. But with all this dignity and glory, and with all this prestige and perfection, he was always in quest of an Abdal (a leader). His Khidr (leader) was Shams-i-Tabriz; if you were associated with him, you would attach no significance to another person and would rend apart the veils of darkness (of sin). His (Shams-i-Tabriz's) glory was veiled even from those who were themselves veiled in the glory of God. He was (in effect) the leader of all those who had established complete communion (with God). Although the saints are hidden from the people, (yet) they constitute the very soul of the people (who are like the body). The visionary saints who were in possession of knowledge and greatness ever since eternity, failed to identify Shams-i-Tabriz, although they endeavoured to discover him. The majesty of God kept him hidden, remote from the sphere of imagination and thought. Since Maulana (Rumi) on account of his loyalty and sincerity was singled out by God, He agreed to reveal his (Shams's) face to him (Rumi) and allow him the full benefit of this special favour (revelation) so that he may not long for another (person) and may completely rid himself of all other attachments. After longing for him for a long time he saw his (Shams's) face and the secrets became transparent for him. He saw what could not be seen by others, and heard what was not communicated to anyone by one. Madly he fell in love with him and lost himself. All conflict born of logic (high and low) was resolved. He asked him to his house saying, 'Listen to the pleading of this darvesh, O King: although my abode is not worthy of you, yet in all sincerity I am your devoted slave, and whatever I possess (at present) and whatever I may happen to possess (in future) is and will remain yours (by the grace of God).

It will be clear from these lines that the chroniclers have sadly missed the spirit of the meeting. They do not really touch the fundamental and get lost in unnecessary details. Shorn of all dramatic elements, the simple fact must be stressed that Rumi, himself on a high spiritual pedestal, was restless and was in quest of a man worthy of his confidence and so also was Shams. Both were men of great spiritual eminence and, when they met, they naturally discovered each other on account of their highly developed sense of intuition. Each of them felt like a traveller who reaches his destination after years of labour and toil. Perfect harmony was established between the two. Both found the long-sought-for confidant in each other, and they opened out their hearts as they would do to no one else. The meeting brought about a unique peace and restlessness. For Rumi it brought the dawn of a new world, a living, pushing force, an *élan vital*, a divine sympathy, a feeling which penetrates the very essence of things. This unique experience of consciousness set off the potential energy stored up in the reservoir. From this day started the real work of Rumi, the work which has made him immortal.

What transpired at the meetings was not known to many but the result of the meetings was too consequential to remain a secret. The learned orthodox professor of theology gave up lecturing and, to the disappointment of a large number of his students, became a rapturous devotee of Shams-i-Tabriz. This excited the jealousy of Rumi's admirers who were suddenly deprived of the learning of an eminent scholar. And what is worse, it excited their anger, for they were shocked to see Rumi flout religious conventions which he had hitherto fervently preached and jealously defended. The person who had always regarded music as undesirable now became a great lover of it. For hours he would listen to music and dance in ecstasy. This departure was as unusual as it was unpleasant for Rumi's admirers. They ascribed this to the evil influence of the new arrival whom they considered a nuisance and a meddlesome freak. But Rumi had been completely enthralled by Shams. He did what he bade him do. He is reported to have said: 'When Shams-ud-din first came, and I felt for him a mighty spark of love lit up in my heart, he took upon himself to command me in the most despotic and peremptory manner. "Keep silent," said he, "and speak to no one." I ceased from all intercourse with my fellows. My words were, however, the food of my disciples; my thoughts were the nectar of my pupils. They hungered and thirsted. Thence ill feelings were engendered amongst them, and a blight fell upon my teacher.'[18]

Shams was by no means *persona grata* to those who loved Rumi and there were thousands of them. Rumi had become dimly aware of the consequences which this jealousy had engendered. He was already entreating Shams to ignore the protests directed against him. 'You are the light of my house,' he cried out; 'do not go away and leave me alone.' There is a childlike simplicity, a magical cadence and a haunting beauty about the lines[19] he is supposed to have addressed to Shams at this time.

بشنیده ام که عزمِ سفر میکنی مکن   مهر حریف و یار دگر میکنی مکن
تو در جهان غریبی و غربت ندیده   قصد کدام خسته جگر میکنی مکن

★ ★ ★

ای مه که چرخ زیر و زبر از برای تست   ما را خراب وزیر و زبر میکنی مکن
کو عهد و کو وثیقه که با ما توکردهٔی   از قول و عهد خویش عبر میکنی مکن
چه وعده میدهی و چه سو گند میخوری   سو گند و عشوه را چه سپر میکنی مکن
ای برتر از وجود و عدم پائگاه تو   این لحظه از وجود گزر میکنی مکن
ای دوزخ و بهشت غلامان امر تو   بر ما بهشت همچوسقر میکنی مکن
اندر شکرستان تو از زهر ایمنم   آن زهر را حریف شکر میکنی مکن
جانم چو کورهٔ پر آتش بست نکرد   روی من از فراق چو زر میکنی مکن
چون روی در کشی تو شود مه زغم سیه   قصد کسوف قرص قمر میکنی مکن
ما خشك لب شویم چو تو خشك آوری   چشم مرا باشك چه تر میکنی مکن

[18] Whinfield, op. cit., p. 107.
[19] Nicholson, op. cit., Ode XXVII.

چـون طاقت عقیلهٔ عشـاق نیستت   پس عقل را چه خیره نگر میکنی مکن

★★★

چشم حرام خوارهٔ من دزد حسن تست   ای جان سزای دزد بصر میکنی مکن

I have heard that thou dost intend to travel: do not so.
That thou bestowest thy love on a new friend and companion: do not so.
Tho' in the world thou art strange, thou hast never seen estrangement;
What heart-stricken wretch art thou attempting? do not so.

* * *

O moon for whose sake the heavens are bewildered,
Thou makest me distraught and bewildered: do not so.
Where is the pledge and where the compact thou didst make with me?
Thou departest from thy word and pledge: do not so.
Why give promises and why utter protestations,
Why make a shield of vows and blandishments? do not so.
O thou whose vestibule is above existence and non-existence,
At this moment thou art passing from existence: do not so.
O thou whose command Hell and Paradise obey,
Thou art making Paradise like Hell-fire to me: do not so.
In thy plot of sugar-canes I am secure from poison;
Thou minglest the poison with sugar: do not so.
My soul is like a fiery furnace, yet it sufficed thee not;
By absence thou art making my face pale as gold: do not so.
When thou withdrawest thy countenance, the moon is darkened with grief;
Thou art intending the eclipse of the moon's orb: do not so.
Our lips become dry when thou bringest a drought;
Why art thou moistening mine eye with tears? do not so.

* * *

My lawless eye is a thief of thy beauty;
O Beloved, thou tak'st vengeance on my thievish sight: do not so.

All these remonstrations notwithstanding, Shams decided to leave Rumi to his jealous friends and left Konya on 21 Shawwal 643 (19 June 1246). He had arrived there on 26 Jumadi II 642 (29 November 1245) so that the period of his stay is 18 months and 20 days and not 120 days as pointed out by some chroniclers. For some time his whereabouts were not known but soon Rumi received a letter from Damascus.[20] According to Aflaki, Rumi wrote four odes to him in the course of his correspondence with Shams. One was in Arabic, the others in Persian. But Shibli quotes Rumi as having written one letter in verse accompanied by a *ghazal* of fifteen verses of which he quotes only two.[21] In one of the *ghazals* sent to Tabriz, Rumi has hinted that he had written five or six of them. The *ghazal* from which Shibli quotes two verses may have been the sixth of this series. Judging from the two verses he has quoted, it seems to be the best of the six *ghazals* addressed to Shams during this period of separation:

بروید ای حریفان بکشید یار ما را بمن آورید حالا صنم گریز پا را
اگر او به وعده گوید که دم دگر بیاید مخورید مکر او را بفریبد او شما را

Begone, O friends, and bring me that friend by persuasion (and otherwise if you deem fit).
Begone forthwith and come back with that evasive beloved.
If he holds forth a promise to come at another time, be not deluded and be not deceived.

According to Farozan Far, Rumi recited this *ghazal* at the time of Sultan Walad's departure for Syria on an expedition to persuade Shams to return to Konya. This seems to be more appropriate. Farozan Far has added another verse:

بـه بهانه هائی شیرین بـه ترانه هائی موزن
بکشید کوئی خانه مه خوب خوش لقا را

Bring that resplendent beauty to my (dark) abode by sweet pretexts and softly spoken words.

It was perhaps this evasive flirtation of Shams which later found expression in a beautiful *ghazal*:[22]

[20] *Damimah Mathnavi Maulana* (Bombay), 1340.
[21] Shibli, op. cit., pp. 13–14.
[22] Nicholson, op. cit., Ode XX.

بگیر دامن لطفش که ناگهان بگریزد
ولی مکش تو چو تیرش که از کمان بگریزد
چه نقشها که ببازد و چه حیلها که بسازد
بنقش حاضر باشد ز راه جان بگریزد
در آسمانش بجوئی چو مه در آب بتابد
در آب چونکه در آئی بآسمان بگریزد
ز لا مکانش بجوئی نشان دهد بمکانت
چو در مکانش بجوئی بلا مکان بگریزد
چو تیرمی برود از کمان چو مرغ گمانت
یقین بدان که یقین وار از گمان بگریزد
از این و آن بگریزم ز ترس نی ز ملولی
که آن نگار لطیفم ز این و آن بگریزد
گریز پای چو بادم ز عشق گل چو صبا ام
گلی ز بیم خزانی ز بوستان بگریزد

★ ★ ★

چنان گریزد از تو که گر نویسی نقشش
ز لوح نقش بپرد و ز دل نشان بگریزد

Grasp the skirt of his favour, for on a sudden he will flee;
But draw him not, as an arrow, for he will flee from the bow.
What delusive forms does he take, what tricks does he invent!
If he is present in form, he will flee by the way of spirit.
Seek him in the sky, he shines in water, like the moon;
When you come into the water, he will flee to the sky.
Seek him in the placeless, he will sign you to place;
When you seek him in place, he will flee to the placeless.
As the arrow speeds from the bow, like the bird of your imagination,
Know that the Absolute will certainly flee from the Imaginary.
It will flee from this and that, not for weariness, but for fear
That my gracious Beauty will flee from this and that.
As the wind I am fleet of foot, from love of the rose I am like the zephyr;
The rose in dread of autumn will flee from the garden.

* * *

He will flee from you, so that if you limn his picture,
The picture will fly from tablet, the impression will flee from the soul.

Sultan Walad succeeded in his mission. In 1247 Shams came back with him. On his way back Sultan Walad walked while Shams rode on horseback. This was probably done under instructions from Rumi whose joy at the re-union can be better imagined than described. His disciples who were responsible for driving out Shams were themselves driven to despondency when they saw their Master suffering miserably on account of the separation which was unwittingly thrust on him by his foolish well-wishers. They soon realised their mistake, apologised and assured him that in case Shams returned they would not stand in his way.

توبه ها می کنیم رحمت کن   گر دگر این کنیم لعنت کن
توبهٔ ما بکن ز لطف قبول   گر چه کردیم جرمها ز فضول

We are (sincerely) repentant, be thou compassionate,
If we repeat our mistake, may we be accursed.
Although we committed sins in frivolity,
Extend to us thy forgiveness.

It was after these solemn assurances that Sultan Walad was sent to Damascus, but when he returned with Shams, the fickle crowd had forgotten all about their promises and old jealousies had already revived. And it is not very difficult to appreciate the hostile attitude of Rumi's admirers towards Shams. He was unpopular with them because: (*a*) it was under his influence that Rumi gave up the professorial gown for a peculiar dress of a darvesh; (*b*) to all appearances Shams did not rigorously follow the Islamic tenets and sometimes he uttered words which ordinary people attributed to irreligion; (*c*) to a casual observer, Shams gave the impression that he did not care much about Islamic discipline. Rumi had established a reputation for piety and learning. It, therefore, hurt the people to see that such a respected scholar had gone 'mad' and had openly acclaimed Shams as his master.[23]

There is little doubt that those who conspired against Shams were the near and dear ones of Rumi. His own son 'Ala-ud-din Muhammad is said to have been implicated in the conspiracy. The poet was perhaps aware of it as he did not attend his son's funeral. The growing jealousy and ill-will around him made the place uncomfortable for Shams and he mysteriously disappeared from the scene. According to Aflaki, he was stabbed by one of the conspirators. He is said to have been in a conference with Rumi when he was called out by someone. As he went out, he faced seven persons, one of whom stabbed him to death. Jami has endorsed this account. On being stabbed, he adds, Shams shouted a slogan at which the party of murderers became unconscious and when they came to, they saw nothing but a few drops of blood. In Daulat Shah's opinion some influential person of Konya engaged a relative of Rumi who killed Shams but he is himself sceptical about this account.[24] Sultan Walad, Rumi's son, does not mention the fact of Shams's murder in his *Mathnawi*. He only alludes to his sudden disappearance. In the absence of convincing evidence to the contrary, one has to accept Sultan Walad's version of the incident. There is, however, no dispute about the year of his disappearance, i.e. 1248.

News spread in Konya that Shams was dead. Rumi refused to believe it. In fact he came out with an emphatic contradiction:

[23] Recall Rumi's *ghazal* with the line beginning:

پیــر من و مــریــد من درد من و دوای من

فــاش بگفتم این سخن شمس مَن و خدای من

[24] *Tadhkirah*, p. 201.

که گفت که آن زندهٔ جاوید بمرد   که گفت که آفتاب امید بمرد
آن دشمن خورشید برآمد بر بام   دوچشم ببست و گفت خورشید بمرد

Who dared say that that Immortal one met his death?
Who dared say that the Sun of hope has set?
Lo! an enemy of the Sun came up to the roof,
Closed his two eyes and exclaimed the Sun had set!

This was apparently an effort to reconcile himself to the new situation. Soon his anxiety grew. He inquired after Shams from every traveller who happened to visit Konya. Anyone who told him that Shams was alive at once became an object of gratitude and reward. One day a traveller told him that he had seen Shams in Damascus. Rumi was so pleased with the news that he took off his robe there and then and gave it to the traveller. A sceptical friend pointed out that it was likely that the traveller was telling a lie in order to please Rumi. He retorted, 'Had I believed the news to be true, I would have given him my life and not my robes'!

Shams was away from Rumi and the agony grew till it became unbearable. Rumi began to devote himself increasingly to dance and music. The contemporary scholars who had great regard for him were shocked at his unconventional life and endeavoured to wean him from it, but Rumi had been completely converted to Shams and there was no room in his life for reservations. He had already become 'notorious' for his new mania – music.

A person who was once considered the last word on religion by his own generation, and who had, according to his own light, ruled out music as undesirable, had now become so enamoured of it that he threw all 'decorum' to the winds, listened to music with rapt attention at odd hours of the day and danced in ecstasy. This is how his own son describes his condition:

روز و شب در سماع رقصان شد   بر زمین همچو چرخ گردان شد
بانگ و افغان او بعرش رسید   ناله اش را بزرگ و خورد شنید
سیم و زر را به مطربان میداد   هر چه بودش بخادمان میداد
يك زمان بی سماع و رقص نبود   روز و شب لحظهٔ نمی آسود
غلغلهٔ، او فتاد، اندر شهر   شهر چه بلکه در زمانه و دهر
کاین چنین قطب و مفتیٔ اسلام   کوست اندر دو کون شیخ و امام
شورها می کند چو شیدا او   گاه پنهان و گاه هویدا او
خلق از وی ز شرع و دین گشتند   همه گان عشق را رهین گشتند
حافظان جمله شعر خوان شده اند   بسوئی مطربان روان شده اند

Day and night he danced in ecstasy,
On the earth he revolved like the Heavens.
His (ecstatic) cries reached the zenith of the skies
And were heard by all and sundry.
He showered gold and silver on the musicians;
He gave away whatever he had.
Never for a moment was he without music and ecstasy,
Never for a moment was he at rest.
There was an uproar (of protest) in the city,
Nay, the whole world resounded with that uproar.
(They were surprised that) such a great Qutb and Mufti of Islam
Who was the accepted leader of the two Universes
Should be raving like a madman –
In public and in private.
The people turned away from religion and faith (on his account)
And went crazy after love!
The reciters of the Word of God now recited (erotic) verses
And mixed freely with the musicians.

Dance and music were by no means an escape from the tribulations of his soul. They were on the contrary an artistic and spiritual expression of the definite advance his personality had made by then.[25]

Dance (only) where you break (mortify) yourself and (when you) tear away the cotton from the sore of lust.
(Holy) men dance and wheel on the (spiritual) battle-field: they dance in their own blood.

[25] *Mathnawi*, Vol. IV, pp. 9–10 (Nicholson's translation).

When they are freed from the hand (dominion) of self, they clap a hand; when they escape from their own imperfection, they make a dance.
From within them musicians strike the tambourine; at their ecstasy the seas burst into foam.
You see it not, but for their ears the leaves too on the boughs are clapping hands.
You do not see the clapping of the leaves: one must have the spiritual ears, not this ear of the body.
Close the ear of the head to jesting and lying, that you may see the resplendent city of the soul.

In music Rumi found solace and composure. In it he found what he calls the 'phantasy of Divine allocution'.

(For) the shrill noise of the clarion and the menace of the drum somewhat resemble that universal trumpet.
Hence philosophers have said that we received these harmonies from the revolution of the (celestial) sphere,
(And that) this (melody) which people sing with pandore and throat is the sound of the revolutions of the sphere;
(But) the true believers say that the influences of Paradise made every unpleasant sound to be beautiful.
Therefore *sama*' (music) is the food of lovers (of God), since therein is the phantasy of composure (tranquillity of mind).
From (hearing) sounds and pipings the mental phantasies gather a (great) strength; nay, they become forms (in the imagination).
The fire of love is made keen (influenced) by melodies.[26]

Rumi was in a terribly perturbed state of mind after his violent separation from Shams who seemed completely to have robbed him of all his composure and peace. There was an instant volcanic eruption and the personality, which once gave the appearance of supreme self-possession and carried itself with poise and dignity, had now become so mercurial that the dynamite of its new found energy would destroy everything which came within close range of its discharge. Rumi was indeed living dangerously in this era of revolution. He was undoubtedly mad, as his contem-

[26] Ibid., Vol. IV, pp. 312-13.

poraries said, but there was a method in his madness which few seemed to discern at that time. This madness found in music the soothing balm so essential for the restoration of the calm which was to follow the storm brought about by the separation from Shams. Although the fire and the fury of the storm had appreciably subsided by 1250, Rumi had yet to take years before he could settle down to a state in which he could muster sufficient courage to recollect the intense experience of this era without causing a serious emotional breakdown in his own personality. The conflict was to continue for some time before it could be finally resolved into the beauty and ringing clarity of the *Mathnawi*. The anguish was there, the disturbance was present and the seething discontentment, which once seemed to throw his whole personality overboard, was now groping its way to a fuller and firmer grasp on the consciousness of Rumi's own development during this crisis. It was in one of these days that Rumi came across a man who offered a complete antithesis to Shams and who was, therefore, of immense help in restoring the tranquillity without which Rumi's personality might have withered away after the terrific blast to which it was suddenly subjected. It was in one of these days that Rumi was dancing about in the streets of Konya when he suddenly arrested his movements and stood intently listening in a street to a musical sound coming from a corner. It was the rhythmic beat of a goldsmith's hammer. Rumi was so completely enthralled by this music that he stood listening to it before the shop, and the goldsmith, in deference to Rumi's state of ecstasy, continued beating the silver leaves. He wasted a good deal of silver but gained more than his weight in gold for he won Rumi's spontaneous friendship and gratitude. For hours the poet sang in praise of the goldsmith who at once became his disciple.

یکی گنجی پدید آمد ازین دکان زر کوبی
زهی صورت زهی معنی زهی خوبی زهی خوبی

I discovered a treasure in the shop of a gold leafmaker,
What a form, what a content, what a beauty, what a grace.

There are at least seventy-one *ghazals* in which the name of this goldsmith, Salah-ud-din Zarkob, appears. Rumi feared that the jealousy of his friends might deprive him once again of a new friend and, in his anxiety to retain him, he married his son to Salah-ud-din's daughter. For nine years, he remained Rumi's *alter ego* and confidant.

The question arises: How could an illiterate goldsmith[27] influence a great Sufi to the extent of retaining his confidence for nine long years? Rumi not only gave him his confidence but loved him to the extent of adoration:

روز و شب میکند سجود اُو را   بر فزونان دین فزود اُو را

Day and night he prostrates himself before him;
He has exalted him above the exalted of the faith.

The question is not difficult to answer. Literary attainments in the eyes of a man of God are no criterion of greatness. He does not attach much importance to the external worth of a man but weighs his inner capabilities:

ما برون را ننگریم و قال را   ما درون را بنگریم و حال را

We see not the form; we need not the objective experience,
We take notice of the content and the subjective experience (only).

[27] In *Walad Namah*, a work by Rumi's son, we read the following about Zarkob:

عامئی محض و ساده و نادان   پیش او نیک و بد بده یکسان
نتـواند درست فـاتحه خـوانـد   گر کند زو کسی سوالی ماند

He did not mould Rumi in a positive manner but supported him in his growth during the most difficult period of his life.[28] The separation from Shams had wrought havoc on Rumi and Zarkob's friendship and devotion during those days acted as a soothing balm. Zarkob describes his own function in Rumi's life in the words of his Master's son:[29]

می برنجند ازین که مولانا   کرد مخصوص از همه تنها
خود ندانسته این که آئینه ام   نیست نقشی مرا معائنه ام
در من او روئی خویش می بیند   خویشتن را چگونه نگزیند ؟

They are offended that the Maulana
Has singled me for his favours,
But they know not that I am but a mirror;
The mirror does not reflect itself (but the one who looks into it);
In me he sees himself;
Then why should he not choose (to see) himself?

Rumi's new mode of life was but an expression of the intense experience during his contact with Shams. Or to be more precise it reflected the perturbation of his soul on losing the company of Shams. He went as far as Damascus inquiring about him from house to house. The whole of Damascus was surprised at a great man searching so desperately for an obscure person who was not known to many in that town. Nobody could therefore help him in his quest. Rumi was completely disappointed till he cried out in despair: 'How long will I search for you from house to house and from door to door? How long will you evade me from corner to corner and from alley to alley?'

[28] For further details about Salah-ud-din Zarkob, see: (*i*) *Kitab Fihi-ma-Fihi*, edited by Farozan Far, pp. 95–96; (*ii*) *Risalah Faridun Sipahsalar*, pp. 134–41; (*iii*) *Walad Namah*, pp. 63–112; (*iv*) *Sharh-i Hal-i-Maulavi* by Farozan Far, pp. 100–111.
[29] *Walad Namah*.

چند کنم ترا طلب ، خانه بخانه در بدر
چند گریزی از برم ، گوشه بگوشه کو بکو

Rumi failed to find Shams but he found something greater. It dawned upon him, as it would dawn upon the restless soul of a prophet, that what he was searching for was his own immortal self.

وصف حسنش که می فزودم من خود همان حسن و لطف بودم من
شیـره از بهر کس نمی جـوشد در پئی حسن خویش می کوشد

Although (apparently) I glorified his beauty, (as a matter of fact),
I was the repository of all that beauty and grace.
The human soul (molten sugar) does not suffer (boil) for others,
In fact it aims at the perfection of its own beauty.

He, therefore, returned to Konya with a unique peace of mind.

Chapter 4

The Miracle of the Muse

Rumi's life appears clearly to divide itself into three phases. Although there can be no rigid division of a man's life into well-defined units, yet for the sake of convenience we may split the sixty-four years of his life into three distinct periods.

The first begins with his birth in 1207 and lasts until the death of his teacher, Burhan-ud-din Muhaqqiq, in 1240. We have referred to it as the period of preparation, for these years of Rumi's life were devoted primarily to the pursuit of knowledge. This, then, was a period of intellectual activity, and, although Rumi embarks on an active career of a teacher and abandons the role of a student after the death of Burhan-ud-din, yet there is no change in the essential nature of his activity until 1244 when he meets Shams-i-Tabriz in Konya. The first phase of his life could be said, therefore, to cover the period between 1207 and 1244.

The second phase begins with the appearance of Shams and lasts with all its immediate results until the death of Rumi's disciple, Salah-ud-din Zarkob, in 1261. The period between 1245 and 1261 could be appropriately called the period of lyrical activity, for most of his time during these fifteen years was devoted to music, dancing and lyrical poetry. The second period was dominated by love as the first was dominated by intellect. The *Divan* belongs to this period.

The third and final phase begins in 1261 when the

work of writing the *Mathnawi* is taken in hand; this was indeed the period of Rumi's immortal contribution and lasts until his death in 1273.

We now propose to deal with the second phase of his life, the period of lyricism and love. We have already dealt with the first phase in which we saw intellect being shattered at the first appearance of love symbolised by Shams. We have seen the revolutionary effect of this impact, for the birth of love did not come without the customary pangs. While Rumi merely suffered a serious change in life, Shams, who was responsible for this change, had to surrender life itself, for he was killed in this glorious attempt at completely changing the course of a great life. The price was heavy indeed, but does love pause to ponder before it offers the supreme sacrifice?

Rumi was thirty-seven when Shams entered his life. For thirty-seven years there is no evidence of his inclination towards poetry. The Muse suddenly appears in the form of Shams and the earliest poems which have been traced belong to the period when Shams left him for the first time, probably in the year 1245. How is it, then, that the man who was destined to be one of the greatest figures in the literature of Persia did not write even a single verse for the best part of his life? The answer is simple. Rumi did not belong to the school of conventional poets who wrote because it was fashionable or useful to do so. There came a stage in his life – an exploding and explosive stage – when he could no longer help being a poet.

He comes, a Moon whose like the sky ne'er saw, awake or dreaming,
Crowned with eternal flame no flood can lay.
Lo, from the flagon of Thy love, O Lord, my soul is swimming,
And ruined all my body's house of clay.
When first the Giver of the grape my lonely heart befriended,
Wine fired my bosom and my veins filled up;
But when His image all my eye possessed, a voice descended:

'Well done, O sovereign Wine and peerless Cup!'
Love's mighty arm from roof to base each dark abode is hewing
'Where chinks reluctant catch a golden ray.
My heart, when Love's sea of a sudden burst into its viewing,
Leaped headlong in, with 'Find me now who may!'
As, the sun moving, clouds behind him run,
All hearts attend thee, O Tabriz's Sun.[1]

The influence of Shams which made Rumi burst into lyricism was so great that it sustained him for nearly seventeen years. Between 1245 and 1261 he wrote about fifty thousand verses.[2] These verses form what is called *Divan-i-Shams-i-Tabriz.* But before we proceed to talk about Rumi's lyricism, we should like the reader to know why a collection of Rumi's verse should be attributed to Shams-i-Tabriz. Is the *Divan* written by Shams-i-Tabriz, as we may well believe from the title? The appearance is quite deceptive and our unsophisticated reader will not be the first to fall a prey to this misunderstanding.

In calling his lyrics the *Divan* of Shams-i-Tabriz, Rumi, of course, uses the name Shams as though Shams and he had become identical and were the same person. Though to us Shams's figure may appear unsubstantial, we need not accept the view put forward by some modern scholars that he is merely a personification of Jalaluddin's poetic mystical genius – an Eastern equivalent for 'the Muse'. Those who adopt this theory must logically extend it to include Salah-ud-din and Hisam-ud-din and can hardly avoid the implication that Sultan Walad created three imaginary characters to play the leading parts in his father's life and in the foundation of the *Mevlevi* Order. Western students of the *Divan* and the *Mathnawi* will recall a celebrated parallel that points to the other way. Did not Dante transfigure the

[1] *Divan*, SP. VII, Tr. by Nicholson, *Rumi, Poet and Mystic* [London, 1950], p. 161.
[2] Shibli, *Swanih Maulana Rum* (India), p. 42.

donn gentil who was the object of his romantic passion into Celestial Wisdom and glorify her under the name of Beatrice?[3]

Professors Browne[4] and Nicholson[5] have no doubt in their minds that the work is the product of Rumi. The *Encyclopaedia of Islam* is equally clear on this point. But all of them dismiss the controversy in a few sentences. They are so sure of their ground that they forget the sceptical reader. Mr Ghulam Dastgir of the Nizam College, Hyderabad (Deccan), has written a series of nine articles in the *Ma'arif* for the year 1936 and has conclusively proved, by citing both external and internal evidence, that the *Divan* was written by Rumi. We will refer the curious reader to the able work by Mr Dastgir which is now available in book form.

The *Divan*,[6] as stupendous in magnitude as it is sublime in content, was the precursor of the celebrated *Mathnawi*, but it is a matter to be regretted that, despite its essential beauty and haunting charm, the *Divan* has not received the attention it deserved at the hands of Rumi's students. We propose, therefore, to deal at some length with the lyrical aspect of Rumi for, without it, one can have no idea of his total personality as it finally emerges at the end of this period of lyrical activity in 1261.

In the old tradition, a *Divan* was supposed to be the proof of a poet's versatile genius. And a versatile genius was he who attempted all forms of poetry, e.g. *ghazal*, quatrain, eulogy, etc. Rumi's *Divan* consists of nothing but *ghazals* and he rigorously refrains from eulogising anyone but his beloved. This in itself is remarkable in an age in which great Sufis like 'Iraqi and Sa'di could not help writing eulogies for

[3] R. A. Nicholson, *Rumi, Poet and Mystic*, p. 22.
[4] *A Literary History of Persia*, Vol. II, p. 519.
[5] *Selected Poems from the Divani Shamsi Tabriz*.
[6] The *Divan* consists of as many as 3500 mystical odes.

their patrons. Rumi was no lover of conventions. He did not become a poet to qualify himself for a place among the *élite*. When he had to become one, he did not adhere to the conventions. Poetry came naturally to him and he wrote only in the form which suited his genius at that time. Besides some 2500 odes, many of considerable length, Rumi composed a large number of *Ruba'is* (quatrains), probably as many as 1600; and ended up with the six books which make up the *Mathnawi*. We are concerned in this chapter, however, with Rumi's *ghazals* – a form which marks the beginning of his poetical career. In choosing this form he did not adhere rigidly to its rules. Before him, the *ghazal* was supposed to deal with certain subjects only, and employ a set diction and a set form. Rumi could not be bound by such rigid rules. He does not believe in poetic subjects and poetic diction. 'The wind of beauty bloweth where it listeth.' It does not seem to create an artificial effect, it is not concerned with creating a certain pattern or the chiselling of words and phrases. Sublime love is the fountain of inspiration which gives it nourishment:

> Without Thee, how should poesy and rhyme dare to come into sight at eve or morn?
> Poesy and homonymy and rhymes, O Knowing One, are the slaves of Thy Command from fear and dread.[7]

Rumi raises every subject that he touches to the heights of sublimity; he uses every word which helps him in the expression of the feeling which is his paramount concern. His poetry, like his life, is an expression of deep sincerity. He rid the *ghazal* of the artificial atmosphere created by his predecessors and gave it a freshness and charm, born of an intense personal experience of love. In his unconscious zeal to break the conventions in the sphere of *ghazal* he probably overshot a little. He used, for instance,

[7] *Mathnawi*, Nicholson's translation, Book III, lines 1493–94.

unfamiliar and heavy words which do not usually fit in even in the grand setting of a *qasidah*[8] and he saw no harm in the use of *Fak-i-Izafi*[9] (elision) which is considered undesirable in Persian poetry.

There is an age-long tradition in *ghazal* that the poet uses his *nom de plume* in the last verse, and a poet has usually one *nom de plume*. Even this restriction seemed abhorrent to Rumi's spontaneity. We see him treading a completely new path. In most of his *ghazals* he uses the name of Shams – his beloved – and refrains from using his own *nom de plume* in traditional manner. On the few occasions that he has done so, he has not stuck to one. He uses Rumi, Mulla-i-Rum, Jalal and Maulana. In fact, it was this departure from tradition that made it so difficult for others to establish the identity of the poet, and the *Divan* has all along been attributed to the person whose name appears so frequently in it. And now to return to his lyrics.

All great lyric poetry is essentially subjective. It is, in fact, the expression of some supreme or some rapturous mood in a poet's life. We have seen in the preceding chapter how intensely Rumi lived in the emotional sphere. That in itself is a good guarantee of sincerity and spontaneity without which no vital work in literature is possible. His intense suscepti-

[8] E.g.

غلط گفتم مسجد های ما را   برون در بود خورشید بو اب
ای آفتاب رخ بنما از نقاب ابر   کان چهرهٔ مشعشع تا بانم آرزوست

[9] E.g.

عاشقان را شمع و شاهد نیست از بیرون خویش
آب انگوری بخورده باده شان از خون خویش
هیچ می دانی چه می گوید رباب
ز اشك چشم و از جگر هائی کباب

bility to music explains the richness of melody so truly characteristic of a lyric. It is not, therefore, surprising to find him amongst the greatest of the world in lyric poetry.

Every student of literature knows that in a study of any lyric we should inquire into 'the character and quality of the emotion which inspires it and the manner in which the emotion is rendered; for a lyric, to be good of its kind, must satisfy us that it embodies a worthy feeling; it must impress us by the convincing sincerity of its utterance; while its language and imagery must be characterised not only by beauty and vividness but also by propriety, or the harmony which in all art is required between the subject and its medium'.[10] Keeping this in view, we will hurriedly glance through the *Divan*. The first thing to consider is the character and quality of the emotion which inspired his poetry. The emotion which was the fountain-head of his inspiration was love; and what is love?

عشق است در آسمان پریدن　　صد پرده بهر نفس دریدن
اول نفس از نفس گسستن　　آخر قدم از قدم بریدن
نادیده گرفتن این جهان را　　مردیدهٔ خویش را ندیدن

★ ★ ★

زان سوئی نظر نظاره کردن　　در کوچهٔ سینها دویدن

This is Love: to fly heavenward,
To rend, every instant, a hundred veils.
The first moment, to renounce life;
The last step, to fare without feet.
To regard this world as invisible,
Not to see what appears to one's self.

* * *

To look beyond the range of the eye,
To penetrate the windings of the bosom![11]

[10] Hudson, *Introduction to the Study of Literature*, p. 97.
[11] *Divan* (Nicholson), p. 136.

Love for Rumi is not what D. H. Lawrence calls an attraction for 'rubber dolls'; it is a sublime and an irresistible urge to discover one's immortal self. It is love and the lover that live to all eternity; everything else is mortal. Not to love is the greatest misfortune that can befall anyone, and to love is to live intensely.

آن روح را که عشق حقیقی شعار نیست
نا بوده به که بودن او غیر عار نیست
در عشق مست باش که عشق است هرچه هست
بی کار و بار عشق بر یار بار نیست

★ ★ ★

عشق است و عاشق است که باقیست تا ابد
دل جز برین منه که بجز مستعار نیست
تا کی کنار گیری معشوق مرده را
جان را کنار گیر که او را کنار نیست

★ ★ ★

نظاره گر مباش درین راه منتظر
والله که هیچ مرگ بتر ز انتظار نیست

'Twere better that the spirit which wears not true love as a garment
Had not been: its being is but shame.
Be drunken in love, for love is all that exists;
Without the dealing of love there is no entrance to the Beloved.

* * *

'Tis love and the lover that live to all eternity;
Set not thy heart on aught else: 'tis only borrowed.
How long wilt thou embrace a dead beloved?
Embrace the soul which is embraced by nothing.

* * *

Be not an expectant looker-on in this path,
By God, there is no death worse than expectancy.[12]

Rumi knows no religion but the religion of love which transcends all barriers of country, creed and

[12] Ibid., p. 51.

colour. He is not the poet of Persia or Rum – he is the bard who sings for the universe, interpreting that which lies dormant in it, without recognition, without use, and without purpose.

چه تدبیر ای مسلمانان که من خود را نمیدانم
نه ترسا نه یهودم من نه گبرم نه مسلمانم
نه شرقیم نه غربیم نه بریم نه بحریم
نه از کان طبیعیم نه از افلاك گردانم

★ ★ ★

نه از هندم نه از چینم نه از بلغار و سقسینم
نه از ملك عراقینم نه از خاك خراسانم

★ ★ ★

مکانم لا مکان باشد نشانم بی نشان باشد
نه تن باشد نه جان باشد که من از جان جانانم
دوئی از خود بدر کردم یکی دیدم دو عالم را
یکی جویم یکی دانم یکی بینم یکی خوانم

What is to be done, O Moslems? for I do not recognise myself.
I am neither Christian, nor Jew, nor Gabr, nor Moslem.
I am not of the East, nor of the West, nor of the land, nor of the sea;
I am not of Nature's mint, nor of the circling heavens.

* * *

I am not of India, nor of China, nor of Bulgaria, nor of Saqsin;
I am not of the kingdom of Iraqain, nor of the country of Khurasan.

* * *

My place is the Placeless, my trace is the Traceless;
'Tis neither body nor soul, for I belong to the soul of the Beloved.
I have put duality away, I have seen that the two worlds are one;
One I seek, One I know, One I see, One I call.[13]

Rumi is a truly great artist. He is not afraid of death, for as a creative artist he draws his inspiration from his own immortal self for which there is neither decay nor death but which, on the other hand, grows and develops continuously. As a painter he is at once

[13] Ibid., pp. 125, 127.

superb and sublime. Every moment he shapes a beauteous form, and it is not a small canvas on which he paints, for his subject is the Immortal Man – the spirit which existed before the universe came into being – the spirit for which the universe was created.

His subject is self – at once limited and beyond all limits. Everything revolves round him; he is the centre of the universe and creation, and it is in his self that he finds the way to Eternity. Such in brief is his conception of love and life, and he sings it aloud with the beat of the drum and invokes you to join him.

ای عاشقان ای عاشقان هنگام کو چست از جهان
در گوش جانم میرسد طبل رحیل از آسمان
نـك سـاربـان بـرخـاسـتـه قـطارهـا آراسـتـه
از ما حلالی خواسته چه خفته اید ای کاروان

★ ★ ★

ای دل سوی دلدار شو ای یار سوی یار شو
ای پـاسبان بیـدار شو خفتـه نشایـد پاسبـان
هر سوی بانگ و مشغله هر کوی شمع و مشعله
کـامشب جهـان حـامله زایـد جهـان جـاودان

O lovers, O lovers, it is time to abandon the world;
The drum of departure reaches my spiritual ear from heaven.
Behold, the driver has risen and made ready the files of camels,
And begged us to acquit him of blame: why, O travellers, are you asleep?

* * *

O soul, seek the Beloved, O friend, seek the Friend,
O watchman, ye wake up: it behoves not a watchman to sleep.
On every side is clamour and tumult, in every street are candles and torches.
For to-night the teeming world gives birth to the world everlasting.[14]

It was a lofty and sublime emotion – and yet not removed from life but the very source of it – which inspired his poetry with love and sympathy. He dares

[14] Ibid., pp. 141, 143.

to unfold the mystery of life, and with love and faith he becomes the master of the universe – the coveted object of creation itself. Such is the quality and character of Rumi's inspiration.

It now remains for us to see the manner in which he renders his emotion. Before we proceed to analyse it, let us read a *ghazal*. And as you read it ask yourself whether it embodies a worthy feeling; whether it impresses you with its convincing sincerity; whether the language and imagery it employs is characterised not only by beauty and vividness but propriety; and, lastly, observe whether there is any harmony between the medium and the subject:

دوش من پیغام کردم سوئی تو استاره را
گفتمش خدمت رسان از من تو آن مه پاره را
سجده کردم گفتم آن خدمت بدان خورشید بر
کو بتابش زر کند مر سنگهائی خاره را
سینهٔ خود باز کردم زخم ها بنمودمش
گفتمش از من خبر کن دلبر خون خواره را
سو به سو گشتم که تا طفلِ دلم ساکن شود
طفل خسپد چون بَجنباند کسی گهواره را
طفل دل را شیر ده ، ما را ز گریه اش وار هان
ای تو چاره کرده هر دم صد چو من بیچاره را
شهر وصلت بوده است آخر ز اول جای دل
چند داری در غریبی این دل آواره را
من خمش کردم و لیکن از پی دفع خمار
ساقیا سرمست گردان نرگس خماره را

Yestereve I delivered to a star tidings for thee:
'Present,' I said, 'my service to that moon-like form.'
I bowed, I said: 'Bear that service to the sun
Who maketh hard rocks gold by his burning.'
I bared my breast, I showed it the wounds:
'Give news of me,' I said, 'to the Beloved whose drink is blood.'
I rocked to and fro that the child, my heart, might become still;

A child sleeps when one sways the cradle.
Give my heart-babe milk, relieve us from its weeping,
O thou that helpest every moment a hundred helpless like me.
The heart's home, first to last, is thy city of union;
How long wilt thou keep in exile this heart forlorn?
I speak no more, but for the sake of averting headache,
O Cup-bearer, make drunken my languishing eye.[15]

The first thing in his lyrics which strikes us is the exceedingly subjective nature of his poetry. And yet, in being extremely subjective, it is truly universal. Our heart returns an echo to his sentiments. He succeeds admirably in completely arresting our sympathy and infusing his own mood into our lives.

Talking of such a poet, Browning said, 'While the subjective poet whose study has been himself, appealing through himself to the absolute Divine mind, prefers to dwell upon those eternal scenic appearances which strike out most abundantly and uninterruptedly his inner light and power, selects that silence of the earth and sea in which he can best hear the beating of his individual heart, and leaves the noisy, complex, yet imperfect exhibitions of nature in the manifold experience of man around him, which serves only to distract and suppress the working of his brain.'

The nature of the emotion which inspired Rumi was such as to make it impossible for him to talk of experiences other than his own. He has, for instance, described his own restless condition at night. Every student of Rumi will know that it is purely a personal account, but how many can say that being personal it has ceased to be universal?

مرغ و ماهی ز من شده حیران — کاین شب و روز چون نمی خسپد
پیش ازین در عجب همی بودم — کـاسمان نگـون نمی خسپـد
آسمان خود کنون زمن خیره است — که چرا این زبون نمی خسپد
عشق بر من فسون اعظم خواند — دل شنید آن فسون نمی خسپد

[15] Ibid., p. 13.

The fishes and fowls are confounded by my wakefulness day and night.
Before this (state of mine) I used to wonder why the vaulted sky does not sleep;
But now the sky itself is amazed at my wretched condition.
Love has cast on me the spell of devotion,
The heart being enthralled by this spell no longer sleeps.

Or again he describes his mood of complete absorption in his prayers. The subject is 'prosaic', the experience is purely personal, but see how Rumi elevates it to great poetic heights:

چو نماز شام بر کس بنهد چراغ و خوانی
منم و خیال یاری غم و نوحه و فغانی
چو وضو ز اشک سازم بود آتش نمازم
در مسجدم بسوزد چو در رسد اذا نی
عجباً نماز مستان تو بگو درست هست آن
که نداند او زمانی نه شناسد او مکانی
عجباً دو رکعت است این عجباً چهارم است این
عجباً چه سوره خواندم چو نداشتم زبانی
در حق چگونه کوبم که نه دست ماندنی دل
دل و دست چون تو بردی بده ای خدا اما نی
بخدا خبر ندارم چو نماز می گزارم
که تمام شد رکوعی که امام شد فلانی

When the lamps are lit and the tables are laid, after the evening prayers,
I am engrossed with the thought of my Beloved, with grief, sorrow and lamentations.
My prayer is fiery for I perform the ablution with my tears.
When the call for prayer comes, the gate of my mosque is set on fire.
Strange is the prayer of the mad (lovers); tell me, is it correct to say prayers like this in complete disregard of time and space?
Strange are these two *rak'ats* and stranger still the fourth one,
How strange, I recited a *sura* without a tongue!
How can I knock at the door of God, since I have neither heart nor hand?

Since you have taken away my heart and hand, give me protection,
O Lord!
By God, I know not as I pray whether somebody has stood up to lead
the prayers or a *ruku'* has ended.

The nature of man's experience in essence remains the same with varying individuals. When Rumi sings of sorrow and grief, of joy and happiness, of love and separation, of success and failure, he sings not only for himself but for mankind. His experience is intense and its vibrations strike the chords of his reader so forcefully that he begins to feel that his own experience has been interpreted to him in beautiful language.

Rumi's universal appeal depends also to a great extent on the fact that he sings essentially of life. In his hand simple experiences become passionate and he communicates them through vivid eloquent imagery. In his poems, the complex principles of philosophy and religion are at once freed from their academic isolation and become a part of the common life of man.

This could be done only by a genius like Rumi. Our poet was later to develop this technique to the extent of writing a very long poem (the *Mathnawi*) with remarkable success. In this chapter, however, we must restrict ourselves to the *Divan* and find some examples from it to illustrate our point. Here, for instance, is the lyric which Sa'di considered to be the best in Persian literature and sent it to Shams-ud-din, the ruler of Shiraz:

هر نفس آوازِ عشق می رسد از چپ و راست
ما به فلك میرویم عزم تماشا كراست
ما بفلك بوده ایم یار ملك بوده ایم
باز همانجا رویم خواجه كه آن شهر ماست
خود ز فلك بر تریم و ز ملك افزون تریم

زین دو چرا نگذریم منزل ما کبریاست
عالم خاك از کجا گوهر پاك از کجا
گرچه فرود آمدیم باز دویم این چه جاست
بخت جوان یار ما دادن جان کار ما
قافله سالار ما فخر جهان مصطفی است

Every moment the voice of Love is coming from left and right.
We are bound for heaven: who has a mind to sight-seeing?
We have been in heaven, we have been friends of the angels;
Thither, sire, let us return, for that is our country.
We are even higher than heaven and more than the angels;
Why pass we not beyond these twain? Our goal is majesty supreme.
How different a source have the world of dust and the pure substance.
Tho' we came down, let us haste back – what place is this?
Young fortune is our friend, yielding up soul our business;
The leader of our caravan is Mustafa, glory of the world.[16]

Here is another lyric – and the number of this kind is legion – which illustrates our point more forcefully.

همرنگ جماعت شو تا لذت جان بینی
در کوی خرابات آ تا درد کشان بینی
در کش قدح سودا هل تا نشوی رسوا
بر بند دو چشم سر تا چشم نهان بینی
بکشائی دو دست خود گرمیل کنار ستت
بشکن بت خاکی را تا روی بتان بنیی

از بهر عجوزی را چندین چه کشی کابین
و ز بهر سه نان تاکی شمشیر و سنان بینی
شب یار همی گردد خشخاش مخور امشب
بر بند دهان از خود تا طعم دهان بینی
نك ساقی بی جوری در مجلس او دوری
در دور در آبنشین تا کی دوران بینی
این جاست ربابنگر جانی ده و صد ستان

[16] Ibid., p. 33.

گرگی و سگی کم کن تا مهر شبان بینی
گفتی که فلانی را ببرید زمن دشمن
رو ترك فلانی کن تا هست فلان بینی
اندیشه مکن الاّ از خالق اندیشه
اندیشهٔ جان بهتر کاندیشهٔ نان بینی
یا وسعت ارض الله در حبس چه خسپیدی
زاندیشه گره کم کن تا شرح جنان بینی
خاموش شو از گفتن تا گفت بری باری
از جان و جهان بگذر تا جان جهان بینی

Make yourself like to the community, that you may feel spiritual joy;
Enter the street of the tavern, that you may behold the wine-bibbers.
Drain the cup of passion, that you may not be shamed;
Shut the eyes in your head, that you may see the hidden eyes.
Open your arms, if you desire an embrace;
Break the idol of clay, that you may behold the face of the Fair.
Why, for an old woman's sake, do you endure so large a dowry,
And how long, for the sake of three loaves, will you look on the sword and the spear?
Always at night returns the Beloved: do not eat opium to-night;
Close your mouth against food, that you may taste the sweetness of the mouth.
Lo, the cup-bearer is not tyrant, and in his assembly there is a circle:
Come into the circle, be seated; how long will you regard the revolution (of time)?
Look now, here is a bargain: give one life and receive a hundred.
Cease to behave as wolves and dogs, that you may experience the shepherd's love.
You said: 'My foe took such a one away from me':
Go, renounce that person in order to contemplate the being of Him.
Think of nothing except the creator of thought;
Care for the soul is better than feeling care for one's bread.
Why, when God's earth is so wide, have you fallen asleep in a prison?
Avoid entangled thought, that you may see the explanation of Paradise.
Refrain from speaking, that you may win speech hereafter;

Abandon life and the world, that you may behold the life of the world.[17]

We need hardly labour at bringing out the beauty of Rumi's diction. One example should do:

این خواجه را در کوئی ما در گل فرو رفته است پا
با تو بگویم حال او برخوان اذا جاء القضا
جبار وار و زفت او دامن کشان می رفت او
تسخر کنان بر عاشقان بازیچه دیده عشق را
ای خواجه سر مستك شدی بر عاشقان خنبك زدی
مست خداوندی خودی کشتی گرفته با خدا
بس مرغ پران در هوا از دامهائی او جدا
می آید از چرخ قضا بر سینه اش تیر بلا

Hard by a master dwells, his feet in mire deep-sunken; of his state I prophesy.
Recite the boding verse, 'Whom doom shall fall.'
Tyrannous he and mighty, and oft he swept
Along in proud magnificence to mock
At lovers; love he deemed an idle play.
He, a besotted fool like thee to scorn
The votaries of love! God's wine has drowned
Thy wits and bidden thee wrestle with thy Lord.
As when a bird his airy flight resumes.
Exultingly, nor dreads the distant lure;
Fate to his bosom speeds the shaft of woe.

The third reason for Rumi's greatness as a lyric poet is his philosophy of life. 'No man was ever yet a great poet without being at the same time a profound philosopher.'[18]

In another chapter we will have an opportunity of discussing his philosophy in some detail, but here it will suffice to say that he was not one of those who advocated the sack-cloth. He saw a glorious destiny for mankind and, what is more, he had an intense

[17] Ibid., pp. 167, 169.

[18] Coleridge, *Biographia Literaria*, Chapter XV

faith in his poetry enabling mankind to reach the glorious goal he saw in his vision. On his own confession he abhorred the idea of writing verses and he only started doing so in the firm belief that thus alone would he be able to interest the poetry-ridden Iranian in the message that he had for mankind.[19] This explains to a large degree the gushing passionate spontaneity of his verse. The protagonists of that vague and shadowy doctrine 'Art for Art's Sake' will hasten to dub Rumi as a preacher. But we never said that, in order to fulfil the conditions of poetic greatness, a poet must, of necessity, write with a conscious ethical aim. At the same time we do not see any reason why we should quarrel with a poet 'who offers us philosophy in the fashion of poetry. We require only that his philosophy shall be transfigured by imagination and feeling; that it shall be shaped into a thing of beauty; that it shall be wrought into true poetic expression; that thus in reading him we shall always be keenly aware of the difference between his rendering of philosophic truth and any mere prose statement of it.'[20] Here, for example, is Rumi as a great poet – a creator and a thinker. Can we blame him for being both at the same time when he gives us a thing of beauty?

صورت گر نقاشم بر لحظه بتی سازم
و آنگه همه بتهارا در پیش تو بگدازم
صد نقش بر انگیزم با روح در آمیزم
چون نقش ترا بینم در آتشش اندازم
تو ساقی خماری یا دشمن هشیاری
یا آنکه کنی ویران بر خانه که بر سازم
جان ریخته شد با تو آمیخته شد با تو

[19] *Fihi-ma-Fihi*, ed. Abdul Majid Daryabadi, published by Maktabat al-Ma'arif, p. 28.
[20] Hudson, op. cit., p. 95.

چون بوی تو دارد جان جان راهله بنوازم
هر خون که ز من روید با خاك تو میگوید
با مهر تو همرنگم با عشق تو انبازم
در خانهٔ آب و گل بی تست خراب این دل
یا خانه در آ ای جان یا خانه بپر دازم

I am a painter, a maker of pictures; every moment I shape a beauteous form,
And then in thy presence I melt them all away.
I call up a hundred phantoms and imbue them with a spirit;
When I behold thy phantom, I cast them in the fire.
Art thou the Vintner's cup-bearer or the enemy of him who is sober,
Or is it thou who mak'st a ruin of every home I build?
In thee the soul is dissolved, with thee it is mingled;
Lo! I will cherish the soul, because it has a perfume of thee.
Every drop of blood which proceeds from me is saying to the dust:
'I am one colour with thy love, I am the partner of thy affection.'
In the house of water and clay this heart is desolate without thee;
O Beloved, enter the house, or I will leave it.[21]

Rumi had a keen ear for melody and music; in fact he was so sensitive on this score that even the rhythmic beats of a goldsmith's hammer made him burst into poetry and ecstasy. Gifted with such a temperament it is no wonder he instinctively selected words and metres which enhanced the beauty of his language. To illustrate this we will only quote one poem and leave the curious reader to the inexhaustible wealth of the *Divan*:

هر لحظه بشکلی بت عیار بر آمد	دل برد و نهان شد
هر دم بلباسی دگر آن یار بر آمد	که پیر و جوان شد
خود کوزه و خود کوزه گر و خود گل کوزه	خود رند سبوکش
خود بر سر آن کوزه خریدار بر آمد	بشکست و روان شد
خود گشت صراحی و می و ساغر و ساقی	خود بزم نیش شد
خورد آن می و سر مست ببازار برآمد	شور دل و جان شد

Trs. Nicholson, *Mathnawi*, p. 135.

رومی سخنی گفت و نگفته است و نگوید کس در همـه عالم
مردود شده آن کـه به انکـار بر آمـد مـردود جهان شـد

Love for Rumi is both a beginning and an end; 'it is the cure of all our ills,' a kind of mania which music helps to create and sublimate. The rapture and ecstasy caused by music enable man to have a glimpse of life and reality. How ecstatic are some his *ghazals*!

Come, O lover! Come, O lover! Let me assuage your suffering.
Let me be your friend and then make your condition better.
Come, O lover! Come, O lover! Surrender to me your heart,
That I may teach you how to win love and make you a beloved like myself.
Come, O lover! Come, O lover! Sacrifice yourself for me
That I may give you my life and make your life happier.
I came again, yet again. Such is lover's mania.
Like a falcon I came. Such is lover's mania.
My divine world became a mortal world, my mortal world divine.
My God's cup became my food. Such is lover's mania.

If you question him any more, he will perhaps say:

Last night, I asked the sage privately
Not to hide from me the secret of the universe.
Quietly he whispered into my ear,
Silent! 'tis something to know but not to utter!

Poetry, art and literature could not, in themselves, be the aim and object of Rumi, for his ambition was not so limited as to be satisfied with a beauteous expression of his own thought; nor did he aim at imparting joy and pleasure to the society in which he was born. His concern was indeed the whole of humanity and no amount of poetry could be regarded as a justification so long as wrong, injustice and intolerance remained. He had indeed a higher object, grander views. Poetry was but a means to an end and the end was nothing less than God Himself!

Rumi recognises one leader, follows one guidance, looks towards one goal. The leader is the Prophet; the guidance is the Holy Qur'an; and the goal is Allah! His belief in the limitless capacities of man is indeed inspiring, his scorn for death and tragic suffering raises you to heights unknown and in his incessant quest for unravelling the mysteries of life he is satisfied with nothing less than Heaven itself. Even that is not considered a prize worth ending the glorious quest of man for he stops at nothing less than the presence of God Himself – and here too this tiny creature displays the unique confidence of holding his own in the presence of the Supreme Reality before which he does not simply wither away! Pessimism and despair do not find any place in Rumi's scheme of life – he weeds out every vestige of fear which arrests the urge for growth and the expression of life. He casts off his phenomenal vesture which veils the divine spark in him and loudly proclaims:

از آب و آتش نیستم و ز باد سر کش نیستم
خاك منقش نیستم من بر همه خندیده ام

I am not of water nor fire, I am not of the forward wind;
I am not moulded clay: I have mocked (transcended) them all.[22]

The truth is independent of outward forms; it shines as brightly in the Heaven as in the mosque or the church; moreover, the religion of the heart, which alone has value, is not the monopoly of any particular creed. In reality all creeds are one:

این زمان و آن زمان بیضه است و مرغی کاندر اوست
مظلم و اشکسته پر باشد حقیر و مستهان
کفر و ایمان دان درین بیضه سفید و زرد را
واصل و فارق میانِ شان برزخ لا یبغیان

[22] Ibid., p. 220

بیضه را چو زیر پر خویش پرورد از کرم
کفر و دین فانی شد و شد مرغ وحدت پر فشان

This world and that world are the egg, and the bird within it
Is in darkness and bruised of wing, contemptible and despised.
Regard unbelief and faith as the white and the yolk in this egg,
Between them, joining and dividing, '*a barrier which they shall not pass.*'
When He hath graciously fostered the egg under His wing.
Infidelity and religion disappear: the bird of Unity spreads its pinions.[23]

For the attainment of this prize, endless endeavour, guided constantly by a courageous faith inspired by love, are the essential requisites. The barque of human life is beset at every stage of its onward voyage with subtle and serious dangers. There can be no smooth sailing save under enlightened and enlightening leadership. Follow the Prophet with love and reason and you can never go wrong! 'If you have eyes, do not walk blindly,' warns Rumi; 'and if you have not eyes, take a staff in your hand. When you have not the staff of prudence and judgement, make the (seer's) eye your leader; and if there is no staff of prudence and judgement, do not stand on every road without a guide. Step in the same fashion as a blind man steps, in order that your foot may escape from the pit and the dog.'[24] 'If anybody goes on the way without a leader, every two days' journey becomes one of a hundred years. Whoever speeds towards the Ka'ba without a guide becomes contemptible, . . . Whoever takes up a trade (or profession) without (having) a teacher becomes a laughing stock in town and country.'[25] In Rumi, the Persian mystical genius found its supreme expression. 'Viewing the vast landscape of Sufi poetry, we see him standing out as a

[23] Ibid., p. 221.
[24] Nicholson, Tr., *Mathnawi*, Book III, lines 276–279.
[25] Ibid., lines 588–590.

sublime mountain peak; the many other poets before and after him are but foothills in comparison. The influence of his example, his thought and his language is powerfully felt through all the succeeding centuries; every Sufi after him capable of reading Persian has acknowledged his unchallenged leadership.'[26]

We have briefly discussed the main reasons for Rumi's greatness as a lyrical poet. We can now consider the chief characteristics of his lyrics.

The first and foremost is his mysticism. And mysticism for our purpose is a mood in which the poet enters the realm Divine, has a certain experience which he relates when he returns to himself. Rumi strongly believed in intuition as a source of knowledge and to him the realm of mysticism was therefore real. At this stage we will not enter into a detailed discussion about the possibility of intuition as we will take up this and allied questions in our chapter on Rumi's thought. Here we will only be content to point out that there is no reason to suppose that thought and intuition are essentially opposed to each other. They spring up from the same root and complement each other. The one grasps Reality piecemeal, the other grasps it in its wholeness. The one fixes the gaze on the eternal, the other on the temporal aspect of Reality. The one is present enjoyment of the whole of Reality; the other aims at traversing the whole by slowly specifying and closing up the various regions of the whole for exclusive observation. Both are in need of each other for mutual rejuvenation. Both seek visions of the same Reality which reveals itself to them in accordance with their function in life. In fact intuition, as Bergson rightly says, is only 'a higher kind of intellect.'[27]

In the annals of literature, it is difficult to find a

[26] Nicholson, *Rumi, Poet and Mystic*, pp. 25–26.
[27] Iqbal, *Reconstruction of Religious Thought in Islam*, pp. 2–3.

greater protagonist of love than Rumi. He did not merely preach it but practised it. In his poetry he resolves everything into the good and the beautiful. Even evil – a seeming incohesion – fits in admirably into the rhythm of life. 'As a mystic he was too much in earnest to care for, even if he observed, the incongruities which draw upon him the censure of fastidious critics. As a poet, he sought to invest the Sufi doctrine with every charm that his genius could inspire.'[28]

Rumi's style 'is a style of great subtlety and complexity, hard to analyse; yet its general features are simple and cannot be doubted. In the *Mathnawi*, where it is fully developed, it gives the reader an exhilarating sense of largeness and freedom by its disregard for logical cohesion, defiance of conventions, bold use of the language of common life, and abundance of images drawn from homely things and incidents familiar to every one. The poem resembles a trackless ocean: there are no boundaries; no lines of demarcation between the literal "husk" and the "kernel" of doctrine in which its inner sense is conveyed and copiously expounded. The effortless fusion of text and interpretation shows how completely, in aesthetics as in every other domain, the philosophy of Rumi is inspired by the monistic idea.'[29]

'In sublimity of thought and grandeur of expression he challenged the greatest masters of song; time after time he strikes a lofty note without effort; the clearness of his vision gives a wonderful exaltation to his verse, which beats against the sky; his odes throb with passion and rapture-enkindling power; his diction is choice and unartificial; at intervals we meet with some splendidly imaginative figure: "a bracelet of bright hair above the bone."'[30]

[28] Nicholson, Tr., *Divan*, p. xlvi.
[29] Nicholson, *Rumi, Poet and Mystic*, p. 22.
[30] Nicholson, *Divan*, p. xlvi.

There are numerous verses written in this state of mind. They are easily the best examples of the mystic nature of his verse. We give some of them below:

(*i*)

زین همرهان سست عناصر دلم گرفت　　شیر خدا و رستم دستانم آرزوست
گفتند یافت می نشود جسته ایم ما　　گفتم آنکه یافت می نشود آنم آرزوست

My heart is weary of these weak-spirited companions;
I desire the Lion of God and Rustam, son of Zal.
They said, 'He is not to be found, we have sought Him long':
I said, 'A thing which is not to be found–that is my desire.'

(*ii*)

می گفت در بیابان رند دهن بریده　　صوفی خدا ندارد او نیست آفریده

With great pertinence remarked a tipsy one in the desert:
A Sufi has no God for he is not created.

(*iii*)

حاصل عمرم سه سخن بیش نیست　　خام بدم ، پخته شدم ، سوختم

The ultimate achievement of my life is summed up in three sentences;
I was raw; I matured; I was burnt out.

The Persian *ghazal* is marked by lack of unity. A verse deals with a single emotion and one is not necessarily connected with the other. 'The butterfly imagination of the Persian flies, half-inebriated as it were, from flower to flower, and seems to be incapable of reviewing the garden as a whole. For this reason, his deepest thoughts and emotions find expression mostly in disconnected verses (*ghazal*), which reveal all the subtlety of his artistic soul.'[31]

With Rumi, however, this is an exception rather

[31] Iqbal, *The Development of Metaphysics in Persia* (Lahore, 1964), p. ix.

than a rule. He is perhaps the foremost Persian poet whose *ghazals* are the expression of a sustained emotion, and are marked by a unity of theme. In his *Divan* one often comes across lyrics to which a title could be easily given.[32] The reason why there is continuity of theme in his lyrics is that he wrote only when he was caught by the Muse in a particular state of mind. We are told by his biographer that most of his *ghazals* were composed extempore, while the poet in a state of trance slowly rotated about a column in the Mevlevi monastery at Konya. Here, for example, is the mood of joy at the union with the beloved:

معشوقه به سامان شد تا باد چنین بادا   کفرش همه ایمان شد تا باد چنین بادا
زان طلعت شاهانه زان مشعلهٔ خانه   بر گوشه چو بستان شد تا باد چنین بادا
غم رفت وفتوح آمد شب رفت و صبوح آمد   خورشید درخشان شد تا باد چنین بادا

Here is the beloved in the full glory of beauty–
May it (this state) continue for ever!
Paganism has been completely converted to faith,
May it (this state) continue for ever!
Owing to that regal beauty, that luminary of my abode,
Every corner finds itself a garden –
May it (this state) continue for ever!
Grief has departed yielding place to happiness,
Night has departed making room for the morn.
Lo! the sun came out in its resplendence.
May this (state) continue for ever!

Rumi is in search of a confidant, a friend with whom he could share his secrets. The wish finds expression in a continuous *ghazal*. The mood is both one of bewilderment and discovery – a paradox: but then paradoxes resolve themselves so beautifully at the hands of Rumi:

[32] An enthusiast from Isfahan has in fact published a selection from the *Divan* and has given a title to each *ghazal*.

کنــاری نــدارد بیــابــان مــا قــراری ندارد دل و جــان ما
جهان در جهان نقش صورت گرفت کدامست ازین نقش ها آن ما
چو در ره ببینــی بــریده سـری که غلطان رود سوی میدان ما
ازو پرس ازو پرس اسرار دل کـزو بشنوی سـر پنهـان مـا
چه بودی که یك گوش پیدا شدی حریف زبان هـای مرغـان ما
چه بودی که یك مرغ پران شدی بـرو طـوق سـر سلیمـان مـا
چه گویم چه دانم که این داستان فزونست از حد و امکـان ما

Our desert hath no bound,
Our hearts and souls have no rest.
World in world has ta'en Form's image;
Which of these images is ours?
When thou seest in the pathway a severed head,
Which is rolling toward our field.
Ask of it, ask of it, the secrets of the heart:
For of it thou wilt learn our hidden mystery.
How would it be, if an ear showed itself,
Familiar with the tongues of our songsters?
How would it be, if a bird took wing,
Bearing the collar of the secret of our Solomon?
What shall I say, what think? for this tale,
Is too high for our limited and contingent being.[33]

And here is the poet who is no more groping in the dark in search of a friend; he has already found the way to him; he is sure of his ground. A Sufi would say that he is in a state of *baqa!*

ما دل اندر راه جان انداختیم غلغـلی اندر جهـان انداختیم
ما ز قرآن گـزیدیم مغـز را پوست را پیش سگان انداختیم
جبه و دستار و علم و قیل و قال جمله در آب روان انداختیم
از کمان شوق تـیر معرفت راست کرده بر نشان انداختیم

We have sacrificed the heart in the cause of this soul;
We have caused a consternation in the world;
We have picked out the essence from the Holy Word,
Throwing the skin to the dogs.

[33] *Divan* (Nicholson), p. 9.

We have totally discarded the mystic's cloak, the scholar's turban, all knowledge and all logic.
With the help of our sure instinct we scored a bull's eye at the first venture.

Sometimes when Rumi cannot express the complete mood in a single *ghazal*, he tries two or three, often in the same rhyme and metre. Occasionally he bursts forth into delightful conversation:

گفتم شها بس قطره ها در هجر تو باریده ام
گفتا چه غم بز قطره را من لولوئی مکنون کنم
گفتم شها بسیار شب دیده نیالودم بخواب
گفتا شبی را صد شبی در عمر تو افزون کنم

I said, 'O Prince, many a tear have I shed in your separation'.
Said he, 'Then why grieve, every tear shall be turned into a precious pearl.'
I said, 'O Prince, many a night have I laid awake.'
Said he, 'For every night so spent, yet shall gain a hundred nights.'

The direct explosive force of expression, the ecstatic fervour and enthusiasm of Rumi's verse is not to be found elsewhere. His lyrics echo beautifully the agonies of a soul madly in love; there is no design or craftsmanship about them; they are the spontaneous, impassioned record of varying experiences. Craftsmanship in art implies insincerity and Rumi is prepared to sacrifice the beauty of his expression for the sincerity of his utterance:

Many prayers are rejected because of the smell thereof: the corrupt heart shows in the tongue.
(But) if thy words be wrong and the meaning right, that wrongness of expression is acceptable to God.

So truly and sincerely does he record his feelings that we feel the pulse of his heart throbbing in our hand; we can almost directly launch into the labyrinthine ways of his mind and follow the track without coming up against a blind alley. Here, for example, we see a lover sincerely in love, being evaded by the beloved. He is tired of his steadfast pursuit and is painfully conscious of the advantage his beloved has over him. The beloved can never appreciate the lover's point of view, for he has never known the agonies of love. 'Would to God he fell in love with a faithless person and spent wakeful nights! Would to God he fell in love with a cruel rake who would completely disregard his feelings! For then alone he would know what it means to love, for then he would understand how I pass my sleepless nights':

ای خداوند یکی یار جفا کارش ده   دلبر عشوه گر و سرکش و خوانخوارش ده
چند روزی ز پی تجربه بیمارش کن   با طبیبان دغا پیشه سرو کارش ده
تا بداند که شب ما به چسان می گذرد   درد عشقش ده و عشقش ده وبسیارش ده

O God, afflict her with a cruel friend,
Coquettish, deceitful and heartless.
Let her pine away (in pain) for a few days,
In the hand of treacherous physicians.
Afflict her with love, more love and still more love
So that she may realise how I pass my nights!

He then entertains the wish that if he were to be the beloved, he would not behave in the way his beloved does. On the other hand he would be responsive – he would willingly confer kisses and remain faithful. How beautifully he expresses this:

گر بدین زاری تو بودی عاشق من هر زمان
بر دلت بخشید می و بوسهٔ بخشید می
ور تو بودی همچو من ثابت قدم درِ راهِ عشق
بر تو هر گز چون تو بر مَن دیگری نگزید می
گرچه بر جور و جفای تو مرا قدرت بدی
یا ز خلقم شرم بودی یا ز حق ترسید می

If you were to love me (as I do) with humility and submission,
I would have condoned the errors of your ways and would have granted you the boon of a kiss.
If you were as constant in love (as I am),
I would not have preferred another one (like you have done).
If I were to command the power of cruelty and tyranny (as you do),
(I would not have exercised it) either in deference to public opinion or out of fear of God.

Rumi is at once direct and effective. The tone sometimes becomes coquettishly tantalising. Take this for example:

بنمای رخ که باغ و گلستانم آرزوست　　بکشای لب که قند فراوانم آرزوست
گفتی ز ناز بیش مرنجان مرا برو　　آن گفتنت که بیش مرنجانم آرزوست
یکدست جام باده و یکدست زلف یار　　رقصی چنین میانهٔ میدانم آرزوست

Show thy face, for I desire the orchard and the rose-garden;
Ope thy lips, for I desire sugar in plenty.
'Vex me no more,' thou saidst capriciously, 'begone'!
I desire that saying of thine, 'Vex me no more.'
In one hand a wine-cup and in one hand a curl of the Beloved:
Such a dance in the midst of the market-place is my desire.[34]

He is deeply aware of all the suffering that love is heir to, and is piercingly delightful in his expression of it. Here, for instance, we see a lover on the horns of a dilemma. He is waiting intently for the beloved but he knows in his heart of hearts that she would not keep her tryst. It happens that she turns up. The lover is shocked into exhilarating confusion. He can hardly believe it. In seething bewilderment he looks about him until he is convinced that she is no mirage:

یار آمد زود زود خلوتیان دوست دوست
دیده نما می کند ، نیست غلط ، اوست اوست !

How successfully he has exploited the dramatic potentialities of the situation and how beautifully he

[34] Ibid., pp. 65–67.

has caught and set aside the fleeting conflict! Only a great lyrical poet could have done it.

Poets, like Hafiz, 'make the mystic terminology . . . serve the function of a mask or a lady's fan in the last century. By tantalising the reader, by keeping him, as it were, suspended between matter and spirit, they pique his ingenuity and double his pleasure. Nearly every line is a play of wit. Love, Wine, and Beauty are painted in the warmest, the most alluring colours, but with such nicety of phrase that often the same ode will entrance the sinner and evoke sublime raptures in the saint.'[35]

But it is not so with Rumi. He does not balance literal and spiritual meanings so equally as to leave the choice uncertain. His words will always bear the profoundest interpretation. He is no juggler with words. Although his metaphors are drawn from every field of Nature and Art, neither Art nor Nature is the subject which they adorn. His verse, in his own words, is the shop for Unity; anything that you see there except the One (God) is an idol.

God is the Saqi and the Wine,
He knows what manner of Love is mine.

His subject is the eternal, immortal man, the man of flesh who can attain to unseen heights of sublimity. Gently he sings to him of love and beauty and he sees him through the travail that follows in the wake of love. To the sick and breaking heart, Rumi imparts a healing comfort; where all the efforts of ancient physicians and sublime philosophers appear to bring nothing but added agony and perplexing anxiety, a word from Rumi produces the unique miracle of peace and comfort. Like a noble comrade he stays with you even when your own shadow is afraid to keep you company, for his is a life dedicated to love which brings about peace, prosperity and dignity of mankind

[35] Ibid., Intro., pp. xxv–xxx.

in the world of reality, and peace, tranquillity and light in the domain of spiritual life.

Doctors we of ancient time
And philosophers sublime,
Roasted flesh and syrup rare,
Face of earth and Sirius star.
For such bones as aching be
Saving liniment are we:
To the sick and breaking heart
Healing comfort we impart.
Earth's physicians soon are fled
When the sufferings are dead;
We do never flee away
But like noble comrades stay.
Hasten then from this abode,
For we take the open road;
Earthly pleasures scarce suffice,
We are folk of Paradise.
Men have argued (but they lied)
That this image does not bide;
One declared we are a tree,
Said another, grass are we.
Yet the rustling of this bough
Proves the breeze is stirring now;
Silent then, O silent be:
That we are, and this are we.[36]

Rumi is at his best in the *Divan*. Here he excels himself as a poet. Most of the 3500 odes and the 2000 quatrains that he wrote must have been sung in the nocturnal sessions in an ecstatic dance. Reminiscent of these intimate and animated sessions is a beautiful ode addressed to the musicians on whom Rumi invokes the blessings of God. The musician has a role to play in the life of a mystic and Rumi is so grateful for the help in spiritual communication that he pleads passionately for this class which was generally looked down upon by the people.

God bless the musicians, he says, with the sweetness of honey, and give their hands strength to play

[36] *Divan* (Tr. A. J. Arberry), p. 202.

on the instruments. They are devoted to love and deserve their rightful place of honour. Their melody has helped revive many a drooping heart: why, then, should they not receive the recognition due to their merit? In a loving tribute to the companions who contributed so significantly to the *sama*ʿ evenings, Rumi says:

خدایا مطربان را انگبین ده   برای ضرب دست آهنین ده
چو دست و پای وقف عشق کردند   تو همشان دست و پای راستین ده
چو پُر کردند گوش ما ز پیغام   تو شان صد چشم بخت شاه بین ده
کبوتر وار نالانند در عشق   تو شان از لطف خود برجِ حصین ده

Dance and music have an important place in Rumi's scheme of things but, removed from the context of contemplation, they cease to sublimate, and in fact tend to be abused as a mere instrument of satisfying one's carnal desires. Rumi is aware of this danger and warns against indiscriminate use of the fine arts by the vulgar and the uninitiated. In their hands *sama*ʿ becomes a mockery and a meaningless exercise:

سماع آرام جان زندگانست   کسی داند که اُو را جانِ جانست
سماع آنجا بکن کانجا عروسیست   نه در ماتم که آن جای خفانست
کسی کو جوهر خود را ندیدست   کسی کان ماه از چشمش نهانست
چنین کس را سماع و دف چه باید   سماع از بهر وصل دلستانست

Rumi is no rhymester. He does not consciously sit down to write a poem. He does not gather his tools about in a workshop. There is no design or craftsmanship about him. He is a man possessed. Poetry simply gushes forth like clear sweet water from a spring. He sings essentially of love. There is a superficial monotony of theme but those who read him today find his odes as fresh, original and inspiring as they must have been some seven hundred years ago when they moved men to rare heights of joy and ecstasy. Thousands of odes in the *Divan* hammer essentially on the same theme but the treatment is so subtle and sincere that it is hard to resist the power, beauty and movement of his verse. The theme recurs, no doubt, but every ode invests old words with a new meaning, unearths a fresh angle, and brings about a deeper and more sensitive perception of the emotion that is love.

انصاف بده که عشق نیکو کار است　　زانست خلل که طبع بد کردار است

تو شهوت خویش را لقب عشق نهی　　از شهوت تا بعشق رهِ بسیار است

Love, you must concede (in all fairness), leads to goodness but the trouble arises because of the evil nature of man.
You style your lust by the name of love. But between love and lust there is a big distance.

The *Divan* is a world of its own. There is nothing objective or scientific about it. Here the concept of time and space changes, the distinction between space and spacelessness disappears. A moment of love is tranformed into eternity. There is no analysis, no explanation, no apologies for the bold assertions that Rumi makes about the intensely subjective experience which transforms his own life. He takes the reader along on his voyage of discovery and gently helps him share his own exhilarating joy and happiness in a complete voluntary surrender to the will and vagaries of his Beloved. There is no attempt to preach, to persuade, to convince. The many moods of love find spontaneous expression in some of the most moving poetry ever written by man. Success to him is as beautiful as failure, sweet union as welcome as the pangs of separation. In his world, good and evil cease to exist. The distinction between ugliness and beauty disappears, the hymn of hate becomes totally unnecessary and irrelevant – there is only the symphony of love, truth and beauty. The veils are lifted, slowly but surely, the old idols crumble like a house of cards, and Rumi guides one on the Path – sure-footed, supremely humble, and allows one a glimpse of the inner mystery and the majesty of Love. It is no empty boast when he says that his heart and tongue have helped many a mind to grasp the secret and mystery of the Soul.

گوشها گشته اند محرم غیب   از زبان و دل ِ سخن ورِ ما

In the odes of the *Divan* one comes across Rumi in all his moods. There are moments of joy and exhilaration, there are moods of sorrow and grief; one sees glimpses of union as one comes across the state of separation, but in all the turmoil and confusion of life one detects a quiet inner conviction, a telling determination to accept the challenge, resolve the conflict and create something truly immortal. With all the apparent agitation and restlessness, the emotional upheaval consequent on the separation from Shams is diverted to creative channels where frustration gives way to a sense of fulfilment and promise. Despite all the agony and pain that Rumi has gone through, one does not come across any shrieking cries in the *Divan*. There are no violent scenes, no loud complaints, no ugly protests, no demonstrative disagreements with the Beloved. On the contrary, he is able calmly to recollect the terrifying experience of the storm which once seemed so completely to sway him off his feet.

The era of scholarship is over. Now love unties the knots that had been tied by intellect. Rumi leaves the world of logic behind him and enters the realm of love. Here the laws are different, the language is not the same, the atmosphere is charged with a lofty intangible feeling. Metaphors and similes suggest a gentle clue but that is about all. Here one does not ask for proofs, there is no dissection of a dead body to discover the secret of life. One simply lives and confronts the reality of life while others seek to escape from it. The whole world sleeps in sweet slumber while Rumi dedicates his wakeful nights to prayer, contemplation and humble prostrations before the Lord. Those alone who have tasted the indescribable pleasure that springs from a sense of communion with one's higher self can appreciate the fervour and enthusiasm with which Rumi describes his frequent encounters with the Beloved.

بحمد الله که خلقان جمله خفتند　　و من بر خالقم برکار امشب
زهی کرو فر و اقبال بیدار　　که حق بیدار و ما بیدار امشب
اگر چشم بخسپد تا سحر گه　　ز چشم خود شوم بیزار امشب

Thank God, people are fast asleep and I am busy tonight with my Creator,
Thank Heavens for the Grace and good fortune.
Truth is wide awake tonight and so am I,
I would be thoroughly disgusted with my eyes were they to close tonight in sleep.

It is impossible to communicate the impact of such spiritual encounters. Silence alone is the answer. Rumi is all too conscious of the limitation of language, for this is the domain of the heart, the spirit.

میجهد شعلهٔ دیگر ز زبانِ دلِ من
تا ترا وهم نیاید که زبانیم همه

Shams-i-Tabriz is of course the hero of the *Divan* though Zarkob comes in for a fair portion of praise. The odes addressed to Shams, however, give some idea of the supreme surrender of Rumi to what he considers the symbol of Perfect Man. Shams is identified with the primeval man; he is Adam, Jesus and Mary, all rolled into one, he is at once the secret and the revealer of mysteries to man; bitterness is rendered sweet by him, he converts disbelief into faith. At his touch a thorn turns into a rose. He is

Rumi's life, his soul, his faith, his belief as well as disbelief. There is nothing higher than him – he is the sovereign of sovereigns and from him Rumi begs a share of faith and fortune:

هم آدم و آن دم تـوئی   هم عیسی و مریم توئی
هم راز و هم محرم توئی   چیـزی بده درویش را
تلخ از تو شیرین میشود   کفر از تو چون دین میشود
خار از تو نسرین میشود   چیـزی بده درویش را
جـانِ من و جانـانِ من !   کفـر من و ایمـانِ من !
سـلطانِ سلطانـانِ مـن !   چیـزی بده درویش را

Shams is invested with all kinds of paradoxical qualities and it is to him that Rumi turns for guidance, help and support in the tortuous task of scaling slippery spiritual heights. Shams is at once his friend, confidant, master and guide. He is the Noah, the Spirit, the Conqueror and the Conquered. He is the light, the revelation. He is at the same time a drop and an ocean. He is both a mercy, grace and a terror. He is in brief a paragon of virtues which reduce desperate paradoxes into a pattern of harmony and unity. It is to him that Rumi turns time and again in the *Divan* for inspiration:

یار مرا ، غار مرا ، عشقِ جگر خوار مـرا
یار توئی ، غار توئی ، خواجه نگهدار مرا
نوح توئی ، روح توئی ، فاتح و مفتوح توئی
سینهٔ مشروح تـوئی ، بر درِ اسـرار مرا
نور توئی ، سور توئی ، دولتِ منصور توئی
مرغِ کهنهِ طور توئی ، خسته بمنقار مـرا
قطره توئی ، بحر توئی ، لطف توئی ، قهر توئی
قند توئی ، رند توئی ، بیش میـا زار مرا

حجرهٔ خورشید توئی ، خانهٔ ناهید توئی
روضهٔ اومید توئی ، راه ده ای یار مرا
روز توئی ، روزه توئی ، حاصل دریوزه توئی
آب توئی ، کوزه توئی ، آب ده این یار مرا
دانه توئی ، دام توئی ، باده توئی ، جام توئی
پخته توئی ، خام توئی ، خام بگذار مرا

The hankering after the ideal, the Perfect Man, is no romantic pursuit. It is an earnest and a serious endeavour. Rumi comes to the conclusion, after years of prayer, mortification and contemplation, that the Perfect Man is no mirage but he is not to be sought in the remote recesses of a cave or the distant heights of a heaven; he is to be found in the depth of one's own self. This was certainly by no means an original discovery but after years of search and struggle a unique consciousness dawned on him, as it dawns on the soul of a prophet, and created in Rumi the power and strength to face a whole hostile world. The vision dissolved doubts, resolved conflicts and created an irresistible urge in him to share his new-found freedom from uncertainty with the rest of mankind. This was the end of lyrical activity. Rumi was now groaning under the weight of a new responsibility – a compulsion that he had now to proclaim the truth and share it with mankind. With a single-minded determination Rumi now addresses himself to the task of spreading the word.

This, then, is the beginning of a new phase – Poetry with Purpose – but before we look at its supreme manifestation – the *Mathnawi* – let us read a few quatrains, a form eminently suited to the expression of philosophic ideas with brevity and effect.

ایدوست بدوستی قرینم ترا   هر جا که قدم نهی زمینیم ترا
در مذهب عاشقی روا کی باشد   عالم تو ببینیم و نه بینیم ترا

O Friend! we are near you in friendship,
Wherever you set foot, we prostrate ourselves like earth.
How is it permissible, in the religion of love,
That we should see your Creation and neglect to see You?

پرورد نباز و نعمت آندوست مرا   بر دوخت مرقع از رگ و پوست مرا
تن خرقه و اندر اُو دلِ ما صوفی   عالم همه خانقاه و شیخ اوست مرا

That Friend brought me up with great care and attention;
He sewed me a garment from skin and veins.
The body is like a cloak and my heart in it like a mystic,
The world is like a monastery and He is my Guide.

علمی که ترا گره گشاید بطلب   زان پیش که از تو جان بر آید بطلب
آن نیست که هست مینماید بگذار   آن هست که نیست بنماید بطلب

Seek the knowledge which unravels mysteries
Before your life comes to a close.
Give up that non-existence which looks like existence,
Seek that Existence which looks like non-existence!

از کفر و ز اسلام برون صحرائیست   ما را بمیان آن فضا سودائیست
عارف چون بدان رسید سررا بنهد   نه کفر نه اسلام ! نه آنجا جائیست

There is a world outside Islam and Disbelief,
We are enamoured of the atmosphere therein.
The mystic lays down his head when he reaches there.
There is neither Islam nor Disbelief in this place.

برهر جائیکه سر نهم مسجود اُو است
بر شش جهت و برون ز شش معبود اُو است
باغ و گل بلبل و سماع و شاهد
این جمله بهانه و همه مقصود اُو است

Wherever I prostrate my head He is the one to whom I bow
In six directions or outside the six, he is the one I worship.
The garden, the rose, the nightingale, music and the beauteous maiden
Are a mere excuse and He alone is the real object.

Rumi attaches great significance to love and there was not a time in his conscious life when he did not have a visible object of love to himself. In the first phase all his loyalty and devotion was given to Burhan-ud-din Muhaqqiq, who was at once his teacher, friend and philosopher. In the second phase we see him completely surrender himself to Shams-i-Tabriz who became the centre of his attention to the complete exclusion of all other loyalties. This was indeed the most violent and the most creative period of his life.

Soon after he regained poise, Rumi transferred his confidence to Salah-ud-din Zarkob, and after his death in 1261 the place is taken up by Hisam-ud-din Chalapi, who retained this position until the death of the Master in 1273.

Rumi was, therefore, never without a confidant for, according to him,[37] it is absolutely essential to have this companionship because a friend gains life and sustenance from the thought of a friend. If the friendship of a mortal man can contribute so much to the development of human personality, how much influence for the good would the friendship of God exert on a man if he were sincerely to cultivate Him? With Rumi this companionship was a constant exercise in courting incessant patience.

In the final period of his life, Hisam-ud-din Chalapi was the recipient of his love and confidence. Rumi was so kind to him that he would send everything he received to Chalapi. Once Ameer Taj-ud-din Mu'tabar sent a present of seventy thousand dirhams to Rumi; he at once sent the whole amount to Chalapi. Sultan Walad drew his father's attention to the utter lack of provisions in the house and complained about Rumi's complete disregard of domestic needs. Rumi retorted, 'If a million saints were to starve within my

[37] See Rumi's views about the nature and importance of a friend, *Mathnawi* Vol. I, pp. 104–05; and *Fihi-ma-Fihi*, p. 109 (Ed. Tehran Farozan Far).

sight and if I had a loaf of bread, by God, I shall send that loaf to Chalapi.'

The fourth, fifth and sixth volumes of the *Mathnawi* start with a mention of Chalapi and it is said that the *Mathnawi* was written at the instance of Hisam-ud-din. This is how the story goes:[38]

Hisam-ud-din learnt that several of the followers of Jalal were fond of studying the *Ilahi Nama* of Hakim Sana'i and *Mantiq-ut-tayr* of 'Attar. He, therefore, sought and found an opportunity to propose that Jalal should indite something in the style of *Ilahi Nama*, but in the metre of *Mantiq-ut-tayr*, saying that the circle of friends would then willingly give up all other poetry and study that alone. Jalal immediately produced a portion of the *Mathnawi*, saying that God had forewarned him of the wishes of the brethren, in consequence of which he had already begun to compose the work. That fragment consisted of the first 18 couplets of the introductory verses.

بشنو از نی چون حکایت می کند   از جداییها شکایت می کند

From reed flute hear what tale it tells,
What plaint it makes of absence's ills.

Rumi and Chalapi spent hours together; often they would work for the whole night on the *Mathnawi* – Jalal dictating and Chalapi taking down the verses and chanting them aloud in his beautiful voice. So closely did he come to be associated with the work that with the death of his wife after the completion of the first volume, the second had to wait for two years.

Rumi's life is full of paradoxes which beautifully resolve themselves in his ever-growing personality. There was a time when he ruled out music as an unhealthy influence, and there came a time when he became the most rapturous devotee to this mania. There was a time, again, when he looked at poets and poetry with a positive disfavour; and there came a time when he himself became the greatest poet that Persia has ever produced! Was he then to throw away this Divine gift for the sake of self-cultivation or was

[38] Whinfield, *Rumi* (London, Trubner's Oriental Series), Intro., p. 88.

he to make a nobler use of this power? Rumi looked at his genius, not as a product of his own efforts, but as a trust from God Who had destined this exile from Khurasan to bring a message of hope and eternal bliss to the people who were living under the delusion of the evasive philosophy of Greece.[39]

Here let us revert to Shams for a while. How do we understand Rumi's love for Shams-i-Tabriz? It is a longing for something that is Rumi's own and yet estranged and unfamiliar. The basic primordial kinship, the essential oneness that he feels with him, is disturbed by an uncertainty, an insecurity that Shams will not remain united with him, that he will go away and leave Rumi with a growing and agonising remembrance. He will be overwhelmed with an image that will seek, when the seeking will sometimes become the begging – the material embodiment, the man of flesh and bone, who is a person in his own right and will not live a life governed and controlled by a seeker and beggar of spiritual alms. It is not only Rumi's liberation from a bond that needed to be snapped by Shams's desertion, but it is also Shams's liberation that he, in his freedom, has given a gift but cannot forever remain bound to the recipient's gratitude. For it is indeed more humiliating, more inhuman for a free man to be a constant object of another person's desire than to desire someone else, persistently, with an aching awareness of one's inner void. Shams had given; Rumi had received. There was nothing more to be achieved by giving permanence to a relationship which in its very nature must be ephemeral if it is to be creative.

The legend has it that Shams was killed by Rumi's followers. Whatever the truth of this statement, symbolically and psychologically it has supreme real-

[39] از خراسانم کشیدی تا بر یونانیان
تا در آمیزم بدیشان تا کنم خوش مذهبی

ity. For Shams had to be killed, in order that Rumi developed his own individuality. Shams as an embodiment of Rumi's aspirations and spiritual needs had to die, had to be psychologically murdered so that Rumi could recognise and accept these aspirations and needs as his own. Psychologically it would be more true to say that Rumi killed Shams. For if he had not killed him, Rumi would have been denounced by him.

For what was Shams to Rumi? A figure that demanded a sacrifice of all that Rumi had regarded as supremely valuable – learning, abstract knowledge and theology. This figure spoke a non-rational language, indeed a non-verbal language, and brought to Rumi's awareness a world that he had never looked at before, but it was there very much alive in his soul. Shams did not create that world; it was already there. Shams only brought it into Rumi's consciousness, primeval and primitive, unburdened with thought and learning. It was the world of feeling that was thus revealed. It was the human in Rumi that had yawned into wakefulness, into a virgin preparing for nuptials. The bridegroom was apparently Shams, who had dared to enter the fairy princess's chamber, but really Shams was only a form that Rumi as the Prince had assumed. Before Shams's disappearance Rumi did not know that he himself was the Prince who had to encounter the Princess in the chamber of his own soul.

When the Prince and the Princess were united in marriage, instinct, with its chthonic and earthly character came to the fore and demanded allegiance as a temporary god. It was at that crucial moment that Zarkob appeared. Zarkob was the instinct-man, the inferior man, the man who worked with his hands, had a shop and amassed money and wealth. There was something else in him also – something alchemical – that he shaped gold into decorative ornaments. These ornaments were meant for buxom maidens whose bodies were awakened to romantic passion with the movements of these bracelets and necklaces. Zarkob's craft was music all over, and no wonder that Rumi began to dance to the rhythm of Zarkob beating the gold. This dancing was the ecstasy of instinct blossoming into awareness. It was the ecstasy of the earth seeking to be united with the Heaven, it was the longing of the serpent to embrace the eagle in its coil, it was the prayer of the void for fulfilment.

Empty form derives substance from instinct. Idea is materialised in emotion. That is why before Rumi meets Zarkob he sings of love, separation, nostalgia for being reabsorbed in unity – the basic primitive and undifferentiated unity. Love seems to him a panacea for all evils, a certain cure for all maladies. It is an obsessive, compulsive eulogy of love, with little or no awareness of adapting love to a cosmic frame of reference. Love is here an empty form devoid of any content. After Rumi meets Zarkob, his feet seem to have come down to earth. He transcends romantic love and begins to see reality as a composite pattern in which many themes participate and coalesce. He starts meditating. The rapture and ecstasy are still there, but one finds them mellowed down with the pale cast of thought. His consciousness no longer revels in the undifferentiated unity of love, but sees it shivering into a multiplicity and variety. Hence one finds in the *Mathnawi* an absence of that lyricism, that primitive, unalloyed passion, that gnawing suffering of separation from the beloved which is a distinctive feature of the *Divan*. One finds in the *Mathnawi* a lame lyricism, almost a crude poetic expression, for metaphysical meditation has asserted itself in Rumi's consciousness. Rumi now thinks of evolution, epistemology, reality, human relations, man's loves and hates; Rumi now consciously exploits mythological forms to express deep truths about human soul. Rumi now seems to be essaying to carve a path through the wilderness created by a clash between light and darkness, good and evil, beauty and ugliness. The early facility of expression, the rhythmic outbursts of melody are gone. Thought chokes the primitive spontaneity of emotive expression. Words come to lips but cautiously, hesitant, lest they should distort truth.

Before Rumi knew Shams he spoke the language of intellect. He talked about theology in prose with a certainty about the distinctions between right and wrong, beautiful and ugly. His lectures called *Fihi-ma-Fihi* contain abstruse discussions about philosophical problems. The rapier-like intellect is throughout in evidence making sharp differentiations, speaking of verities, metaphysical and moral, more through ego than through feeling. The ultimates were his intellectual concern but they did not touch his soul or move his heart. Prose is a real instrument of ratiocination, of logical thought. And Rumi was a master craftsman in the art of expression in prose.

With the appearance of Shams the thought-patterns were broken asunder. Logic was thrown to the winds and prose as a medium of expression was mistrusted. Ego, whose aim is survival and adjustment, became powerless against the torrent of feelings which overwhelmed Rumi like a sudden volcano erupting into a quiet abode of peaceful citizens. These feelings brought Rumi very near death, acquainted him with the agony and overturned the apple-cart of social adaptation. His value-system was now in a chaotic state. The distinction between right and wrong, good and evil, was no longer clear; in fact it seemed irrelevant to living, and unrelated to experiencing. The mass of feelings that had burst forth in consciousness had no room for the delicate though strict differentiations forged by intellect. It was a compulsive dictate of feeling which governed Rumi's life. He was in no state to question it or to seek for the reasons of these dictates. The feeling itself was its own sanction; it could not go beyond itself to find another ground. And when Rumi's feelings sought expression it was not expression in prose but in poetry – in intense and charged lyricism, wild and primitive with rapture and abandon. It was more like the primitive death-dance taking the shape of poetry than any mild or feeble inspiration wrought into words by cogitation.

When this phase was over, when the devouring mother had torn Rumi to bits and pieces, when the separation from Shams had brought forth all its aches and pains, that is when Rumi was dead with agony, that he was reborn with a new promise of awakened sensuousness. He was like an infant growing and developing but uniting in himself both the opposites – ego and feeling. His mode of expression was again poetry, but it was poetry whose strains and themes were no longer romantic but had been woven into a sober metaphysics. Both the form and the substance of the *Mathnawi* show a heaviness which is naturally correlated with the depth and range of Rumi's thought at this stage.

On his own confession[40] he failed to attract the attention of the people of Rum to the message that he was charged to give them. The cold prose of his lectures seemed to animate but a few hearts, the rigid code of his morality seemed to change but a few souls. But Rumi was determined to discharge his trust and if he could not do so by dint of cold prose, he would not hesitate in using the warmth and beauty of poetry if that could help him win over the people to the truth of his message. He sang, therefore, a full-throated song to attract the people round him and the success that he achieved was indeed phenomenal. While singing of love and life Rumi did not forget for a moment that the medium of his expression was but a means to an end. He was certainly not in love with his own voice and he was too great to take the tree for the woods. He

[40] See *Fihi-ma-Fihi* (Ed. Farozan Far), p. 289.

is not at all proud of the excellence of his verse, in the traditional manner of his contemporaries,[41] but freely confesses that he uses it only as an aid to sell his wares for which unfortunately there was no ready market and all the devices of salesmanship had to be used, therefore, to create the demand for a commodity called love.

The *Mathnawi* is a product of this period which brought us a stirring message. We need to understand it as much or perhaps even more than the people of Rum did some seven hundred years ago. We will make an attempt, therefore, to scan the *Mathnawi* with a view briefly to culling the thought of Rumi for a reader who has neither the inclination nor the leisure to go to the original sources.

[41] Not infrequently Rumi declares that poetry for him is not an achievement to be proud of. See these verses, for example:

شعر چه باشد بر من تاکه از آن لا ف زنم
هست مرا فن دگر غیر فنون شعرا

شعر چو ابریست سیه من پس آن پرده چو مه
ابر سیه را تو توان ماه منور بسما

چون باشد آن سعادت یابم ز خود فراغت
این گفتن و نوشتن ارزان و خوار ماند

من پیش ازین می خواستم گفتار خود را مشتری
اکنون همی خواهم که تو از گفت خویشم واخری

Chapter 5

The Message of the *Mathnawi*

And now we come to the *magnum opus* of Rumi. The *Mathnawi* was hailed as a unique revelation of esoteric truth long before Jami called it 'the Qur'an in Persian,' and said of the poet, 'though he is not a Prophet, he has a Book':

نیست پیغمبر ولی دارد کتاب

I

Rumi entitled his collection of odes *Divan-i-Shams-i-Tabriz,* the *Mathnawi* he calls *Husami Namah* – the Book of Husam. Shams was the hero of the *Divan*, Husam-ud-din is invoked as the inspiring genius of the *Mathnawi*. Rumi took nearly twelve years to dictate 25,700[1] verses to Husam-ud-din. The modern reader demands a summary which he can dispose of in an hour. This is not possible. Even the best of summaries would do serious damage to the work. We could only attempt an outline, often using the words and employing the idiom of the author.

In his own day Rumi recorded the contemporary critic as saying that the *Mathnawi,*

* All references in this Chapter are from R. A. Nicholson's translation of the *Mathnawi,* e.g. I, 4 means that verse 4 from Book I has been referred to.

[1] *The Encyclopaedia Britannica* (1952 edn., Vol. XIX, p. 658) mentions 30,000 to 40,000 couplets.

. . . is the story of the Prophet and (consists of) imitation;

(That) there is no mention of (theosophical) investigation and the sublime mysteries towards which the saints make their steeds gallop;

(That) from the stations of asceticism to the passing away, . . . step by step up to union with God,

(It contains not) the explanation and definition of every station and stage, so that by means of the wings thereof a man of heart (a mystic) could soar.

He dismisses the criticism by saying:

When the Book of God (the *Qur'an*) came (down), the unbelievers railed likewise at it too,

Saying, 'It is (mere) legends and paltry tales; there is no profound inquiry and lofty speculation. . . .'[2]

Rumi is aware of the massive contribution he is making. In the prose introduction of Book IV, without being unduly immodest he says, 'it is the grandest of gifts and the most precious of prizes; . . . It is a light to our friends and a treasure for our (spiritual) descendants.' He is now a poet with a purpose. He asks,

Does any painter paint a beautiful picture for the sake of the picture itself . . . ?

Does any potter make a pot in haste for the sake of the pot itself and not in hope of the water?

Does any bowl-maker make a finished bowl for the sake of the bowl itself and not for the sake of the food?

Does any calligrapher write artistically for the sake of writing itself and not for the sake of the reading?[3]

In the last volume of the *Mathnawi*, referring to his critics, Rumi complains that the 'sour people are making us distressed,'[4] but what is to be done? The message must be delivered. 'Does a caravan ever turn back from a journey on account of the noise and clamour of the dogs?'[5] 'If you are thirsting for the spiritual Ocean,' says Rumi, 'make a breach in the

[2] III, 4233–38.
[3] IV, 2881, 2884, 2885, 2886.
[4] VI, 33.
[5] VI, 12.

island of the *Mathnawi*. Make such a great breach that at every moment you will see the *Mathnawi* to be only spiritual.'[6]

The *Mathnawi* begins dramatically with a metaphorical song in which the reed, parted from the reed-bed, complains of separation:

Every one who is left far from his source wishes back the time when he was united with it.[7]

بر کسی کو دور ماند از اصل خویش   باز جوید روزگار وصل خویش

The source of all existence is God and to Him shall we all return, as the Qur'an puts it:

انا لله و انا الیه راجعون

In other words, the basis of all existence is spiritual. The entity called man is the most beautiful creation of God Who has created him in His own image and has breathed in him part of His own spirit. The spirit, the soul, is something which is not veiled from the body, the link between the two is intimate and the integrated personality, the self, which emerges out of the Cosmic self, has no difficulty in recognising it.

Body is not veiled from soul, nor soul from body, yet none is permitted to see the soul.[8]

تن ز جان و جان ز تن مستور نیست   لیك کس را دیدِ جان دستور نیست

The consciousness of the soul, the spirit, is animated by Love, not logic.

'Tis the fire of Love that is in the reed, 'tis the fervour of Love that is in the wine.[9]

آتش عشقست کاندر نی فتاد   جوشش عشقست کاندر می فتاد

The Creation of the World is an act of God. God decreed Be, and it is (کن فیکون). We are since floating

[6] VI, 67–68.   [7] I, 4.   [8] I, 8.   [9] I, 10.

about in space and non-space. Pure Unity expressed itself in the creation of the phenomenal world and we are trying to recapture our original purity, our original Unity. In the process a myriad of contradictions have come into play. Oil has been formed from water and now it has become an opposite entity. The two do not mix together. The rose sprang from thorn and both of them are at war today. Who is imploring help against whom? The existent from the non-existent? What is the conflict between good and evil or are these categories which are illusory and baseless?

The marvel is that this colour arose from that which is colourless: how did colour arise to war with the colourless?[10]

این عجب کین رنگ از بی رنگ خاست   رنگ با بی رنگ چون در جنگ خاست

God, having created the Universe, did not contain Himself in spatial dimensions.

I am not contained in earth or heaven or even in the empyrean – know this for certain, O noble one;

(But) I am contained in the true believer's heart: oh, how wonderful! If thou seekest Me, search in those hearts.

He (God) said (also), '*Enter among My servants,* thou wilt meet with a Paradise. . . .'[11]

در زمین و آسمان و عرش نیز   من بگنجم این یقین دان ای عزیز
در دل مومن بگنجم ای عجب   گر مرا جوئی در آن دلها طلب
گفت ادخل فی عبادی تلتقی   جنةً من رویتی یا متقی

Man is the microcosm who has enchanted the macrocosm (the universe) in his small frame. There are a hundred unseen worlds within him.

Thou alone art the (whole) community, thou art one and a hundred thousand.

اُمت وحدی یکی و صد هزار

[10] I, 2470.   [11] I, 2654–56.

This mystery is not unravelled, however, by intellect. The saints who are the 'intellect of intellect'[12] reveal this mystery to the seeker. The foolish say about the Prophet, 'He is a man, nothing more,' but they fail to see in him the spark that illuminates. It is in the company of saints and seers that our perception of reality is sharpened. Our desires yield to an act of faith and a unique consciousness dawns on the soul of man:

The eye of Ahmad (Mohammed) was cast upon an Abu Bakr: he by a single act of faith became a Siddiq.[13]

چشم احمد بر ابـوبکری زده　　اُو ز یك تصدیق صدیقی شده

'I came to this court in quest of wealth: as soon as I entered the portico I became (a spiritual) chief.'[14]

من برین در طالب چیز آمدم　　صدر گشتم چون بدهلیز آمدم

The limitation of Reason is beautifully brought out in the story of the grammarian who represents discursive knowledge and the boatman who is a simple child of God. The man of knowledge, full of self-conceit, turns to the boatman and asks him if he ever studied grammar. 'No', replies the boatman and the proud grammarian pronounces the verdict: 'You have wasted half your life.' The poor boatman took the chiding with silent grief. A little later the boat was caught in a storm. The boatman asked the man of knowledge: 'Do you know how to swim?' 'No,' replied the grammarian. The boatman said: 'Now you have lost *all* your life!'

Rumi drives home the point that the most learned scholar could be the most ignorant in a discipline which he has not learnt. The discipline of the spirit is another field:

If in the world thou art the most learned scholar of the time, behold the passing-away of this world and this time!

[12] I, 2498　　[13] I, 2688.　　[14] I, 2796.

We have stitched in (inserted) the (story of the) grammarian, that we might teach you the grammar of self-effacement.

In self loss, . . . thou wilt find the jurisprudence of jurisprudence, the grammar of grammar, and the accidence of accidence, [i.e. the cream and essence of these sciences].[15]

کر تو علامهٔ زمانی در جهان   نك فنای این جهان بین وین زمان

مردِ نحوی را از آن در دوختیم   تا شما را نحو محو آمو یم

فقهٔ فقه و نحوِ نحو و صرفِ صرف   در کم آمد یابی ای یارِ شگرف

Sense-perception, which is a key to the physical sciences, cannot lead to the lofty heights of the Spirit.

The pinion of your thought has become mud-stained and heavy because you are a clay-eater: clay has become to you as bread.

Bread and meat are (originally) clay: eat little thereof, that you may not remain in the earth, like clay.

When you become hungry, you become a dog: you become fierce and ill-tempered and ill-natured.

When you have eaten your fill, you have become a carcase: you have become devoid of understanding and without feet (inert), like a wall.

So at one time you are a carcase and at another time a dog: how will you run well in the road of the lions (follow the saints)?

Know that your only means of hunting is a dog (the animal soul): throw bones to the dog but seldom,

Because when the dog has eaten its fill, it becomes rebellious: how should it run to the goodly chase and hunt?

Want of food was leading the Arab to that (exalted) court, and (there) he found his fortune.[16]

پر فکرت شد گل آلود و گران   زآنك گِل خواری ترا گِل شد چونان

نان گلست و گوشت کمتر خور ازین   تا نمانی همچو گِل اندر زمین

چون گر سنه می شوی سگ می شوی   تند و بد پیوند و بدرگ می شوی

چون شدی تو سیر مرداری شدی   بی خبر بی پا چون دیواری شدی

پس دمی مردار و دیگر دم سگی   چون کنی در راه شیران خوش تگی

آلت اشکار خود جز سگ مدان   کمترك انداز سگ را استخوان

15 I. 2845–47.

16 I. 2871–80.

زآنك سگ چون سیر شد سر کش شود   کی سویٔ صید و شکارِ خوش دود
آن عرب را بی نوایی می کشید   تا بدان درگاه و آن دولت بدید

And it is to this Arab, the Prophet of Islam, that Rumi looks for inspiration. Choose a guide, he suggests, for without one the journey is fraught with danger.[17]

It is necessary to have a guide, a leader, a companion who will help one to tread this delicate path and discover the true nature of existence. In seeking such a guide Rumi warns:

Since there is many a devil who hath the face of Adam, it is not well to give your hand to every hand.

The vile man will steal the language of dervishes, that he may thereby chant a spell over . . . one who is simple.

The work of the (holy) men is (as) light and heat; the work of vile men is trickery and shamelessness.[18]

چون بسی ابلیس آدم روی هست   پس بهر دستی نشاید داد دست
حرفِ درویشان بدزدد مردِ دون   تا بخواند بر سلیمی زآن فسون
کارِ مردان روشنی و گرمیست   کارِ دونان حیله و بی شرمیست

Having chosen a guide surrender to his higher enlightened judgment. If he scuttles a boat, do not speak a word, if he kills a boy, do not tear your hair. Be patient. Be not faint-hearted. The hand of the Guide is the hand of God. But there are dangers and pitfalls. The story is told of a scribe who wrote down the Revelation that the Prophet had dictated to him and then said, 'So I too am one upon whom Revelation has descended!' The meddling fool was led astray by this presumption.

As a means of preventing these dangers, '*Guide us*' comes in every (ritual) prayer,

That is to say, 'O God, do not mingle my prayer with the prayer of the erring and the hypocrites.'

[17] I, 2943. [18] I, 316–20.

Especially, O Master, (you must avoid) the analogy drawn by the low senses in regard to the Revelation which is illimitable.

If your sensuous ear is fit for (understanding) the letter (of the Revelation), know that your ear that receives the occult (meaning) is deaf.[19]

از بـــرای چـــارهٔ ایــن خـــوفهـــا   آمـد انـدر بـــر نمـازی راهـــدنـا
کـین نمـازم را میـآمیـز ای خـــدا   بـا نمـازِ ضـالـین و اهـــلِ ریـا
خاصه ای خواجه قیاس حسِ دون   اندر آن وحیی که هست از حد فزون
گوشِ حس تو بحرف از در خودست   دان که گوشِ عیب گیر تو کرست

There is no contradiction, no conflict between the earthly and the heavenly life. One leads to the other. Neither is to be shunned. Neither is more holy or more desirable. Both are part of a unity. Both are inseparable. You do not say 'No' to this world and wait in quiet contemplation for the next. You cannot run away from life and conquer it. Rumi calls Time a cutting sword.[20]

'The Sufi,' he says, 'is the son of the (present) time, O Comrade.' He exhorts, 'It is not the rule of the Way to say "To-morrow".'[21]

صوفی ابن الوقت باشد ای رفیق   نیست فردا گفتن از شرطِ طریق

Life is the most fatal gift of man and he cannot reduce it to naught by postponing the acceptance, the responsibilities, the dangers and the difficulties that go with it. It is now and here that he has to wrestle with them. He has to wade through a river of blood. It is out of this turmoil, tribulation and trial that he will emerge steeled and fortified in his resolve to arrive at the higher reaches of his ego:

The purpose of this (severe) discipline and this rough treatment is that the furnace may extract the dross from the silver.

The testing of good and bad is in order that the gold may boil and bring the scum to the top.[22]

[19] I, 3391–95. [20] I, 132. [21] I, 133. [22] I, 232–33.

بهر آنست این ریاضت وین جفا تا بر آرد کوره از نقره جفا
بهر آنست امتحانِ نیک و بد تا بجوشد بر سر آرد زر زبد

Good and evil, pain and pleasure, are words employed by man who is gravely limited by his intellect, and who is arrogant in presuming knowledge of Reality. But the man who treads the path of the spirit soon realises the danger involved in judging life from the analogy of his own limited experience. The light to recognise these limitations comes like a flash and the limitations are wiped out; new vistas of thought open up and a vision of Reality dawns on man who is unable to communicate its intensity, depth and beauty to others who are governed by the limitations of human language, values and emotions. Words take on a unique significance, a completely original meaning in the minds of those that receive their answers from a source of inspiration. To Moses it appeared that Khadir was stained by lust, covetousness and passion. He could not see the good that wore the aspect of evil – the scuttling of the boat, the killing of a young boy. The man intoxicated with Divine Reason appeared mad to him; his imagination screened from him the inner meaning of acts.

Logic and Intellect are limited. It is only inspiration, revelation, an act of grace from God which illuminates the mind of man who then begins to see the world in an entirely different perspective. In the history of mankind, men of learning who 'sharpened the intelligence and wits,' as Rumi puts it, did not inspire humanity to any great endeavour. Neither did kings, nor men of power. It was the prophets and seers, men who made no claims to formal knowledge and authority, who captured the hearts of men and raised them to heights of effort and achievement:

The myriads of Pharaoh's lances were shattered by (the hand of) Moses (armed) with a single staff.

Myriads were the therapeutic arts of Galen: before Jesus and his (life-giving) breath they were a laughing-stock.
Myriads were the books of (pre-Islamic) poems: at the word of an illiterate (prophet) they were (put to) shame.[23]

صد هزاران نیزهٔ فرعـون را   در شکست ازموسیٔ بایك عصا
صد هزاران طب جالینوس بود   پیش عیسی و دمش افسوس بود
صد هزاران دفتر اشعار بود   پیش حرف اُمیی اش عار بود

The man who is a slave to words and depends on his senses alone will soon discover there are other categories of understanding.

Our speech and action is the exterior journey: the interior journey is above the sky.
The (physical) sense saw (only) dryness, because it was born of dryness (earth): the Jesus of the spirit set foot on the sea.
The journey of the dry body befell on dry land, (but) the journey of the spirit set foot (took place) in the heart of the sea.

* * *

The waves of earth are our imagination and understanding and thought; the waves of water are (mystical) self-effacement and intoxication and death.[24]

سیر بیر و نیست قول و فعل ما   سـیر بـاطن هست بـالای سـما
حس خشکی دید کز خشکی بزاد   عیسیٔ جـان پـای بـر دریـا نهاد
سیر جسم خشك بـر خشکی فتاد   سـیر جـان پـا در دل دریـا نهاد

★ ★ ★

موج خاکی وهم و فهم و فکرماست   موج آبی محو و سکرست و فناست

It is Reason which distinguishes man from the lower animals. Reason and understanding must be used; and it is painful to use them. But to avoid pain one cannot sink to the level of an unthinking animal. But Reason alone will not lead to an understanding of Reality – on the voyage of discovery the role of Reason changes. Man's understanding is his teacher, his

[23] I, 527–29.   [24] I, 570–75.

guide, up to a stage. After the stage is reached it becomes his pupil, his tool.

The understanding says, like Gabriel, 'O Ahmad (Mohammed), if I take one (more) step, it will burn me;
Do thou leave me, henceforth advance (alone): this is my limit, O sultan of the soul!'[25]

عقل چون جبریل گوید احمدا   گر یکی گامی نهم سوزد مرا
تو مرا بگذا زین پس پیش ران   حدِ من این بود ای سلطانِ جان

A stage arrives when identification between the will of the ego and the will of the Cosmic Ego becomes so complete that all the dialectical debate about free-will and predetermination becomes totally irrelevant and superfluous. There is no compulsion left in the Law because it becomes one's own command, freely imposed on oneself; not a set of rules framed by someone else and inflicted on us to discipline our wayward vagaries:

The prophets are necessitarians in regard to the works of this world, (while) the infidels are necessitarians in regard to the works of the next world.
To the prophets the works of the next world are (a matter of) freewill: to the foolish the works of this world are (a matter of) freewill.[26]

انبیا در کارِ دنیا جبری اند   کافران در کارِ عقبی جبری اند
انبیا را کارِ عقبی اختیار   جاهلان را کارِ دنیا اختیار

The man of God, while not frowning upon this world, is able to see it in a perspective which creates in him a sense of detachment; he is able to live on earth without sullying himself with mud, he is able to swim in the middle of the ocean without wetting his garments! Pain becomes joy and bondage becomes freedom. Air and earth and water and fire become (His) slaves.[27]

[25] I, 1066–67. [26] I, 637–38. [27] I, 837–38.

چون بخواهد عین غم شادی شود عــین بــنــد پــای آزادی شــود
باد و خاك و آب و آتش بنده اند با من و تو مرده با حق زنده اند

This is by no means a state of annihilation of the self, as the mystics have it; it is a state of illumination, of the discovery of one's own higher potential, and in such a state quietism and withdrawal do not replace reflection and exertion. Trust in God is the basic quality of a believer, but he cannot abandon the need of exertion and acquisition:

The Prophet said with a loud voice, 'While trusting in God bind the knee of thy camel.'[28]

گفت پیغــمبــر بــآواز بلــنــد بــا توکــل زانوی اُشــتر ببنــد

God is not idle and inactive for a moment. How can man be?[29]

کل یوم هــو فی شانٍ بخــوان مر ورا بی کار و بی فعلی مدان

If you are putting trust in God, put trust (in Him) as regards (your) work: sow (the seed), then rely upon the Almighty.[30]

گــر توکــل میکنی در کارکن کشت کن پس تکیه بر جبار کن

. . . it is better to struggle vainly than to lie still. . . .
In this way be thou even scraping and scratching . . . until thy last breath do not be unoccupied for a moment.[31]

. . . . . کــوشش بیهــوده بــه از خفتگی
اندرین ره می تراش و می خراش تــا دم آخــر دمی فــارغ مبــاش

Rumi is a creative evolutionist. He denies the metamorphosis of the body in any shape. Evolution to him is the metamorphosis of the spirit. When man's spirit becomes the ape-spirit, his body is debased:[32]

28 I, 913. 29 I, 3071. 30 I, 947.
31 I, 1819–22. 32 V, 2594–95.

اندرین اُمت نه بـد مسخ بـدن   لیك مسخ دل بود ای ذوالفطن
چون دل بو زینه گردد آن دلش   از دل بوزینه شد خوار آن گلش

The spirit existed when there were neither names nor things that are named. Love is the evolutionary principle of all existence. Adam was given knowledge of all the names and yet he fell from grace. He tried to interpret for himself the meaning of the command. And in doing so he exposed the hollowness of intellect. Interpretation amounts to intellectual arrogance. When the Prophet said, 'I pass the night with my Lord, He gives me food and He gives me drink,' he was referring metaphorically to the spiritual food. We should accept this saying without any perverse interpretation because interpretation amounts to an alteration of the meaning and is a rejection of the gift. The interpreter regards the real or original meaning as faulty or inadequate and begins to use his reason to aid and to explain. The view that it is faulty arises from the weakness of his own understanding. He fails to realise that the Universal Reason is higher than his own. He should abuse his dull brain and not the Reality which he fails to comprehend.[33]

زانـك تـاویلست وا داد عـطا   چونـك بینـد آن حقیقت را خـطا
آن خطا دیدن ز ضعف عقل اُوست   عقل کل مغزست و عقل ما چو پوست
خویش را تاویل کن نه اخبار را   مغـز را بـد گـوی نی گلزار را

The priorities of a man of God become crystal clear. The confusion, the chaos created by contradictions, the bewildering bedlam of opposites, the strains and stresses of conflicting loyalties merge into a smooth symphony of consciousness, which creates a unity, an integrated whole, a totality of ego which takes a myriad of seeming contradictions in a sweep.

[33] I, 3740–45.

What is this world? To be forgetful of God; it is not merchandise and silver and weighing-scales and women.

As regards the wealth that you carry for religion's sake 'How good is righteous wealth (for the righteous man)!' as the Prophet recited.

Water in the boat is the ruin of the boat, (but) water underneath the boat is a support.[34]

چیست دنیا از خدا غافل بدن   نی قماش و نقره و میزان و زن
مال را کز بهر دین باشی حمول   نعم مالٌ صالحٌ خواندش رسول
آب در کشتی هلاکِ کشتی است   آب اندر زیرِ کشتی پشتی است

Personal experience of a personal God Who is the cause of all creation, fortifies, sublimates and transforms the personality of man; the vicegerent of God who until this moment was receiving commands from the king; henceforth he delivers commands to the world. Until now the stars were influencing him; henceforth he is the ruler of the stars:[35]

تا کنون فرمان پذیرفتی ز شاه   بعد ازین فرمان رساند بر سپاه
تا کنون اختر اثر کردی در اُو   بعد ازین باشد امیر اختر اُو

Before this experience his wish was father to the thought. All his thinking, his logic, his arguments were directed at weaving a rationale for his lazy life. But with the dawn of faith, desire for easy living disappears and so does the need for a wilful corruption of the Divine Message which has been altered and interpreted through the ages to suit the imagined convenience of man. Generation after generation has tampered with the meaning of the Message and the motive has all along been to find a way, a justification for rejecting what is considered inconvenient and troublesome for a class of people. Man's own selfish desire for comfort, power and luxury has always locked the gate of Truth. The sublime meaning has been degraded and perverted to serve desire. Reason is hidden by the world of phenomena; vanity and the

[34] I, 983–85.   [35] I, 1075–76.

pursuit of one's basic desires appear as progress from a lower to a higher plane; one's own limited intellect seems to be the arbiter of all truth, but once this veil is removed the scale of values changes and we perceive with little difficulty that all we were pursuing as the paragon of progress was a mere will-o'-the-wisp, an illusion, a mirage. We begin to see that the treasures of Qar'un (Korah) did not last; we begin to understand that the mighty empires of kings did not endure for they were based on vanity and exploitation but we see also that the message of the Prophets has lasted and still proclaims the Truth which man, in his vanity, continues to ignore. And yet this is human. We who are descendants of Adam are legitimately proud of the fact that knowledge was vouchsafed to him. He was taught all the names of things, even those that did not yet exist. In his exuberance to interpret for himself the meaning of the one prohibition that was imposed on him, he invited the consequences of the Fall, but he averted the wrath by recognising that he had made a mistake and he asked for forgiveness. It was the consciousness of having committed a mistake that redeemed his soul. To err is human, but the moment we become conscious of erring the corrective process comes immediately into play:

Adam, (cast out) from Paradise and from above the Seven (Heavens), went to the 'shoe-row' for the purpose of excusing himself.

If thou art from the back of Adam and from his loins, be constant in seeking (forgiveness) amongst his company.

Prepare a desert of heart-fire (burning grief) and eye-water (tears): the garden is made open (blooming) by cloud and sun.

What dost thou know of the taste of the water of the eyes? Thou art a lover of bread, like the blind (beggars).

If thou make this wallet empty of bread, thou wilt make it full of glorious jewels.[36]

[36] I, 1635–40.

آدم از فردوس و از بالای هفت پای ما چان از برای عذر رفت
گر ز پشت آدمی و ز صلب او در طلب هی باش هم در طلب او
ز آتش دل و آب دیده نقل ساز بوستان از ابر و خورشیدست باز
تو چه دانی ذوق آب دیدگان عاشق نانی تو چون نا دیدگان
گر تو این انبان زنان خالی کنی پُر ز گوهرهای اجلالی کنی

We can receive the Light either from Adam or, like him, direct from the source. In this process of transmission a hundred lamps are lit and the quality of light has not suffered in the least.

To an Adam He in His own person showed the (Divine) Names; to the rest He was revealing the Names by means of Adam.

Do thou receive His light either from Adam or from Himself: take the wine either from the jar or from the gourd (cup), . . .

* * *

When a lamp has derived (its) light from a candle, every one that sees it (the lamp) certainly sees the candle.

If transmission (of the light) occurs in this way till a hundred lamps (are lighted), the seeing of the last (lamp) becomes a meeting with the original (light).[37]

آدمی را او بخویش اسما نمود دیگرانرا زآدم اسما می گشود
خواه از آدم گیر نورش خواه ازو خواه از خم گیر می خواه از کدو

* * *

چون چراغی نور شمعی را کشید هرك دید آنرا یقین آن شمع دید
همچنین تا صد چراغ ار نقل شد دیدن آخر لقای اصل شد

Discursive reason arrogates to itself functions which do not belong to it. Its function is only partial and unless it learns to recognise its limitations it is likely to lead astray. Intellect, though useful, has to be supplemented with intuition.

[37] I, 1943–48.

When the lover (of God) is fed from (within) himself with pure wine, there reason will remain lost and companionless.

Partial (discursive) reason is a denier of Love, though it may give out that it is a confidant.[38]

عاشق از خود چون غذا یابد رحیق   عقـل آنجـا گم بمـانـد بی رفیق
عقـل جزوی عشق را منکـر بود   گرچه بنماید کـه صاحب سـر بود

To realise the highest in one's self one has to make a beginning by waging war on all that hinders our growth – greed, cupidity, avarice and hatred. The parable of the Rumi and Chinese painters in Book I of the *Mathnawi* beautifully describes the situation.

The Chinese said: We are better artists; the Rumis claimed: Power and excellence belong to us. The Chinese and the Rumis began to debate. The Rumis retired from the debate. The Chinese demanded a room to create their work of art. There were two rooms with door facing door. The Chinese took one, the Rumis the other. The Chinese demanded a hundred colours for their painting. The Rumis said no colour was needed for theirs; they would merely remove the rust. They shut the door and went on burnishing. When the Chinese had finished their work, the king entered the room and saw the pictures there. The beauty of the creation was incredible. After that he came towards the Rumis. They simply removed the intervening curtain. The reflexion of the Chinese pictures struck upon the walls which had become clear and pure like the sky. The king was wonder-struck. All that he had seen in the Chinese room seemed infinitely more beautiful in the other room and yet the Rumis had not used a colour, not a brush; they had merely removed the rust from the stained walls.

The moral of the parable is then driven home:

[38] I, 1981–82.

The Greeks, O father, are the Sufis: (they are) without (independent of) study and books and erudition.

But they have burnished their breasts (and made them) pure from greed and cupidity and avarice and hatreds.

That purity of the mirror is, beyond doubt, the heart which receives images innumerable.

They that burnish (their hearts) have escaped from (mere) scent and colour: they behold Beauty at every moment without tarrying.

* * *

They [the Sufis] have relinquished the form and husk of knowledge, they have raised the banner of the eye of certainty.

Thought is gone, and they have gained light: they have gained the throat (core and essence) and the sea (ultimate source) of gnosis.

Death, of which all others are sore afraid, this people (the perfect Sufis) are holding in derision.

None gains the victory over their hearts: the hurt falls on the oyster-shell, not on the pearl,[39]

رومیان آن صوفیانند ای پدر   بی ز تکرار و کتاب و بی هنر
لیک صیقل کرده اند آن سینها   پاك از آز و حرص و بخل و کینها
آن صفای آئینه لا شك دلست   کُو نقوش بی عدد را قابلست

★ ★ ★

اهل صیقل رسته اند از بُو و رنگ   هر دمی بینند خوبی بی درنگ
نقش و قشر علم را بگذاشتند   رایت عین الیقین افراشتند
رفت فکر و روشنایی یافتند   نحر و بحر آشنایی یافتند
مرگ کین جمله ازو در وحشت اند   می کنند این قوم بر وی ریش خند
کس نیابد بر دلِ ایشان ظفر   بر صدف آید ضرر نی بر گهر

II

The world is one thought emanating from the Universal Intellect. The intellect is like a king, the ideas are his envoys. The first world is the world of probation, the second world is the world of recompense. If a man commits a sin, that accident becomes a substance,

[39] I, 3483-96.

namely, chains and prison. If a man performs a good act, that accident becomes a role of honour. This accident with the substance is like egg and bird: this is produced by that, and that by this, in succession. Why, then, have these accidents of ours not produced any substance? The answer is that Divine Wisdom has kept it concealed in order that this world of good and evil may be a mystery, for if the substantial forms of thought were to become manifest, then this world of ours would be like the Resurrection. And who commits sin and wrong at the Resurrection? But God has veiled the retribution of evil only from the vulgar, not from His own elect.

God, then, has shown to me the retribution of work and myriads of the (substantial) forms of actions.[40]

حق بمن بنمود پس پاداش کار   وز صورهای عملها صد هزار

Life is constant activity. One cannot be inactive for a moment. The craving for action is there in order that our inward consciousness should come clearly into view; 'to be inactive is like the death-agony. This world and that world are for ever giving birth: every cause is a mother, the effect is born (from it) as a child. When the effect was born, that too became a cause, so that it might give birth to wondrous effects. These causes are generation on generation, but it needs a very illumined eye (to see all the links in the chain).'[41]

The universe is a series of causes. Every cause, on account of its being both an essence and form (the two are inseparable), is both a cause and an effect, an agent and a patient; and every effect (so called), on account of its being an essence and a form, is also both a cause and an effect. And since Reality is One, now regarded as Essence, now as Form, it follows that it is both a cause and an effect at the same time, and that

[40] II, 991. [41] II, 996–1002.

everything that is called a cause on entering into a causal relation with anything else which is called an effect is at the same time an effect of its own effect, on account of that effect being in virtue of its essence a cause. What it all amounts to is that God, Who is the only Cause, is immanent in both causes and effects. It is immaterial whether we call a particular cause a cause of a certain effect or an effect of this effect (itself being regarded as a cause). This notion of causation has an important bearing on all acts of 'becoming,' for all creation is striving at nothing but 'becoming'. Every particle of the universe is desiring to express itself.

Heaven says to the earth, 'Welcome! To thee I am (in the same relation) as the iron and the magnet.'

In (the view of) the intellect, heaven is man and the earth woman: whatever that (heaven) casts forth this (earth) fosters.

* * *

Therefore regard earth and heaven as endowed with intelligence, since they do the work of intelligent beings.

Unless these two sweethearts are tasting (delight) from one another, then why are they creeping together like mates?

Without the earth how should roses and *arghawan*-flowers grow? What, then, would be born of the water and heat of heaven?

The desire (implanted) in the female for the male is to the end that they may perfect each other's work.

God put desire in man and woman in order that the world should be preserved by this union.

He also implants the desire of every part for another part: from the union of both an act of generation results.

Likewise night and day are in mutual embrace: (they are) different in appearance, but (are really) in agreement.[42]

آسمان گوید زمین را مرحبا   با توام چون آهن و آهن ربا
آسمان مرد و زمین زن در خرد   هرچ آن انداخت این می پرورد

★ ★ ★

پس زمین و چرخ را دان هوشمند   چونك كار هوشمندان می كنند

[42] III, 4403–17.

گر نه از هم این دو دلبر می مزند   پس چرا چون جفت در هم می خزند
بی زمین کی گل بروید و ارغوان   پس چه زاید ز آب و تاب آسمان
بهر آن میلست در ماده بنر   تا بود تکمیل کار همدگر
میل اندر مرد و زن حق زآن نهاد   تا بقا یابد جهان زین اتحاد
میل هر جزوی بجزوی هم نهد   ز اتحاد هر دو تولیدی زهد
شب چنین با روز اندر اعتناق   مختلف در صورت اما اتفاق

Many Sufis have conceived the universe in Neoplatonic fashion as a series of emanations from God, the One Real Being, each successive stage reflecting the one immediately above it and gradually becoming more and more remote from Reality. Most interpreters have sought to expound the *Mathnawi* in terms of the pantheistic system associated with Ibn al-ʿArabi, but this is doing grave injustice to Rumi. He is essentially a poet and a mystic, not a philosopher and logician.

Rumi believes everything is striving to reach its original source. 'The desire of the body for green herbs and running water is because its origin is from those; the desire of the soul is for Life and for the Living One, because its origin is the Infinite Soul. The desire of the soul is for wisdom and the sciences; the desire of the body is for orchards and meadows and vines. The desire of the soul is for ascent and exaltedness; the desire of the body is for grain and means of procuring fodder. . . . Whenever any one seeks, the soul of the object sought by him is desiring him. (Whether it be) man, animal, plant or mineral, every object of desire is in love with everything that is without (has not attained to) the object of desire. . . . But the desire of the lovers makes them lean, (while) the desire of the loved ones makes them fair and beauteous. The love of the loved ones illumines the cheeks; the love of the Lover consumes his soul.'[43]

[43] III, 4435–45.

While everything strives to return to its origin, no origin resembles its product. 'Semen is (the product) of bread, (but) how should it be like bread? Man is the product of semen, (but) how should he be like it? The Jinn is (created) from fire, (but) how should he resemble fire? The cloud is (produced) from vapour, but it is not like vapour. Jesus was produced from the breath of Gabriel (but) when was he ever like him in form. . . ? Adam is (made) of earth, (but) does he resemble earth? No grape ever resembles the vine.'[44]

There is a terrible conflict amongst the parts of the Universe. Consider the four elements. Each 'is a destroyer of the other . . . water is a destroyer of the flames (of fire). Hence the edifice of creation is (based) on contraries.'[45] This conflict is reflected in the mind of man. The states of mind and body are mutually opposed. Man is incessantly struggling with himself. There is a grievous war being waged in himself. 'Reciprocal destruction is inflicted by (every) contrary on its contrary: when there is no contrary, there is naught but everlastingness. He (God), who hath no like, banished contraries from Paradise, saying, "Neither sun, nor its contrary, intense cold, shall be there."'[46]

The orthodox hold that God is beyond comparison, that in His absolute unity He is remote and different from all created things, and that the qualities ascribed to Him in the Qur'an are not to be understood in the sense in which they are applicable to any of His creatures. Pantheistic Sufis, while accepting the doctrine of Divine transcendence (*tanzih*), regard it as only half of the truth: the whole truth, they say, consists in combining *tanzih* with *tashbib*, the doctrine of Divine immanence. The former doctrine, by itself, leads to the duality of God and the world; the latter, by itself, is polytheism. Rumi contrasts the 'bat-like' eye of the sense with the 'eye of the heart,'[47]

[44] V, 3980–85. [45] VI, 45–50. [46] VI, 56–57. [47] II, 47 ff.

and declares that those who are blind to spiritual things virtually occupy the position of the Mu'tazilites, the philosophers, who denied that it is possible for the Faithful to see God either in this world or the next. But Rumi believes that the Faithful see God both in this world and in Paradise. Even in this world Paradise and Hell and the Resurrection are shown by immediate vision. A saying is attributed to 'Ali:

> 'I saw my Lord;
> I do not worship a Lord whom I have not seen!'

Rumi says: So long as you are under the dominion of your senses and discursive reason, it makes no difference whether you regard God as transcendent or immanent, since you cannot possibly attain to true knowledge of either aspect of His nature.[48] The appearance of plurality arises from the animal soul, the vehicle of sense-perception.[49] The 'human spirit' is the spirit which God breathed into Adam,[50] and that is the spirit of the Perfect Man. Essentially it is single and indivisible, hence the Prophets and saints, having been entirely purged of sensual affections, are one in spirit, though they may be distinguished from each other by particular characteristics.[51]

'The world of creation is endowed with (diverse) quarters and directions, (but) know that the world of the (Divine) Command and Attributes is without (beyond) direction. . . . No created being is unconnected with Him: the connexion . . . is indescribable, because in the spirit there is no separating and uniting, while (our) thought cannot think except [in terms] of separating and uniting.'[52] Intellect is unable completely to comprehend this reality for it is in bondage to its own limitation of thinking in categories it has coined for itself. That is why the Prophet

[48] II, 68–69. [49] IV, 411, 425, *sqq*, 477 *sqq*. [50] Qur, xv, 29.
[51] I, 325; II, 188. [52] IV, 3692-96.

enjoined: 'Do not seek to investigate the Essence of God.'[53]

In the Proem of Book V, Rumi says to God:

Thy dignity hath transcended intellectual apprehension: in describing thee the intellect has become an idle fool.

(Yet), although this intellect is too weak to declare (what thou art), one must weakly make a movement (attempt) in that (direction).

Know that when the whole of a thing is unattainable the whole of it is not (therefore to be) relinquished.

If you cannot drink (all) the flood-rain of the clouds, (yet) how can you give up water-drinking?

If thou wilt not communicate the mystery, (at least) refresh (our) apprehensions with the husk thereof.[54]

The man who has seen the vision is alone unique and original; and he cannot give expression to his vision for there are no words to describe the experience which is impossible to communicate. When the Prophet left Gabriel behind and ascended the highest summit open to man the Qur'an only says that 'Then He revealed to His servant that which He revealed.'[55] What he saw is not explained; it cannot be explained and it cannot be described. A stage arrives when silence becomes the height of eloquence! And yet we cannot remain content with knowledge borrowed from others. We must strive to experience for ourselves that unique indescribable vision. Our bane is that we see with borrowed light and colour and we think it is our own. Rumi asks God 'what fault did that orchard commit,' that it has been stripped of the beautiful robes and has been plunged into the dreary destruction of autumn? The reply comes:

'The crime is that he put on a borrowed adornment and pretended that these robes were his own property.

We take them back, in order that he may know for sure that the stack is Ours and the fair ones are (only) gleaners;

That he may know that those robes were a loan: 'twas a ray from the Sun of Being. . . .

[53] IV, 3700. [54] V, 15–19. Italics ours. [55] liii, 11.

Thou art content with knowledge learned (from others): thou hast lit thine eye at another lamp.

He takes away his lamp, that thou mayst know thou art a borrower, not a giver.'[56]

The question arises: what is the purpose of making an image and casting in it the seed of corruption? Is destruction, then, a prelude to construction? Rumi answers:

The ignorant child first washes the tablet, then he writes letters upon it.

(So) God turns the heart into blood and abject tears, then He writes the (spiritual) mysteries upon it. . . .

When they lay the foundation of a house (to rebuild), they dig up the first foundation.

Except at night there is no unveiling of the moon: except through heartache do not seek your heart's desire. . . .

This eternal conflict seeks expression in the creation of man. God endowed man with infinite purity and then set up against him a contrary. He made two banners, white and black: one was Adam, the other was Iblis.

In the second period Abel arose, and Cain became the antagonist of pure light. Then the period of Nimrod arrived. He became the antagonist and adversary of Abraham. Thus it came down to Pharaoh and Moses. So it went on till the period of Mustafa and Abu Jahl. The conflict continues.

Every created thing is in the act of becoming, growing, developing. There is constant movement and activity. 'Every herb that has a propensity for (moving) upwards is in (the state of) increase and life and growth. When the propensity of one's spirit is upwards,' (you are) 'in (the state of) increase'; 'when it has turned its head towards the earth, (it is) in (the state of) decrease and dryness and failure and disappointment,' for '"God loves not those that sink." '[57]

[56] V, 979–93. [57] II, 1812–15.

Man has already passed through a series of deaths to attain his present stage. Death has always resulted in a higher stage. Why should he now be afraid of it?

I died to the inorganic state and became endowed with growth, and (then) I died to (vegetable) growth and attained to the animal.
I died from animality and became Adam: why, then, should I fear? When have I become less by dying?
At the next remove I shall die to man, that I may soar and lift up my head amongst the angels;
And I must escape even from (the state of) the angel: *everything is perishing except His Face.*
Once more I shall be sacrificed and die to the angel: I shall become that which enters not into the imagination.
Then I shall become non-existence: non-existence saith to me (in tones loud) as an organ, *Verily unto Him shall we return.*[58]

از جمادی مردم و نامی شدم   وز نما مردم بحیوان برزدم
مردم از حیوانی و آدم شدم   پس چه ترسم کی ز مردن کم شدم
حملهٔ دیگر بمیرم از بشر   تا برآرم از ملائك پر و سر
و ز ملك هم بایدم جستن زجو   کل شی هالك الا وجهه
بارِ دیگر از ملك قربان شوم   آنچ اندر وهم ناید آن شوم
پس عدم گردم عدم چون ارغنون   گویدم که انا الیه راجعون

It is this conviction that stamps out the fear of death from the mind of man. He then lives dangerously, he becomes a reckless vagabond, a seeker of death.

(I am) not the vagabond who gets small money into his palm, (but) the nimble vagabond who would cross this bridge (to the world hereafter) –
Not the one who cleaves to every shop; nay, but (the one who) springs away from (phenomenal) existence and strikes upon a mine (of reality).
Death and migration from this (earthly) abode has become as sweet to me as leaving the cage and flying (is sweet) to the (captive) bird.[59]

[58] III, 3901–06.   [59] III, 3949–51.

منبلی نی کو بکف پول آورد   منبلی چستی کزین پل بگذرد
آن نه کو بر هر دکانی برزند   بل جهد ان کون و کانی برزند
مرگ شیرین گشت و نقلم زین سرا   چون قفصِ هشتن پریدن مرغ را

In form man is the microcosm; in fact he is the macrocosm. 'Externally the branch is the origin of the fruit,' but 'intrinsically the branch came into existence for the sake of the fruit. If there had not been desire and hope of the fruit,' the gardener would not have planted the root of the tree. 'Therefore in reality the tree was born of the fruit,' though in appearance the fruit was born of the tree. The thought that is idea, 'which is first, comes last into actuality, in particular the thought that is eternal.'[60]

Rumi divides existence into three classes. God created angels and set reason in them. He created beasts and set lust in them. He created the sons of Adam and set both reason and lust in them. The first class is entirely reason and knowledge and munificence. The angel is absolute light and lives through the love of God; he is therefore immune from any conflict. The second class is devoid of knowledge. They are also free, therefore, from the strains and stresses experienced by man. Half of man is of the angel and half of him is ass. Angel and beast are at rest from war and combat while man is engaged in torment, a painful struggle with adversaries.

Again, there are three communities of man. One has become absolutely submerged and, like Jesus, has 'attained unto the (nature of) angel.' Their form is Adam, 'but the reality is Gabriel' – they have 'been delivered from anger and sensual passion and (vain) disputation.' The Prophets rank higher than angels.

'The second sort have attained unto (the nature) of asses: they have become pure anger and absolute lust.' The third kind are 'half animal, half (spirit-

[60] IV, 520–30.

ually) alive and endowed with guidance. Day and night in strife and mutual struggle,' their 'last (state) battles with the first.'[61]

We are thus half-men in search of a whole man. We must, therefore, seek an entirely intelligent person and clutch him 'as the blind man clutches the guide.' The half-intelligent one 'becomes wholly dead in (devotion to) the man of (perfect) intelligence, that he may ascend from his own low place to the (lofty) heights.'[62]

And the whole man is a saint. 'His form has passed away and he has become a shining mirror. . . . If you spit (at it), you spit at your own face; and if you strike at the mirror, you strike at yourself. And if you see an ugly face . . .; 'tis you; and if you see Jesus and Mary, 'tis you.' The saint is simple and pure – he places your image before you.[63]

Man is like the water of the river. When it becomes turbid, you can't see its bottom. The bottom of the river is full of jewels and full of pearls. Take heed, warns Rumi, do not make the water turbid, for it is originally pure and free. The spirit of man resembles air; when it is mixed with dust, it veils the sky, and prevents the eye from seeing the sun. When its dust is gone, it becomes pure and undefiled.

Moses asks God: 'Thou didst create the form: how didst Thou destroy it again?'

God asks Moses to sow some seeds in the earth. When Moses had sown and the seed-corn was complete and its ears had gained beauty and symmetry, he took the sickle and was cutting the crop when a voice from the Unseen cried out: 'Why dost thou sow and tend some seed-corn and now art cutting it when it has attained to perfection?' Moses replied that he was doing so in order to separate the grain from the straw. The moral of the story is that amongst the created beings are pure spirits and there are also

[61] IV, 1498–1532. [62] IV, 2188–98. [63] IV, 2140–43.

spirits that are dark and muddy. All 'shells are not in one grade: in one (of them) is the pearl and in another the bead.' The object of creation is manifestation.

He (God) said: 'I was a hidden treasure': hearken! Do not let thy (spiritual) substance be lost: become manifest![64]

The story of man's spiritual ascent is indeed fascinating. First he came into the clime of inorganic things passing into the vegetable state. Many years he lived in the vegetable state, and forgot the inorganic state because of the opposition between the two states. 'And when he passed from the vegetable into the animal state, the vegetable state was not remembered by him at all.' From the animal state he came towards humanity. Thus he advanced 'from clime to clime . . . till he has now become intelligent and wise and mighty. He hath no remembrance of his former intelligences . . .; from this (human) intelligence' he has to make a migration 'that he may escape from this intelligence full of greed and self-seeking and may behold a hundred thousand intelligences most marvellous. Though he has fallen asleep and become oblivious of the past,' he cannot for ever remain in this state of self-forgetfulness. In this world, which is the sleeper's dream, the sleeper panics 'that it is really enduring, till on a sudden there shall rise the dawn of Death and he shall be delivered from the darkness of opinion and falsehood.'[65]

Rumi calls Dawn the 'lesser resurrection.'

Our sleep and waking are two witnesses which attest to us the significance of death and resurrection.
The lesser resurrection has shown forth the greater resurrection; the lesser death has illumined the greater death.[66]

هست ما را خواب و بیداریٔ ما   بر نشانِ مرگ و محشر دو گـوا
حشر اصغر حشرِ اکبر را نُمـود   مرگِ اصغر مرگ اکبر را ز دود

[64] IV, 3000–29. [65] IV, 3637 *sqq*. [66] V, 1787–88.

In the *Mathnawi* Rumi sets forth clearly the doctrine of the Divine origin of the soul, its descent to the material world, its life on earth, and its ultimate return to its true home. This doctrine may have its source in the Neoplatonic theory of emanation and the psychology of Aristotle and Plotinus, but Rumi invests his ideas about creative evolution of man with a power and feeling all his own. The world was created in order that the Perfect Man – the soul of the world – might be evolved. It is in selfless and humble service to mankind that man discovers his highest potential. Contrive in the way of God, he urges, 'that you may gain the position of a prophet; . . . contrive that you may be delivered from your own contrivance; contrive that you may become detached from the body. Contrive that you may become the meanest slave (of God). . . . Never . . . practise foxiness and perform service with the purpose of (gaining) lordship. . . . Renounce power and adopt piteous supplication: (the Divine) mercy comes towards piteous supplication.'[67]

Rumi believes that in every age after Muhammad, the last of the Prophets, there arises a supreme saint (*Qutb*) who, together with the hierarchy subordinate to him, acts as the touchstone whereby truth and falsehood are discriminated. So long as the world endures, this process of testing will go on. Rumi makes a sharp distinction between the twelve Shi'ite Imams, descendants from 'Ali, of whom the last vanished mysteriously but is expected to reappear as the Mahdi at the end of the world, and the uninterrupted succession of great Sufi saints, who have no common ancestry except their purely spiritual descent from the Prophet. The relation of the saint submerged in mystical union with the Light of God to Reason, whether universal or particular, is the same as that of Muhammad to Gabriel, who was unable to

[67] V, 469–74.

partake with the Prophet in the ultimate realisation of Unity.

He [the Prophet] said to Gabriel: 'Hark, fly after me.'
He (Gabriel) said, 'Go, go; I am not thy companion (any farther).'
He [the Prophet] answered . . ., 'Come, O destroyer of veils: I have not yet advanced to my zenith.'
He [Gabriel] replied, 'O my illustrious friend, if I take one flight beyond this limit, my wings will be consumed.'[68]

گفت اُو را هین بپر اندر پَیَم   گفت رَو رَو من حریف تو نیم
باز گفت اُو را بیا ای پرده سوز   من باوج خود نرفتستم هنوز
گفت بیرون زین حد ای خوش فرّ من   گر زنم پَری بسوزد پَر من

Our ceaseless activity arises from the duty laid upon us of manifesting the Divine consciousness which is the ground of human nature. Since God is always working in the heart, the body cannot be idle. God says, 'Albeit I know thy secret, nevertheless declare it forthwith in thine outward act.' Rumi addressing Husam-ud-din, the hero of the *Mathnawi*, asks: 'Inasmuch as thou art seeing, why dost thou seek speech from me?' and in reply to his own question quotes Abu Nuwas: 'Give me wine to drink and tell me it is (wine).'[69]

When the 'self' has 'passed away' (*fana'*) it persists (*baqa'*), not as an individual, but as the Universal Spirit, the Perfect Man, bearing the 'Mark of God's feet on his dust'. There are numerous eloquent passages in the *Mathnawi* describing the Perfect Man. We will quote only a few to conclude this section.

From every quarter they hear the cry of the oppressed and run in that direction, like the Mercy of God.
Those buttresses for the breaches of the world, those physicians for hidden maladies,
Are pure love and justice and mercy; even as God, they are flawless and unbribed.

* * *

[68] IV, 3802–04. [69] IV, 2077 *sqq*.

. . . medicine seeks naught in the world but pain (which it should cure).

Wherever a pain is, the remedy goes there: wherever a lowland is, the water runs there. . . .

Bring the sky under thy feet, O brave one! Hear from above the firmament the noise of the (celestial) music![70]

بانگِ مظلومان ز هر جا بشنوند   آن طرف چون رحمتِ حق می دوند
آن ستونهای خلل هائی جهان   آن طبیبانِ مرض های نهان
محض مهر و داوری و رحمتند   همچو حق بی علت و بی رشوتند

★ ★ ★

- - - - - - - -   در جهان دارو بخوید غیر درد
هر کجا درد ی دوا آنجا رود   بر کجا پستیست آب آنجا دود

★ ★ ★

چرخ را در زیرِ پا آر ای شجاع   بشنو از فوقِ فلك بانگِ سماع

The wind becomes a bearer for Solomon, the sea becomes capable of understanding words in regard to Moses.

The moon becomes able to see the sign in obedience to Ahmad (Mohammed), the fire becomes wild-roses for Abraham.

The earth swallows Qarun (Korah) like a snake; the Moaning Pillar comes into (the way of) righteousness.

The stone salaams to Ahmad (Mohammed); the mountain sends a message to Yahya (John the Baptist).

(They all say), 'We have hearing and sight and are happy, (although) with you, the uninitiated, we are mute.'[71]

باد حمالِ سلیمانی شود   بحر با موسی سخن دانی شود
ماه به احمد اشارت بین شود   نار ابراهیم را نسرین شود
خاك قارون را چون ماری درکشد   کوه یحیی را پیامی می کند
ما سمیعییم و بصیریم و خوشیم   با شما نامحرمان ما خامشیم

The man transcending space, in whom is the Light of God – whence (what concern of his) is the past, the future or the present?

His being past or future is (only) in relation to thee: both are one thing, and thou thinkest they are two.

One individual is to him father and to us son: the roof is below Zayd and above 'Amr.

[70] II, 1934–42. [71] III, 1015–25.

The relation of 'below' and 'above' arises from those two persons: as regards itself, the roof is one thing only.

These expressions are not (exactly) similar to that (doctrine of spiritual timelessness): they are a comparison: the old words fall short of the new meaning.[72]

لامکانی که درو نور خداست   ماضی و مستقبل و حال از کجاست
ماضی و مستقبلش نسبت بتوست   هر دویك چیزند پنداری که دوست
یك تنی اُو را پدر ما را پسر   بام زیرِ زید و بر و عمرو آن زبر
نسبتِ زیر و زبر شد ز آن دو کس   سقف سوی خویش یك چیزست و بس
نیست مثلِ آن مثالست این سخن   قاصر از معنیٔ نو حرف کهن

Man is the substance, and the celestial sphere is his accident; all things are (like) a branch or the step of a ladder: he is the object.

* * *

Thou art the sea of knowledge hidden in a dewdrop; thou art the universe hidden in a body three ells long.

* * *

Since every atom of that World is living and able to understand discourse and eloquent,

They (the prophets) have no rest in the dead world, for this (worldly) fodder is only fit for the cattle.

* * *

. . . this (bodily part) is within Time, while that (spiritual part) is beyond Time.

This which is in Time endures till death, while the other is the associate of everlastingness and the peer of eternity.[73]

جوهرست انسان و چرخ اُو را عرض   جمله فرع و پایه اند و اُو غرض

★ ★ ★

بحر علمی در نمی پنهان شده   در سه گز تن عالمی پنهان شده

★ ★ ★

[72] III, 1151–55.   [73] V, 3575, 3579, 3591–92, 3606–07.

آن جهان چون ذره ذره زنده اند   نکته دانند و سخن گوینده اند
در جهان مرده شان آرام نیست   کین علف جز لایق اَنعام نیست

* * *

جزو جزوش را تو بشمر همچنین   این درون وقت و آن بیرونِ حین
این که در وقتست باشد تا اجل   وآن دگر یارِ ابد قرنِ ازل

III

Rumi calls sense-perception the way of asses.

راهِ حس راهِ خرانست ای سوار[74]

He dubs those in thrall to sense-perception as Mu'tazilites or philosophers. There is no point in describing God as formless or formed. Whether he transcends forms or is immanent in forms is mere intellectual exercise – the point is that you must liberate yourself from Form before you begin to have some idea of Reality. Unless you are freed from sense-perception, you can perceive little.

The Sufi's book is not (composed of) ink and letters: . . .
The scholar's provision is (consists of) pen-marks . . .: what is the Sufi's provision? Footmarks.[75]

دفتری صوفی سواد و حرف نیست   جز دل اسپید همچون برف نیست
زاد دانشمند آثارِ قلم   زاد صوفی چیست آثارِ قدم

The heart of the scholar is a wall, an impediment; for the gnostic it is a door, an opening. Every human expression is a symbol of a particular state and there is nothing absolute where the description of Reality is concerned.

'I am God [Truth]' on the lips of Mansur was the light (of truth):
'I am Allah' on the lips of Pharaoh was a lie.
In the hand of Moses the rod became a witness (to the truth), in the hand of the magician the rod became (worthless as) a mote in the air.[76]

[74] II, 48. [75] II, 159–60. [76] II, 305–06.

بود اناالحق در لب منصور نور   بود انا الله در لب فرعون زور
شد عصا اندر کفِ موسی گوا   شد عصا انـدر کفِ ساحـر هبا

One cannot, therefore, rest content with the form; one must seek the inner meaning of forms. The outward form passes away, the inner reality remains for ever. These shells of bodies we see in the world are not all living; there is not a pearl in every shell. We have to open our eyes and look into the heart of each shell before we can find a pearl.

How can the philosopher, the believer in sense-perception, deny the power of thought, something which is intangible and is yet so potent? Is it not true that by one thought that comes into the mind, a hundred worlds are overturned in a single moment? Then, why in your foolishness, asks Rumi, does the body seem to you a Solomon, and thought only as an ant? The material world in your eyes is awful and sublime: you tremble and are frightened at the clouds and the thunder and the sky, while in regard to the world of thought you are indifferent as a witless stone. The reason for this indifference is that you are a mere shape and have no portion of intelligence. From ignorance you deem the shadow to be the substance, hence the substance to you has become a plaything.

Sense-perception is merely the beginning. It is not to be deprecated as a source of knowledge. But one has to move on and not rely entirely on this fragile tool. The light of sense draws towards earth; the Light of God bears aloft. Since sensible things are a lower world, the Light of God is compared to the sea, and the light of sense to a dewdrop. 'The light of sense is hidden notwithstanding its grossness: how (then) should not that radiance be hidden which is so pure (and subtle)?'[77]

Reason, by its proper nature, is a seeker of the end.

[77] II, 1293–99.

The intellect that is vanquished by flesh becomes the flesh. Because of the diverse difference in appearance and reality, intellect is always at war with the senses. This is an eternal struggle. The infidels regarded the Prophet as only a man since they failed to see the prophetic nature in him. The sensuous eye is blind in that it sees the foam and not the sea, it sees the present and no tomorrow.

The danger of taking appearance as reality without striving to discover the deeper truth is brought out beautifully in the story of Moses and the shepherd. Moses hears a simple shepherd pour out his heart to God in his own imperfect way. 'Where are you, O God,' he says, 'that I may become Thy servant and sew Thy shoes, comb Thy head, . . . wash Thy clothes and kill lice and bring milk to Thee; . . . that I may kiss Thy little hand and rub Thy little foot, . . . when bedtime comes I may sweep Thy little room.' 'What babble is this?' demands Moses who is simply infuriated at the shepherd's description of God. 'You have become an infidel,' Moses charges, 'the stench of your blasphemy has made the (whole) world stinking. Why do you indulge in doting talk and familiarity?' For this stern rebuke Moses is taken to task by God:

. . . Thou hast parted My servant from Me.
Didst thou come . . . to unite, or didst thou come to sever?

* * *

I have bestowed on every one a (special) way of acting: I have given to every one a form of expression.

* * *

I am independent of all purity and impurity, of all slothfulness and alacrity. . . .

* * *

In the Hindoos the idiom of Hind is praiseworthy; in the Sindians the idiom of Sind is praiseworthy.

I am not sanctified by their glorification (of Me); 'tis they that become sanctified. . . .

I look not at the tongue and the speech; I look at the inward (spirit) and the state (of feeling).

* * *

The religion of Love is apart from all religions: for lovers (the only) religion and creed is – God.[78]

وحی آمد سوی موسی از خدا　　بندهٔ ما را ز ما کردی جدا
تو برای وصل کردن آمدی　　یا خود از بهر بریدن آمدی

★ ★ ★

هر کسی را سیرتی بنهاده ام　　هر کسی را اصطلاحی داده ام

★ ★ ★

ما بری از پاك و ناپاکی همه　　از گرانجانی و چالاکی همه

★ ★ ★

هندوان را اصطلاح هند مدح　　سندیان را اصطلاح سند مدح
من نگردم پاك از تسبیحشان　　پاك هم ایشان شوند و در فشان
ما زبان را ننگریم و قال را　　ما درون را بنگریم و حال را
ملت عشق از همه دینها جداست　　عاشقان را ملت و مذهب خداست

Conventional knowledge is a borrowed thing. We rest at ease in the belief that it is ours, but this is apparently a deception which we perpetrate on ourselves.

I have tried far-thinking (provident) intellect, henceforth I will make myself mad. . . .

Often have I tried (sound) intelligence; henceforth I will seek a nursery for insanity. . . .

In our city there is nobody of intelligence except Yonder man who appears to be mad.[79]

Since conventional knowledge is learnt as a bait for popularity, not for the sake of spiritual enlighten-

[78] II, 1750–70. [79] II, 2332–39.

ment, the seeker of religious knowledge is just as bad as the seeker of worldly knowledge. Such knowledge is good for debate; it is used to impress people, to indulge in disputation and argument. It is robust at the time of disputation but it is dead and gone when it has no customer!

Expression in words always fails to convey the meaning; hence the Prophet said: 'Whosoever knows God his tongue falters!'

Speech is (like) an astrolabe in (its) reckoning; how much does it know of the sky and the sun?[80]

Satan has knowledge, intelligence, wit and argumentative ability. Even Adam who learnt the names from God could not prevail in argument with Iblis, but does that make Satan the man of God?

How, then, does one arrive at Truth? There is much discord and perplexity amidst doctrines. How is one to know? The philosopher gives an explanation, the scholastic theologian invalidates his statement. And someone else jeers at both of them. Rumi believes the truth to be this:

. . . All these (various persons) are not in the right; nor (again) are this herd entirely astray,

Because nothing false is shown without the True: the fool bought (desired) spurious coin in the hope of (its being) gold.

If there were no current (genuine) coin in the world, how would it be possible to issue false coins?

Unless there be truth, how should there be falsehood? That falsehood receives brilliance (prestige and reputation) from truth. . . .

Do not say, then, that all these utterances are false: . . .

Do not say, then, that all (this) is phantasy and error: without truth phantasy exists not in the world.

Truth is the Night of Power (which is) hidden among the other nights. . . .

Not all nights are (the Night of) Power.[81]

Inasmuch as truth and falsehood have been mingled

[80] II, 3014. [81] II, 2927–36.

one needs a picked touchstone to test the good coin from the bad.

There are some assertions whose truth is attested by their very nature. If at midnight, for example, a kinsman says, '"I am near you: come now, be not afraid of the night,"' you do not ask for a proof. The two assertions you accept because you recognise the voice of your own relative. But an 'uninspired fool who in his ignorance does not know a stranger's voice from his own kinsman's' will hesitate to accept the statement. To him the words of his relative 'are (mere) assertion: his ignorance has become the source of his disbelief.' Or, for example, 'one whose mother-tongue is Arabic says in Arabic, "I know the language of the Arabs." The very fact of his speaking in Arabic is (evidence of) the reality (of his assertion), although his saying (that he knows) Arabic is (only) an assertion.' When you say to a thirsty man: 'Here is water,' will he ask you to produce some testimony and proof that it is drinkable? When a mother cries to her suckling babe, does he ask for proof of her being his mother before he takes comfort in her milk? Similarly, 'when a prophet utters a cry from without, the soul of the community falls to worship within, because never . . . will the soul's ear have heard from any one a cry of the same kind as his. That stranger (the soul), by immediate perception of the strange (wondrous) voice, has heard from God's tongue (the words), "*Verily I am near*"' and has responded without seeking proofs.[82]

From sense-perception one must progress to soul-perception. The five senses are linked with one another because all of them have grown from one root. The strength of one becomes the strength of the rest. Seeing with the eye increases speech; speech increases penetration in the eye. When one sense has perceived things that are not objects of sense-percep-

[82] II, 3572–3600.

tion. that which is of the invisible world becomes apparent to all the other senses. It is, as it were, one sheep of the flock jumping over a stream and the rest following on each other's heel.

The body is manifest, the spirit is not. Intellect is more concealed than the spirit. If you see a movement, you know that the one who moves is alive; but you do not know that he is full of intellect until regulated movements appear. The spirit of Divine inspiration is more concealed than the intellect. The intellect of the Prophet was not hidden from anyone, but his spirit of prophethood was not apprehended by everyone. The intellect of Moses was troubled by seeing the reasonable actions of Khadir. His actions seemed unreasonable to Moses, since he did not have his state of inspiration.[83]

Man is superior to animals because he has the faculty of reason. 'The more knowledge one has, the more (spiritual) life one has.' The spirit of the angels is higher than the spirit of man because it is exempt from the common sense. And 'the spirit of mystical adepts is more than (that of) the angels. . . . For that reason Adam is their object of worship: his spirit . . . is greater than their being. . . . Since the spirit (of the perfect saint) has become superior and has passed beyond the utmost limit (reached by man and angel), the soul of all things has become obedient to it.'[84]

There is only one Reality; it is recognised in different ways by different people who call it by different names. A Persian, an Arab, a Turk and a Greek are shown fighting in a story over the purchase of grapes. They all want to buy grapes but they refer to them by different names. The Persian wants *angur*, the Arab is looking for *'inab*, the Turk seeks *uzum*, and the Greek insists on *istafil*. They 'began fighting . . . because they were unaware of the hidden meaning of the names. In their folly they smote each other with

[83] II, 3236–80. [84] II, 3326–34.

their fists: they were full of ignorance and empty of knowledge.'[85]

The intellectual man likes to tie himself in knots. We are addicted to subtle discussions; we are exceedingly fond of solving problems. We tie knots and try to undo them. We create our own snare and make rules to undo the fastenings of a snare in order that our intelligence may become sharp and perfect in skill. Our life is spent in dealing with knots:

> 'Tis no wonder, indeed, for the flying bird not to see the snare and (so) fall into destruction;
>
> The wonder is that it should see both the snare and the net-pin and fall (into the snare) willy-nilly.
>
> (With) eye open and the ear open and the snare in front, it is flying towards a snare with its own wings.[86]

'Do not struggle with knots,' advises Rumi, 'lest thy wings and feathers be snapped asunder one by one through this vain display (of effort) on thy part. . . . The difficulty over *angur* and '*inab* was not solved by the contest between the Turk, the Greek, and the Arab. Until the spiritual Solomon, skilled in tongues, shall intervene, this duality will not disappear.'[87]

Sense-perception is extremely limited. The world-view of an embryo in the mother's womb is not the same as that of a thinking adult. 'If any one were to say to the embryo in the womb, "Outside is a world exceedingly well-ordered, a pleasant earth, broad and long, wherein are a hundred delights . . . mountains and seas and plains, . . . a sky very lofty and full of light, sun and moonbeams and a hundred stars"; . . . it (the embryo), in virtue of its present state, would be incredulous. . . .' Its perception has not seen anything of the kind and he would not believe the news of a world bigger and better than the one he knows. The moment, however, the child is born he begins to be less sceptical and as his perception increases he

[85] II, 3685–90. [86] III, 1647–49. [87] II, 3733–42.

begins to believe what once appeared absolutely incredible to him. You come across the same story of disbelief when a man of God speaks to the common folk and gives them tidings of a much bigger, better and eternal world. Even as, in the case of the embryo, his own limited perception debars man from conceding the existence of anything which he cannot conceive.[88]

'If a child does not see the various aspects of reason, will a rational person,' asks Rumi, 'ever abandon reason? And if a rational person does not see the various aspects of Love, (yet) the auspicious moon of Love does not wane':

> Joseph's beauty was not seen by the eye of his brethren, . . .
> The eye of Moses regarded the staff as wood; . . .
> The eye of the head was in conflict with the eye of the heart: the eye of the heart prevailed.[89]

Rumi compares Reality to an elephant in the dark. A man feels it with the palm of his hand. The hand falls on the trunk. He thinks the elephant is like a water-pipe. The hand of another touches its ear; to him it appears to be like a fan. Another handles its leg and comes to the conclusion that the elephant is like a pillar. Yet another lays his hand on its back and says that it is like a throne! If there had been a candle in each one's hand, says Rumi, the difference would have gone out of their words. The eye of sense-perception, he argues, is like the palm of the hand: the palm has no power to reach the whole of the elephant.[90]

The futility of dialectical approach – hair-splitting – is brought out beautifully in a parable. An old man who has chosen a new bride goes to a top hair-dresser and asks him to pick out his white hairs. That 'pick them out' is dialectics. The barber cut off his beard

[88] III, 50–70. [89] V, 3931–35. [90] III, 71–73.

and laid the whole of it before him for he had no time for splitting hairs.[91]

Rumi gives another example. 'A certain man slapped Zayd on the neck; he (Zayd) at once rushed at him. . . .' The assailant said: 'Answer a question before you strike me back.' ' "I struck the nape of thy neck, and there was the sound of a slap: . . . was this sound caused by my hand or by the nape of thy neck?" ' Zaid had no leisure to indulge in this reflection because he was suffering from pain; he that feels the pain has no such thought; he that is without pain can afford to indulge in the luxury of hair-splitting.[92]

The Mu'tazilites hold that all intellects were originally equal and that experience or education 'makes them more or less, so that it makes one person more knowing than another'. Rumi considers this a false doctrine. He believes that people's intellects differ in their original nature and that the superiority that stems from anyone's 'nature is even better than the superiority that is (the result of) endeavour and reflection.'[93]

'Sense-perception is captive to the intellect,' and 'intellect is captive to the spirit. The spirit sets free the chained hand of the intellect and brings its embarrassed affairs into harmony.'[94] 'That which one look perceives, 'tis impossible . . . to show it forth by the tongue. That which intellectual apprehension sees in one moment, 'tis impossible during years to hear it by the ear.'[95] 'The philosopher is in bondage to things perceived by the intellect; (but) the pure (saint) . . . rides as a prince on the Intellect of intellect.'[96]

The intelligent man begins to distinguish between form and reality. The serpent's egg resembles the sparrow's egg, the seed of the quince resembles the seed of the apple, but the intelligent man recognises the difference. Here again there is a difference

[91] III, 1376–80. [92] III, 1380–85. [93] III, 1540–44.
[94] III, 1824–25. [95] III, 1994–95. [96] III, 2527–28.

between the saint and the scholar. The latter has learned things by rote, while the source of the former's knowledge is the Spirit. One is like David, the other is a mere echo.

Between the true knower and the blind imitator there are (great) differences, for the former is like David, while the other is (but) an echo.
The source of the former's words is a glow (of feeling), whereas the imitator is one who learns things (by rote).[97]

از محقق تا مقلّد فرق هاست کین چون داودست و آن دیگر صداست

منبع گفتار این سوزی بود وآن مقلّد کهنه آموزی بود

There is a difference between knowing a thing by comparison and convention, and knowing the quiddity of that thing. The scholastic theologian says,

'This is far (from reasonable) and deeply involved (in error): do not listen to an absurdity without some explanation.'

The Sufi replies:

'To thee, O inferior one, that which is above your spiritual state seems absurd.'
The visions which are now revealed to you, is it not the case that at first they seemed absurd to you?[98]

Speaking philosophically, both affirmation and negation are possible at the same time. 'It is possible to deny and affirm the same thing.' The flame of a candle is non-existent in the presence of the sun though in formal calculation it exists. Its essence is existent; if you put cotton on it, it will burn, '(but) it is (really) non-existent: it gives you no light. . . . When you throw an ounce of vinegar into two hundred maunds of sugar, . . . the flavour . . . is non-existent, (though) the ounce exists (as a) surplus when you weigh.'[99]

[97] II, 493–94. [98] III, 3654–55. [99] III, 3658–75.

Galen the Greek philosopher, is quoted by Rumi as having stated, '"I am content that (only) half of my vital spirit should remain, so that I may see the world through the arse of a mule."' He has obviously, like his class, 'deemed all except this sensible world to be non-existence and has not perceived in non-existence a hidden resurrection.' That embryo, too, is unaware of a world outside the womb of the mother; like Galen it is also unfamiliar with the world he cannot perceive. 'It does not know that the humours which exist (in the womb) are supplied (to it) from the external world, even as our elements in this world obtain a hundred supplies . . . from the City beyond space.'[100]

Rumi talks of opinion, knowledge and certainty. 'Knowledge is inferior to certainty, but above opinion. . . . Knowledge is a seeker of certainty, and certainty is a seeker of vision. . . . Knowledge leads to vision . . . [which] is immediately born of certainty, just as fancy is born of opinion.'[101]

Whilst nothing is better than life, life is precious; when a better appears, the name of life becomes a slippery (futile) thing.

The lifeless doll is as (dear as) life to the child until he has grown up to manhood.

This imagination and fancy are (like) the doll: so long as you are (spiritually) a child, you have need of them;

(But) when the spirit has escaped from childishness, it is union (with God): it is done with sense-perception and imagination and fancy.

There is no confidant (familiar with this mystery), that I should speak without insincerity (reserve). I will keep silence.[102]

When knowledge strikes on the heart (is acquired through mystical experience), it becomes a helper; when knowledge strikes on the body (is acquired through the senses), it becomes a burden.

علم چون بر دل زند یاری شود　　علم چون بر تن زند باری شود

But when you carry this burden well, the burden will be removed and you will be given (spiritual) joy.

[100] III, 3061–81. [101] III, 4120–25. [102] III, 4110–14.

لیك چون این بار را نیکو کشی بار بر گیرند و بخشندت خوشی

Beware! Do not carry this burden of knowledge for the sake of selfish desire (but mortify yourself), so that you may ride on the smooth-paced steed of knowledge.

هین مکش بهر هوا این بار علم تا شوی راکب تو بر رهوار علم

Thou hast pronounced the name: go, seek the thing named.

اسم خواندی رو مسمّی را بجو

Make thyself pure from the attributes of self, that thou mayst behold thine own pure untarnished essence.[103]

خویش را صافی کُن از اوصاف خود تـا ببینی ذات پـاك صـاف خـود

There are three stages of certain knowledge – the knowledge of certainty (علم اليقين), the vision of certainty (عين اليقين) and the intuitive actuality of certainty (حق اليقين). The last is the highest. In such a state:

In the ear's hearing there is transformation of equalities, in the eye's seeing there is transformation of essence.

If your knowledge of fire has been turned to certainty by words (alone), seek to be cooked (by the fire itself) and do not abide in the certainty (of knowledge derived from others).

There is no intuitive (actual) certainty until you burn; (if) you desire this certainty, sit down in the fire.[104]

در شنـود گوش تبـدیل صفـات در عیـان دیـدهـا تبـدیـل ذات
ز آتش اُر علمت یقین شد از سخن پختگی جُو در یقین منزل مکن
تا نسوزی نیست آن عین الیقین این یقین خواهی در آتش در نشین

The way to certainty is not the way of reason. One seeks no proof in the presence of that which stands proved in front of one's eyes.

(Suppose that) a sun has come to speech (and says), 'Arise! for the day has risen; jump up, do not dispute!'

(And suppose that) you say, 'O sun; where is the evidence?' – it will say to you, 'O blind one, beg of God (that He give you) an eye.'

[103] I, 3447–61. [104] II, 859–61.

If any one seek a lamp in bright daylight, the very fact of seeking it announces his blindness.

* * *

To say in the midst of day 'Where is the day?' is to expose yourself.[105]

آفتابی در سخن آمد که خیز   که بر آمد روز بر جه کم ستیز
تو بگویی آفتابا کُو گواه   گویدت ای کُور از حق دیده خواه
روزِ روشن هر که اُو جوید چراغ   عینِ جستن کوریش دارد بلاغ

* * *

در میانِ روز گفتن روز کُو   خویش رسوا کردنست ای روز جُو

The beloved said, 'If this is for my sake, (to read) this at the time of (our) meeting is to waste one's life.

I am here beside thee, and thou reading a letter! This, at any rate, is not the mark of (true) lovers.'[106]

گفت معشوق این اگر بهر منست   گاهِ وصل این عمر ضائع کردنست
من به پیشت حاضر و تو نامه خوان   نیست این باری نشانِ عاشقان

There is a difference, and a fundamental one, between the philosopher and the mystic. The philosopher is content with a syllogism. He multiplies links consisting of logical proofs. The mystic, on the contrary, flees from the proof. If to the philosopher the smoke is a proof of the fire, to the mystic it is sweet to be in the fire without smoke, especially the Fire of God, which is nearer to him than the smoke. To him every proof that is without a spiritual result is vain for he is considering the final result of man.[107]

Intelligence is of two kinds – acquisitive and intuitive. The former is acquired 'from book and teacher and reflexion and . . . memory, and from concepts, . . . and . . . virgin sciences . . . [and] your intelligence becomes superior to . . . others [who have not taken the trouble to study]. The other intelligence is the gift of God: its fountain is in the midst of the soul. . . . The

[105] III, 2719–24. [106] III, 1408–09. [107] V, 568–72.

acquired intelligence is like the conduits which run into a house from the streets: (if) its (the house's) water-way is blocked, it is without any supply (of water).' The other flows like a fountain from within yourself.[108]

'Without a touchstone, imagination and reason are not clearly distinguished. . . . The *Qur'an* and the (spiritual) state of the Prophets are this touchstone. . . . Imagination belongs to Pharaoh, the world-incendiary; Reason to Moses, the Spirit-enkindler.'[109]

Rumi deprecates borrowed knowledge and exhorts independent thinking:

> (If) you have an eye, look with your own eye: do not look through the eye of an ignorant fool.
>
> (If) you have an ear, hearken with your own ear: why be dependent on the ears of blockheads?
>
> Make a practice of seeing . . . without blindly following any authority: think in accordance with the view of your own reason.[110]

In the beginning of Vol. I of the *Mathnawi* there is the story of a sick girl who is pining away and her disease cannot be diagnosed through the conventional methods until an inspired physician divines that the cause of her suffering is love.

The king in this allegory is the Spirit (*ruh*) which loves the soul (*nafs*) and desires to purify her. But though she has a certain affinity with him, she is not disposed to exchange her own world for a better. This indisposition is symbolised by the illness that overtakes her and separates her from the king. Thereupon the intellect (*'aql*), which is the vizier of the Spirit, intervenes in the guise of a physician but succeeds only in aggravating the soul's malady. The Spirit, perceiving that intellectual remedies are of no avail, turns humbly to God, confesses its helplessness, and prays for help. God sends Beauty (*jamal*), which appears to the spirit in the likeness of a Saint (*wali*),

108 IV, 1960–67. 109 IV, 2301–07. 110 VI, 3342–44.

and the king says to him, 'Thou art my beloved in reality; not the heart (*dil*) that claimed to be able to heal itself.' Then the heart, in agreement with the spirit, gives the soul (*nafs*) in marriage to her beloved, namely, sensual desire (*hawa*); but after a time the heart gradually administers to Desire the potion of gnosis (*'irfan*), so that it wastes away and becomes hateful in the eyes of the soul and finally dies. Thus does the soul that commands to evil (*nafs-i-ammarah*) attain to the blessedness of the soul at peace (*nafs-i-mutma'innah*). To such a soul comes this beautiful invitation from God: 'Thou, O soul at peace! return to thy Lord well pleased (with Him and) He well pleased (with thee). So enter thou among My chosen servants, and enter thou My Garden.'[111]

Rumi describes the thrill and bliss of responding to such a call:

For a long while I was seeking the image of my soul, (but) my image was not displayed (reflected) by any one.

The soul's mirror is naught but the face of the friend, who is of yonder country. . . .

I saw my own image in thine eyes!

I said, 'At last I have found myself: in his eyes I have found the shining Way.'

My image cried out from your eye, I am you, you are Me – in complete Union.

نقش جانِ خویش می جُستم بسی   هیــچ می ننمُـود نقشم از کسی
آئینـهٔ جـان نیست اِلاّ روی یـار   روی آن یاری که باشد ز آن دیار
دیدم اندر چشمِ تو من نقش خود   . . . .
گفتم آخـر خـویش را من یـافتم   در دو چشمش راهِ روشن یـافتم
نقشِ من از چشمِ تـو آواز داد   کــه منم تـو تــو منی در اتحـاد

Most of those destined for Paradise are simple God-fearing men. The clever ones are caught in the mischief of philosophy, the simple ones perform their

[111] Qur., xxx, 28–31.

duties and save themselves and the society from discord. They do not know the philosophy of the poor-tax but they pay it; they do not split hairs about the motives and meanings of prayers, they simply say their ritual prayer. The philosopher kills himself with thinking; the more he thinks, the less he finds.[112]

Knowledge did not profit Samiri who made the golden calf; Qarun gained little by his alchemy; Bu'l-Hakam (the Father of Wisdom) became Abu Jahl (the father of ignorance) from his knowledge. He went to hell on account of his unbelief. 'Knowledge consists in seeing fire plainly, not in prating that smoke is evidence of fire.'[113]

Rumi defines justice as putting a thing in its right place, and injustice as putting it in its wrong place. 'Nothing is vain that God created.' Nothing is absolutely good nor is anything absolutely evil. The usefulness and harm of each thing depend on where you place it. That is why knowledge is necessary and useful.[114]

Moses and Pharaoh have the same arms, the same head, the same figure, yet one is celestial, the other contemptible. Knowledge is necessary to distinguish one from the other.[115]

The highest Reality is not an external object; it lies deep within man himself. Knowledge is necessary to perceive it – not discursive knowledge which clouds the vision, but esoteric knowledge which illuminates.

'I am not contained in the heavens or in the void or in the exalted intelligences and souls;

(But) I am contained, as a guest, in the true believer's heart, without qualification or definition or description.

From this mirror (appear), at every moment fifty (spiritual) wedding-feasts: hearken to the mirror, but do not ask (Me) to describe it.'[116]

[112] VI, 2356–57. [113] VI, 2502–05. [114] VI, 2596–99.
[115] VI, 3006–07. [116] VI, 3072-77.

The man whose search culminates in such a consummation, the seeker whose heart responds to such a call, the traveller on the Path who gains this goal – such a man indeed is a gnostic, the soul of religion and the essence of piety. In him knowledge attains its highest illumination for he is both the revealer of mysteries and that which is revealed:

He is our king to-day and to-morrow: the husk is for ever a slave to his goodly kernel.

* * *

For *lawlaka* (but for thee) is (inscribed) on his (imperial) sign-manual: all are (included) in his bounty and distribution.
If he did not exist, Heaven would not have gained circling motion and light and (the dignity of) being the abode of the angels;
If he did not exist, the seas would not have gained the awe (which they inspire) and fish and regal pearls;
If he did not exist, the earth would not have gained treasure within and jasmine (flowers and verdure) without.[117]

شاهِ امروزینه و فردای ماست   پوست بنده، مغزِ نغزش دایماست

★ ★ ★

ز آنك لولاکست بر توقیعِ اُو   جمله در انعام و در توزیعِ اُو
گر نبودی اُو نیابیدی فَلك   گردش و نور مکانیٔ مَلَك
گر نبودی اُو نیابیدی بحار   هیبت و ماهی و در شاهوار
گر نبودی اُو نیابیدی زمین   در درونه گنج و بیرون یاسمین

IV

The one quality which marks out Rumi from conventional Sufis is his repudiation of the sackcloth – his utter opposition to quietism, withdrawal and escape. His emphasis on effort and constant activity is overwhelming. God is not idle and inactive for a moment. How can man be? Even vain struggle is better than idleness. Life is nothing but constant activity;

[117] VI, 2094-2106.

and cessation of activity is synonymous with death.[118]

اندرین ره می تراش و می خراش　　تا دمِ آخر دمی فارغ مباش

Rumi states the argument for and against quietism in a dialogue between the lion and the beast in the *Mathnawi*. His own view is that faith in Divine providence implies active exertion for spiritual ends.[119]

He goes to the extent of suggesting that in one's iconoclastic pursuit of dynamic living one should not stop short of the image of God Himself!

'Break God's image (but only) by God's command; cast (a stone) at the Beloved's glass, (but only) the Beloved's stone!'[120]

نقشِ حق را هم بامرِ حق شکن　　بر زجاجهٔ دوست سنگِ دوست زن

To struggle against Destiny is the destiny of man. To fight Nature is the nature of man. Rumi finds it difficult to extol the virtues of passivity and poverty. The great Sufis, it is true, were destitute and poor, but for most men poverty, in the words of the Prophet, almost comprises an infidelity that brings the soul to perdition.

O thou rich man who art full-fed, beware of laughing at the unrighteousness of the suffering.[121]

He exhorts the poor to work and not rely on a miracle happening on their behalf to bring them riches for none ever reaped until he sowed something. Do not say to yourself:

So-and-so suddenly found a treasure; I would like the same:
One must earn a living so long as the body is able. . . .
Do not retire from work, that (treasure), indeed, is following behind (the work).[122]

[118] I, 1819–24. [119] II, 975–91. [120] I, 3079.
[121] I, 517–18. [122] I, 731–35.

They only live who dare. One must take life by the forelock and not seek to run away from it. Life has its dangers and risks as it has its rewards. Unless you jump in the fire you cannot hope to convert it into a garden. It is the quality of reason to pause and ponder. Love takes a plunge. Safety is the slogan of cowards.

O blamer (of lovers), safety be thine! O seeker of safety, thou art infirm.

My soul is a furnace: it is happy with the fire; 'tis enough for the furnace that it is in the fire's house.[123]

One must seek and search, for how else does one find? This seeking, Rumi calls a blessed motion:

. . . this search is a killer of obstacles on the Way to God.

This search is the key to the things sought by thee; this (search) is thy army and the victory of the banners.

This search is like chanticleer crowing and proclaiming that the dawn is at hand.[124]

And this search cannot be postponed until tomorrow, for who ever knew he would see another dawn? Only this moment belongs to us. We must therefore struggle now and here. The Sufi, he calls 'the son of time', who clasps time.

صوفی ابن الوقت باشد در مثال

And what has a poor man to lose that he should not plunge into life? Why should he hesitate? But this destitute man is simply terrified. 'He possesses nothing, (yet) he has dread of thieves. Bare he came and naked he goes, and (all the while) his heart is bleeding on account of the thief.'[125]

عور می ترسد که دامانش برند   دامنِ مردِ برهنه کَی درند
مردِ دنیا مفلس است و ترس ناك   هیچ اُو را نیست از دزدانش باك
اُو برهنه آمد و عریان رود   وز غم دزدش جگر خون میشود

[123] II, 1375. [124] III, 1442–45. [125] III, 2632–33.

He exhorts this hesitant, halting man to rid himself of fear and realise his potential which knows no limits. He challenges him to 'make a circuit of heaven without wing and pinion, like the sun and like the full-moon and like the new moon.'[126]

He instils faith, courage and confidence in this creature who falters and fumbles and is afraid to face himself:

You are your own bird, your own prey, and your own snare; you are your own seat of honour, your own floor, and your own roof.

The substance is that which subsists in itself; the accident is that which has become a derivative of it (of the substance).[127]

مرغ خویشی صید خویشی دام خویش   صدر خویشی فرش خویشی بام خویش
جوهر آن باشد که قائم با خودست   آن عرض باشد که فرعِ اُو شدست

In Rumi's view the Divine call to Prophecy signifies struggle. It means coming out into the open to accept the challenge. Muhammad was called upon to abandon the quiet solitude of the cave and emerge into the open.[128]

وقتِ خلوت نیست اندر جمع آی

He was asked to wage war against the forces of tyranny; to destroy the order that was based on injustice and exploitation and create a new world; to 'make a resurrection ere the Resurrection'.

Since thou art the upright-rising Israfil (Seraphiel) of the time, make a resurrection ere the Resurrection.

O beloved, if any one say, 'Where is the Resurrection?' show thyself, saying 'Behold, I am the Resurrection.'[129]

چون تو اسرافیل وقتی راست خیز   رستخیزی ساز پیش از رستخیز
هر که گوید کُو قیامت ای صنم   خویش بنما که قیامت نک منم

Rumi comes down with a heavy hand on the fake Sufis who had misled the people, over centuries, into

[126] IV, 1105. [127] IV, 807–08. [128] IV, 1463. [129] IV, 1479–80.

the belief that quietism and withdrawal were virtues which led to inner bliss and happiness. 'With these base scoundrels,' charges Rumi, 'Sufism has become patching [of the garment of wool] and sodomy, and that is all.'[130]

The degenerate Sufi, Rumi dubs as 'that vain hypocritical impostor, a trap for the fools and a noose for (leading into) error.' He calls him 'a braggart, a lick-platter and a parasite. . . The licence practised by these people,' he warns, 'has become notorious: 'tis an indulgence enjoyed by every scoundrelly evil-doer.'[131]

He repudiates their teaching by asserting emphatically:

In our religion the right thing is war and terror [majesty]; in the religion of Jesus the right thing is (retirement to) cave and mountain.[132]

مصلحت در دین ما جنگ و شکوه   مصلحت در دین عیسی غار و کوه

There is no monkery in Islam. '(If) thou hast no lust, there can be no obedience (to the Divine command). There can be no self-restraint when thou hast no desire; when there is no adversary, what need for thy strength? Hark, do not castrate thyself . . . for chastity is in pawn to . . . lust.'[133]

There is nothing wrong with wealth and property. What is wrong is that you should earn it through unlawful means and use it for unlawful purposes.

علم و حکمت زاید از لقمهٔ حلال   عشق و رقّت زاید از لقمهٔ حلال

Effort is ordained. 'Our movement (exertion) and . . . our acquisition is a key to that lock and barrier. Without the key there is no way to open the door: bread without endeavour is not (according to) God's law.'[134]

[130] V, 363–64. [131] VI, 2057–66. [132] VI, 494.
[133] V, 575–78. [134] V, 2385–87.

جهد کن تا مست و نورانی شوی

'The way of the *Sunnah* is to work and earn'[135]:

راهِ سنت کار و مکسب کرد نیست

While pleading passionately for struggle and strife, and espousing eloquently the virtues of incessant activity, Rumi concedes that the gnostics appear lazy to the common man who is deceived by appearances and fails to perceive that:

They have made laziness their prop . . . since God is working for them.
The vulgar do not see God's working.[136]

The parasites, the pretenders, the hypocrites seek to copy this aspect alone without essaying to scale the spiritual heights that such saints attained after wading through rivers of blood.

Rumi views the world of Reason and Reality as an ocean in which the forms of phenomenal existence are waves that rise in rapid and continuous succession, only to fall back the next moment and disappear for ever; or bowls floating on the surface of the deep that are submerged as soon as the water fills them. Such is the relation of individuals to the Divine ground of being haunted by forms and, unconscious of the Spirit in ourselves, we vainly seek rest. The few who find it are Perfect Men.[137]

All changes have arisen from the hours: he that is freed from the hours is freed from change.[138]

جمله تلوینها ز ساعت خاستست   رست از تلوین که از ساعت برست

Much confusion was caused in the public mind by the advocates of that decadent, fatalist philosophy that sought to place a premium on quietism, withdrawal and retirement from life on the plea that man

[135] V, 2424. [136] VI, 4886–88. [137] I, 1109–48. [138] III, 2074.

is but a small inconsequential creature in the scheme of the universe and that his destiny is determined even before he is born. There is nothing he can do to frustrate the stars and his struggle and endeavour to improve his lot are doomed to failure. Resignation emerges as the supreme virtue. Waiting rather than striving becomes the rule of life. Rumi cannot possibly accept such a situation which reduces the vicegerent of God to a state of complete impotence.

Rumi rejects the concept of a static world, a finished product which is incapable of change and development. On the contrary, he believes that the world has only the semblance of duration; in truth, all phenomena are annihilated and re-created at every moment by the eternal manifestation of Divine Energy. The Prophet said, 'the world is but a moment,' i.e. a flash of Divine illumination. But in our minds this immediacy produces the illusion of Time and we deem the world enduring. The truth cannot be learnt except through the highest mystical experience, that of the saint in timeless union with God.[139]

Time is an arbitrary category of understanding. The Sufi surpasses this limitation. He is not of Time, 'for "with God is neither morn nor eve": there the past and the future and time without beginning and time without end do not exist: Adam is not prior nor is Dajjal (Antichrist) posterior. (All) these terms belong to the domain of the particular (discursive) reason . . . they are not (applicable) in the non-spatial and non-temporal world. Therefore he [the Sufi] is the son of the "moment" by which is to be understood only a denial of the division of time (into several categories), just as the statement "God is one" is to be understood as a denial of duality, not as (expressing) the real nature of unity.'[140]

It is in this context that Rumi asserts that such riddles as free-will and determinism are not to be

[139] I, 1142-49. [140] VI, heading, p. 408.

solved by intellect. Only perfect love harmonises every discord. Unity and Love replace the vulgar notions of freedom and necessity which represent Man either as the rival of the Almighty or as His involuntary scapegoat.[141]

Adam loved God; Iblis did not. Both acknowledged their sin, but while Adam took the blame on himself, Iblis held God responsible. The infidel takes refuge in the Necessitarian plea that if he commits evil, it is because the Almighty did not create him good; but the believer imputes his sins to himself and thanks God for washing them away.[142]

There are laws of Nature which are immutable and there are others which are subject to change. There are qualities which are fundamental, there are others which are accidental.

If you bid a stone become gold, 'tis futile; (but) if you bid copper become gold, the way . . . exists.

If you bid sand become clay, it is incapable . . ., (but) if you bid earth become clay, that is possible.[143]

The man of God shirks neither work nor effort. He freely submits himself to the will of God. His entire life is dedicated to the purpose of God which is essentially to help man evolve his own personality until he reaches a stage which is marked by complete and total identity between the will of man and the will of God. This is the explanation of the Qur'anic verse:[144]

ما رمَيتَ اذ رمَيتَ و لكنّ الله رمى

revealed at the battle of Badr when the Prophet threw a handful of gravel in the faces of the Quraysh who immediately fled before the Muslim onslaught.[145]

Such a man in whom God has supreme confidence cannot be cynical. On the contrary,

[141] I, 1446. [142] II, 2549-50. [143] 2909–12.

[144] Qur'an, vii, 18. [145] I, 615.

We are ever fresh and young and gracious, unfaded and sweet and laughing and debonair.

To us a hundred years are the same as a single hour, for long and short (time) is a thing disjoined from us.

* * *

When there is no day and night and month and year, how should there be satiety and old age and weariness?[146]

Happy indeed is the understanding that is undimmed:[147]

ای خنک عقلی که باشد بی غبار

Rumi is a believer in free-will, the capacity of man to choose his actions for himself. Choice he calls the salt of devotion; otherwise there would be no merit in prayer and piety. The 'celestial sphere revolves involuntarily; (hence) its revolution has neither reward nor punishment. . . . "*We have honoured* Man,"' says the Qur'an.[148] The honour lies in the fatal gift of free-will. The reins of free-will are in the hands of man.[149]

Human action is both a cause and an effect. Man, in so far as he acts freely, incurs retribution hereafter; but this, though from one point of view is a direct consequence of the action with which it corresponds in quality, may also be regarded as the final cause and eternal form of the action, pre-existent in God's knowledge, like the idea of a house in the mind of the architect. Looked at in this way, retribution is a Divine manifestation of the form immanent in all that appears under the form of human action or, in other words, a transformation of the appearance into its underlying reality. Hence there can be no true similarity between them: they differ as accident and substance.[150]

[146] III, 2936–41. [147] III, 3263. [148] xvii, 72.
[149] III, 3287–89. [150] III, 3445–63.

A man of God is not compelled. He freely chooses to submit to God.

In sooth the end of free-will is that his free-will should be lost here.
The free agent would feel no savour . . . if at last he did not become entirely purged of egoism.[151]

'God's assignment of a particular lot to any one does not,' in Rumi's view, 'hinder . . . consent, and will and choice. . . . In battle the pusillanimous from fear for their lives have chosen the means of flight . . .; the courageous, also from fear for their lives, have charged towards the ranks of the enemy. Rustams (heroes) are borne onward by (their) fear and pain; from fear, too, the man of infirm spirit dies within himself.'[152]

Beyond doubt we possess a certain power of choice. If we did not, command and prohibition would lose all meaning. Reward and rebuke would be pointless. The power of choice and the instinct to choose are latent in the soul. The power to choose good or evil is increased manifold by inspiration and suggestion. The Devil will say on the Day of Reckoning: 'I was merely presenting objects of desire to you. I did not force them on you.' And the angel will say: 'I told you that sorrow would be increased in consequence of this indulgence in sensual joy. Both the Devil and the Spirit who present objects of desire to us exist for the purpose of actualising the power of choice. There is an invisible power of choice within us; when it sees two alternative objects of desire it waxes strong.'

Our sense of guilt is evidence of free-will. If there were not free-will, what is this shame? And what is this sorrow and guilty confusion and abashment? Addressing those who believe in *jabr*, compulsion, Rumi asks:

151 IV, 399–406. 152 IV, 2912–20.

How should one make merry who is bound in chains? When does the captive in prison behave like the man who is free?

And if you consider that your foot is shackled. . . .

Then do not act like an officer (tyrannously) towards the helpless, inasmuch as that is not the nature and habit of a helpless man.[153]

The plain fact, Rumi tells the votaries of predeterminism, is that

In every act for which you have inclination, you are clearly conscious of your power (to perform it),

(But) in every act for which you have no inclination and desire, in regard to that (act) you have become a necessitarian, saying, 'This is from God.'[154]

To Rumi, Necessitarianism is more shameful than the doctrine of absolute Free-Will, because the Necessitarian is denying his own inward sense. The believer in absolute free-will says: 'There is smoke, but no fire; there is candle-light, but no candle.' The Necessitarian plainly sees the fire but for the sake of denial he says it does not exist. It burns his clothes, yet he says: 'There is no fire'; thread 'stitches his raiment,' (yet) he says, 'There is no thread.' Rumi dubs the doctrine of Necessity as Sophisticism or Scepticism. He regards the Necessitarian as worse than the believer in absolute Free-Will whom he calls an infidel. The infidel says: 'The world exists but there is no Lord.' The Necessitarian says: 'The world is really naught.' Both are in a tangle of error.[155]

Rumi argues that the entire Qur'an consists of commands and prohibitions and threats of punishment. Whoever saw commands given to a marble rock? Does any wise man, does any reasonable man do this? Does he show anger and enmity to brickbats and stones? 'If none but God have the power of choice,' he asks, 'why do you become angry with a man who has committed an offence (against you)? Why do you gnash your teeth at a foe? Why do you regard the sin

[153] I, 630–33. [154] I, 635–36. [155] V, 2967–3015.

and offence as (proceeding) from him? . . . (In the case of) a man who steals your property, you say, . . . "Arrest him, . . . make him a captive"; and (in the case of) a man who visits your wife, a hundred thousand angers shoot up from you. (On the contrary), if a flood come and sweep away your household goods, will your reason bear any enmity towards the flood? And if the wind came and took off your turban, when did your heart show any anger against the wind? The anger within you is a clear demonstration of (the existence of) a power of choice (in Man).' Even animals have this sense. 'If a camel-driver goes on striking a camel, the camel will attack the striker . . . [for] he has got some notion of the power of choice (in Man). Similarly a dog, if you throw a stone at him, will rush at you, . . . [not the stone]. Since the animal intelligence is conscious of the power of choice (in Man),' it is strange, to say the least, that man should seek to deny it. In fact, inward consciousness of man is more evident than his senses. One can bind the senses and prevent them from functioning but it is impossible to bar the way to the experiences of inward consciousness. Do or don't, command and prohibition, discussions and debate are all proofs of the power of choice. The thought, 'Tomorrow I will do this or that,' is a proof of the power of choice.[156]

Preordination and predestination do not annual the power of choice. A thief pleaded to the magistrate, 'That which I have done was decreed by God.' The magistrate retorted: 'That which I am doing is also decreed by God.'[157]

God's '(universal) power of choice brought (our individual) powers of choice into existence.' His power of choice makes our power of choice. 'Every created being has it in his power to exercise authority over the form (that is) without free-will.... The carpenter has authority over a piece of wood, and the artist has

[156] V, 3020–52. [157] V 3058–59.

authority over (the portrait of) a beauty; the iron-smith is a superintendent of iron'; the builder has control over his tools. The power forcibly exercised by man over inanimate objects does not deprive them of their inanimate nature. Similarly, the power exercised by God 'over (our) acts of free-will does not deprive any act of free-will of that (quality).' Without man's will his 'unbelief does not exist at all,' for involuntary unbelief is a contradiction in terms.[158]

Accountability can follow only from choice. Every action has the effect and consequence appropriate to it. Determinism would make nonsense of God; it would dismiss Him from office. There would be no mercy, no pardon, for any sinner, there would be no grace, no hope through piety. God would be rendered absolutely powerless. All that He would be able to say in response to our prayers and insistent entreaties is: 'Sorry. The affair has gone out of My hands: do not approach Me so often, do not entreat Me so much.'[159]

Rumi ends this lucid exposition by a characteristic qualification: 'This difficult and controversial matter cannot be decided except by real love that has no further interest in it – and that is God's grace. There is a disputation (which will continue) till mankind is raised from the dead.' Love ends all argument![160]

V

'Then what is love?' asks Rumi, and he answers his own question:

The sea of Not-Being: there the foot of the intellect is shattered.
Servitude and sovereignty are known: loverhood is concealed by these two veils.
Would that Being had a tongue, that it might remove the veils from existent beings![161]

[158] V, 3086–3124. [159] V, 3132–53.
[160] V, 3213–14. [161] III, 4723–25.

پس چه باشد عشق دریای عدم در شکسته عقل را آنجا قدم
بندگی و سلطنت معلوم شد زین دو پرده عاشقی مکتوم شد
کاشکی هستی زبانی داشتی تاز هستان پردها برداشتی

Again, Rumi poses the question:

The intellect (was) simply bewildered, saying 'What is love and what is ecstasy?
(I know not) whether separation from Him or union with Him is the more marvellous?'[162]

عقل حیران که چه عشقست و چه حال تا فراق أو عجب تر یا وصال

Love truly expresses itself in service. Service is a means of gaining, growing and developing. 'The servant of God desires to be freed from Fortune; the lover . . . nevermore desires to be free.' The servant is always seeking reward, a 'robe of honour and a stipend; all the lover's robe of honour is his vision of the Beloved.'

Love is not contained in speech and hearing: Love is an ocean whereof the depth is invisible.

* * *

Love makes the sea boil like a kettle; Love crumbles the mountain like sand.
Love cleaves the sky with a hundred clefts; Love unconscionably makes the earth to tremble.[163]

در نگنجد عشق در گفت و شنید عشق دریاییست قعرش ناپدید
* * *
عشق جوشد بحر را مانند دیگ عشق ساید کوه را مانند ریگ
عشق بشکافد فلك را صد شکاف عشق لرزاند زمین را از گزاف

Love is not lust nor is it phantasy and imagination. The bane of this gate is sensuality and lust; else, draught on draught of spiritual knowledge is to be found here. Adam took one step in sensual pleasure:

[162] III, 4717. [163] V, 2728–36.

he fell from his high place. The creative power of love is determined by the greatness of the object desired. A 'mother, distraught (with grief) beside the grave of a child newly dead, utters heart-felt words earnestly and intensely: the inanimate (corpse) seems to her to be alive. She regards that dust as living, . . . as having an eye and an ear. To her at the moment . . . every atom of the earth in the grave seems to have hearing and intelligence.' This is the magic worked by love! 'Fondly and with tears she lays her face, time and again, on the fresh earth of the grave. . . . (But) when some days pass in mourning, the fire of her love sinks to rest.' Rumi drives home the point:

> Love for the dead is not lasting: keep your love (fixed) on the Living One who increases spiritual life.[164]

Love is the motive force of all creation. It transforms the quality of life:

> By love bitter things become sweet; by love pieces of copper become golden;
> By love dregs become clear; by love pains become healing;
> By love the dead is made living; by love the king is made a slave.
> This love, moreover, is the result of knowledge: who (ever) sat in foolishness on such a throne?
> On what occasion did deficient knowledge give birth to this love?[165]

Rumi makes no distinction between the gnostic (*'arif*) and the lover (*'ashiq*). For him love and knowledge are inseparable and co-equal aspects of the same reality.

Love, whether its immediate object be Divine or human, real or phenomenal, leads ultimately to the knowledge of God. All earthly beauty is but the reflexion of Heavenly Beauty, and as the reflexion fades away we turn our eyes towards the height whence it came.[166]

Woman is the highest type of earthly beauty, but

[164] V, 3260–72. [165] II, 1529–32. [166] I, 111.

earthly beauty is nothing except in so far as it is a manifestation and reflexion of Divine attributes.[167]

That which is the object of love is not the form.[168]

'Tis the draught of (Divine) beauty – (mingled) in the lovely earth – that thou art kissing with a hundred hearts day and night.[169]

When Iblis desired God to give him a means of temptation that should be irresistible, he was shown the beauty of woman and was amazed by the revelation of Divine glory:

'Twas as though God shone forth through a thin veil.[170]

Sweeping aside the veil of form, Rumi beholds in woman the eternal Beauty which is the inspirer and object of all love, and regards her, in her essential nature, as the medium *par excellence* through which that uncreated Beauty reveals itself. From this point of view she is the focus for the Divine *tajalli* and may be identified with the life-giving power of its ray. From another point of view woman is the cause of Adam's fall. Rumi recalls wistfully:

(Both) my first and my last fall were caused by woman, since I was spirit – and I became body.[171]

اول و آخــر هبــوطِ من ز زن چونك بودم روح و چون گشتم بدن

This is not a happy thought about woman. This is why perhaps he never fell in love with one. His devotion and dedication to Shams-i-Tabriz is well known. After him came Salah-ud-din Zarkob who was followed by Hisam-ud-din Chalapi. These three men were the centre of Rumi's adoration and attention. It is through them that he strives to discover the Perfect Man – the central theme of the *Divan* and the *Mathnawi*. These men are only milestones on the Way.

167 III, 554 *sqq.*; V, 985 *sqq.* 168 II, 703. 169 V, 374.
170 V, 954 *sqq.* 171 VI, 2799.

They lead to the Prophet Muhammad who, as the Logos, is the archetype and final cause of creation. In him the supreme idea of humanity is realised.[172]

The World-Idea, the Divine Consciousness, is realised in Muhammad, the last of the Prophets, who therefore is the final cause of creation, according to the *Hadith-i-Qudsi*: *lawlaka la-ma khalaqtu'l-aflaka* ['but for thee I would not have created the heavens']. Hence the description of the Prophet as *khawjah-i-lawlak*. Were it not for Muhammad (the Perfect Man), the object of creation would not have been realised, since God would not have been known to Himself in and through the Perfect Man by whom all His attributes are made manifest.

The Prophet attained perfection through love, not reason, not through a studied pursuit of knowledge. Adam won signal honour through love and Iblis was rejected though he had all the intelligence.

He that is blessed and familiar (with spiritual mysteries) knows that intelligence is of Iblis, while love is of Adam.

Intelligence is (like) swimming in the seas: he (the swimmer) is not saved: he is drowned at the end of the business.

* * *

Love is as a ship for the elect: seldom is calamity (the result); for the most part it is deliverance.[173]

داند او کو نیک بخت و محرمست　　زیرکی ز ابلیس و عشق از آدمست

زیرکی سباحی آمد در بحار　　کم رهد غرقست او پایانِ کار

* * *

عشق چون کشتی بود بهرِ خواص　　کم بود آفت بود اغلب خلاص

It is Love which makes the world go round. The wheeling heavens are turned by waves of Love. If there had not been Love, there would be no existence. Love, says Rumi, is an infinite ocean, on which the

[172] I, 2060.　　[173] IV, 1402–04.

heavens are but a flake of foam. Were it not for Love the world would remain inanimated, a mass of frozen dead matter. It is Love alone which breathes the warmth and glow of life, which makes an inorganic thing into a plant, which produces the Breath that makes Mary deliver the miracle of Christ.

عشق بحری آسمان بر وی کفی   چون زلیخا در هوای یوسفی
دورِ گردونها ز موجِ عشق دان   گر نبودی عشق بفردی جهان
کی جمادی محو گشتی در نبات   کی فدای روح گشتی نامیات
روح کی گشتی فدآی آن دمی   کز نسیمش حامله شد مریمی

Love indeed is that radiance and warmth which animates, quickens and sublimates everything it touches. It imparts a glow of feeling, a faith which transforms the quality and character of life. In fact life is not possible without love.

If there had not been Love, how should there have been existence? How should bread have attached itself to you and become (assimilated to) you?

The bread became you: through what? Through (your) love and appetite; otherwise, how should the bread have had any access to the (vital) spirit?

Love makes the dead bread into spirit: it makes the spirit that was perishable everlasting.[174]

Love solves all the mysteries of the world; it is at once an ailment and a matchless cure. 'The lover's ailment is separate from all other ailments: love is the astrolabe of the mysteries of God.'[175]

علّتِ عاشق ز علّتها جداست   عشق اصطرلابِ اسرارِ خداست

Rumi hails Love with a fervour and beauty which is impossible to communicate:

Hail, O love, that bringest us good gain – thou that art the physician of all our ills.

[174] V, 2012–14. [175] I, 110.

The remedy of our pride and vainglory, our Plato and our Galen!
Through Love the earthly body soared to the skies: the mountain began to dance and became nimble.[176]

شاد باش ای عشقِ خوش سودای ما   ای طبیب جمله علّتهای ما
ای دوای نخوت و ناموس ما   ای تو افلاطون و جالینوس ما
جسمِ خاك از عشق بر افلاك شد   کوه در رقص آمد و چالاك شد

The final and the supreme objective is indeed God. Corporealists and anthropomorphists cannot form a spiritual conception of God. They invest Him with bodily attributes. But real love transcends all duality. When Mansur Hallaj declares his mystical union with God he says:

Thy spirit is mingled in my spirit even as wine is mingled with pure water.
When anything touches Thee, it touches me. Lo, in every case Thou art I![177]

The good Muslims executed him in 309 A.H. Rumi says in a similar state:

Sometimes I say to thee, "Tis thou,' sometimes, "Tis I': whatever I say, I am the Sun illuminating (all).[178]

گه تونی گویم ترا گاهی منم   هر چه گویم آفتابِ روشنم

Humility is the hall-mark of lovers. Respect and reverence is called for. Rumi warns those who tend to be familiar:

For-as-much as praise and prayer were vouchsafed to you, through making that prayer your heart became vainglorious.
You regarded yourself as speaking . . . with God. Oh, (there is) many a one that becomes separated (from God) by this opinion.
Although the King sit with you on the ground, know yourself and sit better (with more decorum and reverence).[179]

Loyalty in love is the first requisite. Rumi picks up

176 I, 23–25. 177 *Tawasin*, 134. 178 I, 1940. 179 II, 339–41.

the falcon as a symbol of loyalty, for every time he soars he comes back to the king:

باز آن باشد که باز آید بشاه

I fly as a moon and sun, I rend the curtains of the skies.
The light of intellects is from my thoughts; the bursting forth of heaven is from my original nature.
I am a falcon, and (yet) the *huma* becomes lost in amazement at me: who is an owl, that it should know my secret?

* * *

I am the owner of the (spiritual) kingdom, I am not a lick-spittle: the King is beating the falcon-drum for me from the shore.[180]

Rumi compares the falcon to the spirit for it soars high, and bodily properties he calls crows and owls:[181]

روح بازست و طبایع زاغ ها   دارد از زاغان و چغدان داغ ها

It is 'a foot-bound broken-winged creature (but) when its self-consciousness is gone and its foot untied, that falcon flies towards the King.'[182]

جان چو باز و تن مرو را کُندهٔ   پـای بسته پَـر شکسته بنـدهٔ
چونك هوشش رفت و پایش بر گشاد   می پَـرد آن بـاز سـوی کیقباد

In love, pain and suffering is a must. 'Love is like the lawsuit; to suffer harsh treatment is (like) the evidence; when you have no evidence, the lawsuit is lost.'[183]

عشق چون دعوی جفا دیدن گواه   چون گواهت نیست شد دعوی تباه

Suffering in love is its own reward. In love, life is completely transformed. Concepts change, values change and words take on another meaning. Mansur sought to annihilate himself and he became immortal; Pharaoh sought to perpetuate his rule and he was drowned. Gallows become a throne and the imperial

180 II, 1159–70. 181 V, 843. 182 V, 2280–81. 183 III, 4009.

court becomes a prison-house. 'A Pharaoh said "I am God" and he was laid low; Mansur said, "I am God" and he was saved. The former "I" was followed by God's curse and the latter "I" by God's mercy. . . .'[184]

گفت فرعونی اناالحق گشت پست　　گفت منصوری اناالحق و برست
آن انا را لعنة الله در عقب　　وین انا را رحمت الله ای محب

The former was provoked by opposition to God, the latter was inspired by submission to God. What appeared supreme defiance on the part of Mansur to people, who only knew the ordinary meaning of words, became in the eyes of God an act of supreme submission.

All this flows from the infinite mercy of God, for man indeed is weak and limited:

We will set fire to the tenement of man and make the thorns (in it) a spiritual garden of roses.
We have sent from the Ninth Sphere (the highest Heaven) the elixir, '*He will rectify for you your actions*.'
What in sooth is Adam's sovereignty and power of choice beside the Light of the Everlasting Abode?
His speaking organ is a piece of flesh; the seat of his vision is a piece of fat;
The seat of his hearing consists of two pieces of bone; the seat of his (intellectual) perception is two drops of blood, that is to say, the heart.[185]

شعله در بُنگاهِ انسانی زنیم　　خار را گلزارِ روحانی کنیم
ما فرستادیم از چرخ نهم　　کیمیا یُصلِح لکُم أعمالَکُم
خود چه باشد پیش نور مُستقر　　کرّ و فرِ اختیارِ بُوالبشر
گوشت پاره آلت گویای او　　پیه پاره منظر بینای او
مَسمعِ او آن دو پاره اُستخوان　　مَدرکش دو قطره خون یعنی جنان

'Love alone cuts disputation short, for it (alone) comes to the rescue when you cry for help against

[184] V, 2035–36.　　[185] V, 1850–54.

arguments. Eloquence is dumbfounded by Love: it dare not engage in altercation.'[186]

In expounding Love, intellect is helpless like an ass in the mire; it is Love alone that can offer the explanation of love. Love is the motive force of all creation and love defies all definition, all description. The price of love is life itself; the lover values love above everything else, for he has not come by it so cheaply that he should consent to throw it away. This power of love has freed him from the bondage of life and he has come by a treasure which cannot be evaluated in terms of gold, power or possessions.[187] To others it may appear something imperceptible, intangible, but to him it is the very essence of life for it has bestowed upon him the consciousness of a world which is hidden from the capricious eyes of those that look only at the exterior, the obvious, the superficial, and have not learnt to penetrate the inner meaning of words. As for Rumi,

What care I though ruin be (wrought)? Under the ruin there is a royal treasure.[188]

VI

And now we enter territory where angels fear to tread. The universe is indeed marked by such power, beauty, order and harmony that man is in danger of worshipping them. In the perishable and the mutable, therefore, man's reason must grasp the evidence for the necessary and transcendent existence of the Creator. The universe is created and is dependent for its continuance upon something else, but the Creator is not dependent upon any other being. The whole creation has proceeded from Him and reverts to Him. He is the First and the Last. He is Self-Existent and Uncreated. He is neither begotten nor He begets, nor has He a partner or associate who shares with Him

[186] V, 3240–41. [187] I, 1468. [188] I, 1744.

His powers. He is unique in all His powers and attributes. All the beautiful names belong to Him, but they are all inadequate in conjuring up the Reality of God. He is Omnipotent, Omniscient. He is the Lord of Unity, absolutely One and Unique, absolutely Self-Sufficient. He is Wise and knows all about everything. There is nothing that is outside His ken. He is kind, Most Merciful, the Lord of Majesty, the Possessor of Power and Authority. He is Most Forgiving, Most Appreciating. He answers the prayers of His servants. He is not aloof, remote and distant. He is close to man. In fact, He is closer to him than his jugular vein.[189] He is at once Manifest and Hidden. He is the Equitable and the Just and his retribution is swift. There is no contradiction in these attributes. Pain and penalty are not inconsistent with Mercy and Forgiveness. The erring servants must revert to the Path by penitence and pain. And death is no destroyer – it is neither a disaster, nor an end to life. It is merely a milestone on the way; it only indicates transition from one world to another. Man passes through a series of deaths before he is able to achieve immortality.

If murder of man by man is the act of God, why does He command retribution (*qisas*)? The question leads to an exposition of the essential unity of the Divine nature under all the diverse modes of its manifestation in the world. In reality the avenging God, says Rumi, is the merciful God; He is Love, and from that infinite source flows every chastisement that He inflicts.[190]

All attributes are merely a feeble attempt at describing the Divine nature, but God in Himself must remain the unexpressed mystery. All things are recognised by their opposites and God alone has no opposite. Human imagination is simply not able to

[189] وَ نَحنُ اَقرب اِلیهِ مِن حَبلَ الورید (Qur., 1, 16).

[190] I, 3854.

comprehend the subtle nature of Godhood. Whatever idea you may form of God in your mind, He is different from that. Like the shepherd in the *Mathnawi* you may use anthropomorphic terms in His praise but remember that none applies. The highest stage of praise is indeed with the heart, not with the tongue. God is independent of all praise, of all purity and impurity, of all slothfulness and alacrity. He is worshipped by believers and infidels alike. But He is not sanctified by their glorification; it is they that become sanctified. God is absolutely Self-Sufficient:

> I am not the four temperaments or the first cause, I am ever remaining in (absolute) control.
> My action is uncaused and upright (independent): I have (the power of) predetermination, (I have) no cause.
> I alter My custom at the time (I choose).[191]

God is 'with' us only in respect of His attributes. His Essence is absolutely One, transcending all 'otherness'. Hence it may be symbolised by the letter *alif* which is a bare perpendicular line devoid of any diacritical mark.[192]

Diverse created beings are spiritually different. They pass through various stages of experience in their perception of Reality:

> One man is beholding a moon plainly, while another sees the world dark,
> And another beholds three moons together. These three persons are seated in one place.
> The eyes of all three are open, and the ears of all three are sharp; they are fastened on thee and in flight from me.
> Is this an enchantment of the eye? Or is it a marvellous hidden grace? On thee is the form of the wolf, and on me is the quality (beauty) of Joseph.
> If the worlds are eighteen thousand and more, these eighteen (thousand) are not subject to every eye.[193]

The varying states of consciousness that make up

[191] II, 1625–26. [192] I, 1514. [193] I, 3752–56.

the inner life of the mystic swing him to and fro between various ways of contemplating Reality. The experience is essentially incommunicable in its subtle and profound effects. All the theories woven round this theme are at best half-truths. The Truth must remain a Mystery. Those who assert the transcendence of God and those who assert His immanence are both bewildered by Him. But one thing is certain. Sense-perception, on which philosophers rely for the knowledge of Reality, cannot lead to the vision of God. Unless you are freed from bondage to sense-perception, you cannot behold images which are not of the material world.

To sharpen the intelligence and wits is not the (right) way: none but the broken (in spirit) wins the favour of the king.[194]

Though God is the only real Agent, normally He acts by means of secondary causes (*asbab*). This 'custom', however, is not invariable; God can at any time make such causes ineffective or decree that they shall produce effects contrary to their nature.

Rumi believes that God is absolutely Self-Sufficient (*ghani*). He does not need the 'slaves' ('*ibad*) whom His mercy brings into existence. The Qur'anic text: 'I created the Jinn and mankind only that they might worship Me,'[195] signifies that they were created in order that by worshipping God they might make themselves perfect.[196]

It behoves the seeker of God, therefore, not to rely entirely on his own strength, but to regard all Sufis as friends and brethren without whose aid he cannot overcome the dangers and temptations that assail travellers on the way.[197]

If anybody goes on the way without a leader, every two days' journey becomes one of a hundred years.

[194] I, 532. [195] I, 156. [196] II, 1755. [197] II, 2150.

Whoever speeds towards the Ka'ba without a guide becomes contemptible.[198]

هر که در ره بی قلاوزی رود　　هر دو روزه راه صد ساله شود
هر که تازد سوی کعبه بی دلیل　　همچو این سر گشتگان گردد ذلیل

Seek the friend of God and God is your friend.[199]

رو بجُـو یارِ خـدایی را تـو زُود　　چون چنان کردی خدا یار تو بُود

One must seclude oneself from strangers, not from friends. 'Since the true believer is a mirror for the true believer, his face is safe from defilement. The friend is a mirror, O my soul!'[200]

When the mirror of your heart becomes clear and pure, you will behold both the image and the image-Maker.

The phantom (seen in mystical vision) of my Friend seemed to me like Khalil (Abraham) – its form an idol, its reality a breaker of idols.[201]

چون خلیل آمد خیالِ یارِ من　　صورتش بُت معنیٔ اُو بُت شکن

'The spirit debarred from everlasting life is exceedingly tormented; the spirit united (with God) in everlasting life is free [and blissful].'[202] And yet the terms 'union' and 'separation,' implying the existence of subject and object, are incompatible with absolute unity.[203] Rumi is uncompromising in his belief in Divine Unity. He postulates a universal Being which may be regarded as the Essence of phenomena. This Being is all that exists; there is nothing else.[204] The multitudinous forms of phenomena produced by the manifestation of various attributes of the One Real Being are compared to shadows which owe their existence to sunlight falling on a wall. Demolish the wall of illusion and all phantoms disappear; and you

[198] III, 588–89.　[199] II, 23.　[200] II, 30-31.　[201] II, 74.
[202] IV, 446.　[203] III, 1340.　[204] I, 606-10.

see nothing but the Sun of Unity.[205] The many are nothing but modes and aspects of the One whence all numbers originate. Even dualists and polytheists admit the existence of the One God. What they are not agreed upon is the number of gods. If their spiritual obliquity were removed, they would perceive the truth and confess the Divine Unity which they now deny.[206]

Rumi is an uncompromising theist. The pantheists contend that part is connected with the whole. Rumi retorts: if this is so, eat thorns, for the thorn is connected with the rose! The part, he asserts emphatically, is not connected with the whole. Were this so, the mission of the Prophets would be meaningless. The Prophets are sent in order to connect the part with the whole; how, then, should they connect them when they are already one body?[207] In clarifying God's relation to created things, Rumi says:

> The parts of the Whole are not parts in relation to the Whole – (they are) not like the scent of the rose, which is a part of the rose.
>
> The beauty of (all) green herbs is a part of the Rose's beauty, the coo of the turtle-dove is a part of that Nightingale. . . .[208]

Rumi rejects the pantheistic idea of emanation and confirms that man remains himself despite his lofty flights to heaven. The Prophet remained a man, a perfect man, despite his ascent to the highest heaven and the personal vision of God. He did not assume divinity on that score. The colour of iron changes in the heat of fire but it remains iron. If iron, in the heat of its new experience, calls itself fire, it is gravely mistaken:

> The colour of iron is lost in the colour of the fire, the iron has assumed the colour of the fire but is iron.
>
> When it becomes red like gold, then its appearance boasts without words: 'I am fire.'

[205] I, 688–89. [206] II, 311–12. [207] I, 2810–12. [208] I, 2905–06.

Glorified by the colour and nature of fire it says, 'I am fire, I am fire.'

'I am fire; if you doubt it, then come and experience by putting your hand on me.'[209]

رنگ آهن محو رنگ آتش است　　ز آتشی می لافد و آهن و ش است
چو به سرخی گشت همچو زر کان　　پس انا النار است لافش بی گمان
شد ز رنگ و طبعِ آتش محتشم　　گـویـد اُو من آتشم من آتشم
آتشم من گر ترا شك است و ظن　　آزمـودن کن دست بـر من بـزن

In the *Mathnawi* God is described as a dyer,[210] as a magician,[211] as a hidden treasure, as a rider hidden by the dust which he raises,[212] as a painter or calligrapher,[213] as a butcher,[214] as the hunter of the soul,[215] as a camel-driver,[216] as a mother,[217] as a dice-player,[218] as a shepherd,[219] as a vine.[220] God is the ultimate source of good and evil and all opposites.[221] The seeming contradictions disappear, the differences dissolve altogether and a man of God perceives nothing but total harmony and utter Unity.

The speaker of the word and the hearer of the word and the words (themselves) – all three become spirit in the end.

The bread-giver and the bread receiver and the wholesome bread become single (denuded) of their forms and are turned into earth,

But their reality, in the three categories, is both differentiated in (these) grades and permanent.

In appearance they have become earth, in reality they have not; . . .

In the spiritual world all three are waiting (for the Divine command), sometimes fleeing from form and sometimes taking abode (in it).[222]

This is the case with mystics. They pass through various states of consciousness. At one stage by

209 III, 3670–73.
210 I, 766, 3954.
211 I, 1447.
212 III, 383–84.
213 II, 2537–39; V, 310–11.
214 III, 3743.
215 IV, 1054.
216 IV, 1102.
217 V, 698.
218 V, 4190.
219 VI, 1835.
220 VI, 4739.
221 I, 298; IV, 2517–27.
222 VI, 72–76.

denying his self-existence the mystic affirms his oneness with God.[223] In the phenomenal world the Divine Attributes of Majesty (*Jalal*) and Beauty (*Jamal*) appear under the form of externality. Only by transcending all the aspects in which the One Essence presents itself to our perception can the mystic's experience of Unity be realised.[224]

The Necessitarian view implies separation between the creature and the Creator, the opposition of two wills, and the subjugation of the weaker. But mystics who know God to be Love and themselves one with Him are not 'compelled'; on the contrary, they enjoy the unconstrained rapture of self-abandonment and the perfect freedom of feeling and acting in harmony with the will of God.[225] By dying to self (*fana'*) the mystic returns, as it were, to his original state of potential existence as an idea in God's consciousness, and realises the Unity of the Divine Essence, Attributes, and Action.[226]

Inasmuch as those united (with God) are absorbed in the Essence, O Son, how should they look upon His Attributes?
When your head is at the bottom of the river, how will your eye fall on the colour of the water?[227]

The states of consciousness vary with the degree of one's spiritual progress. The piety of the vulgar is sin in the elect; the unitive state of the vulgar is a veil in the elect.

That which is the very essence of grace to the vulgar becomes wrath to the noble favourites (of God).
Much tribulation and pain must the vulgar endure in order that they may be able to perceive the difference.[228]

Rumi believes that a vision of God is possible both in this world and the next. And this vision is direct.

223 I, 1759. 224 I, 498. 225 I, 1463.
226 I, 762. 227 II, 2813–14. 228 IV, 2982–83.

And after the direct vision of God the intermediary is only an inconvenience.

For, O (my) companion in the Cave, these intermediary words are, in the sight of one united (with God), thorns, thorns, thorns.[229]

Prayer is the pathway to God. And this prayer is no mere posture of the body; it shakes the entire spirit and transforms the whole being of man. But not every man who prostrates himself becomes the recipient of grace. 'The wages of (Divine) mercy are not the (allotted) portion of every hireling.'[230]

At one stage it dawns on the mystic that:

This uttering of praise (to Him) is the omission of praise on my part, for this (praise) is a proof of (my) being, and being is a sin.

It behoves (us) to be not-being in the presence of His being: in His presence what is (our) being? Blind and blue.[231]

(Confronted) with such an all-conquering Lord, how should any one not die (to self), unless he be a vile wretch?[232]

In such a mood of surrender Rumi discovered individuality in non-individuality.[233] But man must emerge from this ecstasy and rapture in order consciously to capture greater heights. From self-negation he must leap forward to self-affirmation. Says Rumi in such a state:

. . . Cease from negating and begin to affirm.

Come, leave off (saying) 'this is not' and 'that is not'; bring forward that One who is Real Being,

Leave negation, and worship only that Real Being.[234]

نفی بهرِ ثبت باشد در سخن   نفی بگذار و ز ثَبت آغاز کُن
نیست اینَ و نیست آن بین وا گذار   آنک آن هستت آنرا پیش آر
نفی بگذار و همان هستی پرست   این در آموزای پدر ز آن تُرکِ مست

In the ultimate reaches of life the subtle difference between existence and non-existence disappears. Both

[229] IV, 2984. [230] II, 1651. [231] I, 517.
[232] I, 530. [233] I, 1735. [234] VI, 640–41.

negation and affirmation are possible at the same time. Both are true. Both are valid.

'Such a non-existent one who hath gone from himself is the best of beings, and the great (one).

He hath passed away (*fana*) in relation to (the passing away of his attributes in) the Divine attributes, (but) in passing away (from selfhood) he really hath the life everlasting (*baqa*).

All spirits are under his governance; all bodies too are in his control.

He that is overpowered in Our grace is not compelled; nay, he is one who freely chooses devotion (to Us).'

In sooth the end of free-will is that his free-will should be lost here.[235]

این چنین معدوم کُو از خویش رفت   بهتـرین هستهـا افتـاد و زفـت
اُو بنسبت بـا صفات حق فنـاست   در حقیقت در فنـا اُو را بقـاست
جمـله ارواح در تـدبـیر اُوسـت   جمله اشبـاح هـم در تـیر اُوست
آنك اُو مغلوب اندر لطف ماست   نیست مُضـطر بلك مختـارِ ولاست
منتـهـای اختیـار آنست خـود   کـه اختیارش گـردد اینجا مُفتقـد

[235] IV, 398–402.

Chapter 6

The Poet as a Thinker

When we talk of Rumi's thought, we should not be taken to mean that he had a systematic and coherent philosophy. His thoughts lie scattered and unconnected like broken threads, but a patient effort can weave them into an almost consistent pattern. The point is that we should not approach Rumi's thought in the same spirit as we approach the thought of a systematic thinker.

Another point of difference between Rumi and systematic thinkers is that, whereas the latter usually support their contentions with arguments, Rumi generally makes assertions and tries to invest them with power by means of analogies.

As Whinfield points out, the *Mathnawi* is an exposition of 'experimental' mysticism, and not a treatise of 'doctrinal' mysticism. Hence Rumi does not set out all this Sufi gnosis with the logical precision of a systematic thinker but rather assumes it all as known to his readers.[1]

Muslim philosophers used to employ *a priori* reasoning in order to establish the truth of metaphysical dogma. This method, however, does not elicit ready approval from the average individual whose mind is not trained for abstract thinking of a high order. Rumi, therefore, employs analogies in order to drive home a subtle point – analogies from this matter-of-fact, sensible world of ours. Analogy used in poetry often assumes the form of a didactic story; and

[1] Whinfield, *Mathnawi*, Introduction, p. xxxv.

a didactic story, in order to be successful, should possess three characteristics: the moral should entice our imagination by its originality, uniqueness and importance; the moral should appear like the 'soul' and the story like the 'body'; and both should be interwoven into each other, and during the perusal of the story the reader should not even think of the moral. It should come as a complete surprise, an original experience.

There are numerous stories in Rumi which aptly illustrate this method.[2] In fact it is the effective employment of this method which has given unique influence and popularity to his *Mathnawi*. For example, here is an interesting story. There was a *muezzin* who had an extremely unpleasant voice. The people of his village offered him a lump sum with the request that he should proceed to Mecca for a pilgrimage. This was obviously a pretext to get rid of him. The *muezzin*, on his way to Mecca, halted in a village. There he went into the mosque and called the faithful to prayers. After a short while, a Zoroastrian came, laden with presents, and asked for the *muezzin*. People were naturally surprised. 'What is it?' they asked. 'What has he done for you that you bring him such valuable presents?' 'I am greatly indebted to him,' said the Zoroastrian; 'he has saved my daughter.' 'How?' came the anxious query, and this is what the Zoroastrian told the curious crowd: 'I have a young and beautiful daughter. Much to my embarrassment, of late she has been showing a growing inclination towards Islam. I tried my best to dissuade her; all the influential members of my community helped in bringing pressure to bear upon her, but our efforts notwithstanding, she persisted in her designs of con-

[2] Of his stories he says in the *Mathnawi*:

ای برادر قصه چون پیمانه است   معنی اندر وی بسان خانه است
دانهٔ معنی بگیرد مرد عقل   ننگرد پیمانه را گر گشت نقل

version. Today she heard the *muezzin* call the faithful to prayers; she was so much disgusted with his voice that she has now decided to abandon her plan. This decision has brought me great relief, and it is in recognition of this unique service that I bring these rich presents to the *muezzin*.'

The moral of this story does not seem to be evident. It becomes evident only when Rumi points it out, and administers an effective rebuke to the so-called Mussalmans who are bringing discredit to their religion by their wrong example.

It is by means of such delightful stories that Rumi discusses and analyses profound truths:

> Now hear the outward form of my story,
> But yet separate the grain from the chaff.

A systematic thinker usually has a set of ideas which he either wants primarily to communicate to others or he wants just to express them in words. Expression in words may *ipso facto* mean communication to others, but a thinker might only aim at expression and not at communication. It seems that Rumi is certainly not a thinker of this type. He does not primarily aim at communication; he is not thinking of conveying his ideas as such. On the contrary, it seems that Rumi is giving expression to an experience or a series of experiences. There is an enormous difference between giving expression to an experience and giving expression to an idea – and this difference is the difference between Rumi and the systematic thinkers. Our experiences do not follow one another like premises in a syllogism. We can deduce one thought from another, but we cannot deduce one experience from another. While reading the *Mathnawi* we find ourselves not in the presence of a mind but in the presence of a personality. Experiences of a personality cannot possess a logical sequence, since logical sequence is a characteristic only of thoughts. Therefore, when thoughts are interwoven with experiences, and it is the expression of experiences which is primarily intended, thoughts have to be scattered and unconnected as they are in Rumi's *Mathnawi*. Any attempt, therefore, to summarise his thought will inevitably damage the spirit of his work.

The nature of Rumi's experience is essentially religious. By religious experience is not meant an experience induced by the observance of a code of taboos and laws, but an experience which owes its being to love; and by love Rumi means 'a cosmic feeling, a spirit of oneness with the Universe.' 'Love,' says Rumi, 'is the remedy of our pride and self-conceit, the physician of all our infirmities. Only he whose garment is rent by love becomes entirely unselfish.' Love, according to him, is the motive force of the universe; it is because of love that everything restlessly travels towards its origin; it is love which animates music and gives a meaning to life. It is in love that the contradictory forces of Nature achieve a unique unity. And love is not logic; it eludes reason and analysis and is best understood by experience. It does not ask why before it makes the supreme sacrifice for the Beloved; it jumps into the battlefield regardless of consequences.

لا اُبــالی عشق بــاشــد نی خـرد　　عقل آن جوید کزان سـود ی برد
نی خــدا را امتحــانی می کنــد　　نی در ســود و زیــانی می زنــد

It is love, not reason, which is heedless of consequences,
Reason pursues that which is of benefit.
(Love) never puts God to the test,
Nor does it weigh profit and loss (in its pursuit).

Love is a mighty spell – an enchantment. Reason dare not stand against it. Love puts reason to silence.

When those Egyptian women sacrificed their reason,[3]
They penetrated the mansion of Joseph's love;
The cup-bearer of life bore away their reason,
They were filled with wisdom of the world without end.
Joseph's beauty was only an offshoot of God's beauty;
Be lost, then, in God's beauty more than those women.[4]

The more a man loves, the deeper he penetrates into the Divine purpose. 'Love is the "astrolabe of heavenly mysteries," the "eye salve" which clears the spiritual eye and makes it clairvoyant'. Rumi compares it to the love of an affectionate child which divines the reasons for its father's severity, and to the love of a lover who finds excuses for the cruelty of his mistress.[5]

Love endures hardships at the hands of the Beloved with pleasure.

Through love thorns become roses, and
Through love vinegar becomes sweet wine.
Through love the stake becomes a throne,
Through love reverse of fortune seems good fortune.
Through love a prison seems a rose bower,
Through love a grate full of ashes seems a garden.
Through love burning fire is pleasing light,
Through love the Devil becomes a Houri.
Through love hard stone becomes soft as butter,
Through love soft wax becomes hard iron.
Through love grief is a joy,
Through love Ghouls turn into angels.
Through love stings are as honey,
Through love lions are harmless as mice.
Through love sickness is health,
Through love wrath is as mercy.
Through love the dead rise to life,
Through love the king becomes a slave.[6]

[3] 'And when they saw him they were amazed at him and cut their hands (Qur'an, xii. 31).

[4] Whinfield, *Mathnawi*, p. 260.

[5] Ibid., Introduction, p. xxviii.

[6] Ibid., p. 80.

And true love, he says, is ashamed to demand proofs of his beloved, and prides himself on trusting her in spite of appearances telling against her. 'Not only is faith generated by love, but, what is more, faith generated by any other motive is worthless. Faith, like that of respectable conformists, growing from mere blind imitation and the contagion of customs, or like that of scholastic theologians, consisting in mere intellectual apprehension of orthodox dogmas and all mere mechanical and routine professions of belief, – is summed up by the poet under the general name of the "yoke of custom" (*taqlid*). They only produce the spiritual torpor called by Dante *accidia*. To be of any value, faith must be rooted and grounded in love. The mere external righteousness generated by *taqlid* – the mere matter-of-course adoption of the virtues of the age, the class, the sect, – is compared to a "veil of light" (formal righteousness) which hides the truth more entirely than the "veil of darkness" (open sin). For self-deluding goodness is of necessity unrepentant, while the avowed sinner is always self-condemned and so advanced one step on the road to repentance.'[7] Love is the essence of all religion. It has three important characteristics:

(1) Any form in which love expresses itself is good – not because it is a particular expression but because it is an expression of love. Forms of love are irrelevant to the nature of religious experience.

(2) Love is different from feelings of pleasure and pain. It is not regulated by any consideration of reward and punishment.

(3) Love transcends intellect. We do not live in order to think; we think in order to live.

Rumi admits the utility of the intellect and does not reject it altogether. His emphasis on intuition as against intellect is explained by the fact that some of his outstanding predecessors had placed an incredible

[7] Ibid., Introduction, pp. xxxii and xxxiii.

premium on reason. Since the tenth century, those Muslim thinkers who are called 'philosophers' entrusted themselves completely to the guidance of Aristotle. Al-Farabi, the tenth-century philosopher, was so fanatical in his admiration of Greek thought that he considered it the final word in wisdom. For him Plato and Aristotle were the 'Imams or the highest authority in philosophy.'[8] For Ibn Rushd, 'that fanatical admirer of Aristotelian logic'[9] (born in Cordova 1126), Aristotle is the supremely perfect man, the greatest thinker, the philosopher who was in possession of infallible truth. It was upon Aristotle that his activity was concentrated and it was because of this that he has been assigned the title of 'the commentator' in Canto IV of Dante's *Commedia*.

Neoplatonism, which wielded such tremendous influence on Muslim thinkers, is theistic in teaching a transcendent God, and pantheistic in conceiving everything, down to the lowest matter, as an emanation of God. It is a 'religious idealism';[10] the final goal of the soul is to find rest in the mind of God, and though this is impossible of attainment in this life, man should prepare for it by keeping his mind on God, by freeing himself from the shackles of the senses.

The doctrine of reason emerged for the first time with Kindi. According to him, all knowledge is acquired by reason; that which lies between is either fancy or imagination. The faith in the capacity of the human mind to attain knowledge had become so great that philosophy itself had become dogmatic. Reason had presumptuously arrogated to itself functions which it was not fit to discharge.

The entire system of philosophy which had been built up in the East on Greek foundation was attacked and shattered by Ghazali. He started a crusade

[8] De Boer, *History of Philosophy in Islam*, p. 102.
[9] Ibid., p. 188.
[10] Thilly, *History of Philosophy*.

against the monopoly of reason in apprehending Reality. Ghazali formulated that *Kashf* (intuition) alone is the surest way to Reality. 'How great is the difference between knowing the definition, causes, and conditions of drunkenness and actually being drunk! The drunken man knows nothing about the definition and theory of drunkenness, but he is drunk; while the sober man, knowing the definition and the principles of drunkenness, is not drunk at all.'[11]

It is against this background that we must consider Rumi's overwhelming emphasis on intuition rather than reason. Rumi gives an important place to knowledge, and makes a clear distinction between 'knowledge' and 'opinion'.

> Knowledge has two wings, Opinion one wing: Opinion is defective and curtailed in flight.
> The one-winged bird soon falls headlong; then again it flies up some two paces or (a little) more.
> The bird, Opinion, falling and rising, goes on with one wing in hope of (reaching the nest).
> (But) when he has been delivered from Opinion, Knowledge shows its face to him: that one-winged bird becomes two-winged and spreads his wings.
> After that, he walks erect and straight, not falling flat on his face or ailing.
> He flies aloft with two wings, like Gabriel, without disputation.[12]

Opinion, imagination or *wahm* is the counterfeit of reason and in opposition to it, and though it resembles reason it is not reason. 'Reason is the contrary of sensuality: O brave man, do not call Reason that which is attached to sensuality. That which is a beggar of sensuality – call it imagination.'[13]

He regards vision as superior to knowledge. 'Knowledge is inferior to certainty, but above opinion. Know that knowledge is a seeker of certainty, and

[11] *Munqidh*, pp. 20–21.
[12] *Mathnawi*, Nicholson's translation, Book III, lines 1510–15.
[13] Ibid., IV, 2301–02.

certainty is a seeker of vision and intuition. . . . Vision is immediately born of certainty, just as fancy is born of opinion.'[14]

Experience shows that truth revealed through pure reason is incapable of bringing that fire of living conviction which personal revelation can bring. That is why pure thought has so little influenced man, while religion has always elevated individuals and transformed whole societies.[15] Even today, 'religion, which in its higher manifestations is neither dogma, nor priesthood, nor ritual, can alone ethically prepare the modern man for the burden of the great responsibility which the advancement of modern science necessarily involves, and restore to him that attitude of faith which makes him capable of winning a personality here and retaining it hereafter. It is only by rising to a fresh vision of his origin and future, his whence and whither, that man will eventually triumph over a society motivated by an inhuman competition, and a civilisation which has lost its spiritual unity by its inner conflict of religious and political values.'[16]

The apparent belittling of the intellect is only a protest against the gross exaggeration of its role in life. Like Goethe, Rumi looks upon Satan as the embodiment of pure intellect, which, though valuable in itself, is likely to become an instrument of terrible destruction without the guiding hands of love. Satan passionately defends himself in his meeting with Amir Mu'aviyah in Vol. II of the *Mathnawi*, and as you read his defence you feel that the sympathetic poet has striven hard indeed to do justice to his hero. Again, Hallaj, in his dialogues, asserts Satan's superiority to Adam and to Moses, though he raises Muhammad above him. For this Satan Rumi has a

[14] Ibid., III, 4120–24.
[15] Iqbal, *Reconstruction of Religious Thought in Islam*, p. 170.
[16] Ibid., p. 189.

soft corner but he realises that unless his powers are wedded to those of Adam, humanity cannot achieve its full development. Iqbal elucidates this point in his *Lectures*:

> The modern man with his philosophies of criticism and scientific specialism finds himself in a strange predicament. His Naturalism has given him an unprecedented control over the forces of nature, but has robbed him of faith in his own future. . . . Wholly overshadowed by the results of his intellectual activity, the modern man has ceased to live soulfully, i.e., from within. In the domain of thought he is living in open conflict with himself; and in the domain of economic and political life he is living in open conflict with others. He finds himself unable to control his ruthless egoism and his infinite gold-hunger which is gradually killing all higher striving in him and bringing him nothing but life-weariness.[17]

Rumi's philosophy is at once a description, an explanation and a justification of his religious experience – where description, explanation and justification should be regarded as different notes combining and merging into a higher unity – Rumi's symphony of Love.

In order to understand Rumi's philosophy,[18] we should begin by understanding what he says about the nature of the self. A spiritual philosophy has to start with the nature of the self, for the only thing which we can call spirit and of which we claim to have an immediate awareness is the self.

Rumi divides Reality into two realms: the Realm of Spirit and the Realm of Nature. Material objects belong to the realm of Nature but soul is the realm of Spirit. Soul is one and undifferentiated – the 'that' of all being. It is what Spinoza calls substance and

[17] Ibid., pp. 186–88.

[18] In a way it is wrong to call Rumi's thought a 'philosophy,' for as a saint he is superior to a philosopher. 'The philosopher is in bondage to things perceived by the intellect: (but) the pure (saint) is he that rides as a prince on the Intellect of intellect. The Intellect of intellect is your kernel, (while) your intellect is (only) the husk; the belly of animals is ever seeking husks'. (*Mathnawi*, III, 2525–28).

defines as 'that which is in itself and is conceived through itself; in other words, the conception which does not need the conception of another thing from which it must be formed.' It is a pertinent question to ask here: How does one (Transcendental) soul differentiate itself into so many (Phenomenal) souls inhabiting the bodies of different human beings? Rumi, true to himself, gives a characteristically spiritual answer. One and many, he says, are categories of understanding. Soul is substance and its nature is super-sensual and super-rational. Therefore the popular belief that the soul was created by God is totally false; soul is itself the Ultimate Reality, how can it be created by something else?[19]

The realm of Nature consists of the attributes of the eternal substance. Spinoza defines an attribute as 'that which the intellect perceives of substance as if constituting its essence'. The most important difference between the realm of Spirit and the realm of Nature is that the former is out of time (since time is a category of understanding) and the latter is in time. Rumi does not tell us clearly whether time is a mode (as Spinoza thought) or a category of understanding (as Kant thought). Khalifah Abdul Hakim is of the view that Rumi used it in the latter sense. It is not clear whether time is itself an attribute of substance or it is the category of time which is an attribute of substance. If time itself is an attribute of substance, then it is as much real as substance – a conclusion which contradicts Rumi's assertion that time is a characteristic only of the phenomenal world and not of the Ultimate Reality. If, on the other hand, time is a category of understanding only, then time, as such, can in no sense be an attribute of substance. This conclusion is quite in accordance with Rumi's utterances about time – but this is certainly a precarious

[19] With the denial of creation, the denial of God as Creator becomes a logical necessity and Rumi boldly faces the consequences.

position to hold. Rumi is a firm believer in evolution. But can evolution and the unreality of time go together?

Evolution, according to Rumi, started with matter. But matter is not what it appears to be. Rumi does not regard matter as 'independent of mind,' 'my body is a product of my soul, not my soul a product of my body.'

قالب از ما هست شد نی ما ازو

It seems, therefore, that Rumi not only regards matter as having been produced by mind but also as being dependent for its existence on mind. Not only that. He regards mind as independent of matter. The question how matter, which is an attribute of the soul, can be also a product of the soul is left unanswered by Rumi. The other question, how matter, which is an attribute of the soul, can be dependent for its existence on the soul, without the soul being dependent for its existence on matter, is also left unanswered.

An attribute is as real as the substance. Attributes without substance are as unreal as substance without attributes. We may even go so far as to say that 'the what' without 'the that' is conceivable but not 'the that' without 'the what'.

Matter is the foundation-stone of Evolution. There was 'fire and water as wind and cloud' until the emergence of a new form of existence – the plant life. From plant life emerged animal life which assumed its highest form (so far) in human life. Rumi does not believe that the process of creative evolution has ended with the emergence of man in the existing spatio-temporal order. He has a contagious faith in the unlimited possibilities of man's development.

Man has developed through a dynamic process of evolution. He has passed through a series of deaths and with every death he has risen higher in the scale of human values. Why should he then fear the death of his body and not rise to a stage of life where death dies itself?

اول جماد بودی آخر نبات گشتی
آنگه شدی تو حیوان این بر تو چون نهانست
گشتی از آن پس انسان با علم و عقل و ایمان
بنگر چه کل شد آن تن کو جزو خا کدانست
زا انسان چو سیر کردی بی شك فرشته گشتی
پیٔ این زمین از آن پس جائت بر آسمانست
باز از فرشتگی هم بگذر برو در آن یم
تا قطرهٔ تو بحری گردد که صد عمانست

First you were mineral, later you turned to plant, then you became animal: how should this be a secret to you?

Afterwards you were made man, with knowledge, reason, faith: behold the body, which is a portion of the dust-pit, how perfect it has grown!

When you have travelled from man, you will doubtless become an angel; after that you are done with this earth; your station is heaven.

Pass again from angelhood; enter that ocean, that your drop may become a sea which is a hundred seas of Oman.[20]

In the beginning 'God was, and there was naught besides Him.' The first thing created was the soul of man which lived and moved and had its being in God. The soul was originally pure; it then fell and can rise only if it flows back to the burning fountain whence it came. God alone is, therefore, a suitable object for man's quest and nothing less will satisfy the yearnings of his soul.

[20] Refer to a fine passage in the *Mathnawi* (278.8, translated by Whinfield, p. 159).

مردم از حیوانی و آدم شدم پس چه ترسم که ز مردن کم شدم ؟
حملهٔ دیگر بمیرم از بشر تا بر آرم از ملائك بال و پر
بار دیگر از ملك قربان شوم آن چه اندر وهم ناید آن شوم !

من آن روز بودم که اسما نبود نشـان از وجـود مسـما نبـود
ز ما شد مسما و اسما پـدید در آن روز کانجا من و ما نبود
نشان گشت مظهر سر زلف یار هنوز آن سر زلف زیبـا نبود

I was on that day when the Names were not, nor any sign of existence endowed with name.

By me Names and Named were brought to view; on the day when there were not 'I' and 'We'.

For a sign, the tip of Beloved's curl became a centre of revelation; as yet the tip of that fair curl was not.[21]

Life is a passage through a series of deaths[22] – which cannot, however, quench its surging flame! It is open to every individual not only to become a saint but to become a prophet for a nation – a highly shocking assertion for the orthodox yet very much consistent with the thought of Rumi.

مکر کن در راه نیکو خدمتی تـا نبوّت یـابی انـدر اُمتی

Evolution takes place, not as Darwinians thought, by 'mechanical and passive natural selection,' but according to the will of the organism to live a higher and fuller life, by assimilating the qualities of the higher organism. 'That a mystic should have shown the way to the scientists and the philosophers, is one of the rarest phenomena in the history of thought. But the mystic neither begins with naturalism nor ends with it. His matter, to start with, is not the matter of the materialists or the Darwinists. It was from the beginning only the outer form of the spirit; it consisted rather of the monads of Leibniz than the atoms of Democritus. Then again Darwin ends with man, but Rumi does not stop there. Nor do the mystic and

[21] The whole of this magnificent ode has been rendered in verse by Prof. Falconer (Forbes's *Persian Grammar*, p. 159). The reader will do well to compare the poems of Henry Vaughan, entitled *The Search* and *The Dwelling Place* (Vol. I, pp. 33 and 241 of the Muses' Library Edition).

[22] 'I have tried it: my death is (consists) in life: When I escape from this life, 'tis to endure for ever. "Kill me, kill me, O trusty friends! Lo, in my being killed is life on life." ' (*Mathnawi*, III, 3838–39).

the scientist agree about the forces that lead to this evolution. Darwin's doctrine consists of struggle for existence, chance variations and natural selection. . . . With Rumi there is no development by chance variations. For him development consists in the creation of an ever-increasing need for expansion and by assimilation into a higher organism.'[23]

But this conception of evolution suffers from three difficulties. Firstly, how can the new species assimilate the other unless it is already in existence? This difficulty has also been pointed out by Dr Hakim, but he brushes it aside with the remark: 'As his [Rumi's] purpose was not scientific so he has neither put nor tried this question.' We are inclined to believe that this conception cuts at the root of the conception of evolution as being creative. If the new species is somehow already in existence, then the whole course of evolution is prearranged. Teleology in this sense, as Bergson has pointed out, becomes inverted mechanism.

Secondly, the conception of a definite cyclic order runs counter to the conception of creative evolution. A truly creative organism is one which has infinite possibilities of growth and expansion and none of the forms it assumes can ever be predicted. We cannot say for certain that man in his development will become an angel. For a creative individual the future exists as an open possibility and like a work of art it is unpredictable. No fixed order of events with definite outlines can, therefore, be visualised consistent with the theory of Creative Evolution.

'Every act of a free Ego creates a new situation and thus offers further opportunities for creative unfolding . . . every moment in the life of Reality is original, giving birth to what is absolutely novel and unforeseeable.'[24] And does not Rumi himself declare:

[23] Khalifa Abdul Hakim, *Metaphysics of Rumi,* (Lahore 1959), pp. 38–40.

[24] Iqbal, op. cit., p. 48.

Every instant I give to the heart a different desire, every moment I lay upon the heart a different brand.
At every dawn I have a new employment.[25]

The third difficulty follows from the second. Rumi admits that evil does not exist for angels and yet he talks of angels as being the next stage in evolution after man. It means that the higher stage of life is bereft of choice and responsibility, two characteristics which constitute the essence of creative individuality.

Everything else, according to Rumi, is controlled by influences outside it; man alone carries his star his destiny within him.

'Tis wonderful that the spirit is in prison, and then, (all that time) the key of the prison is in its hand!
That youth (the spirit) is plunged in dung from head to foot, (whilst) the flowing river is (almost) touching his skirt.[26]

This world is a stage where man – the principal actor – continues his experiment in living. In the words of the Qur'an he is the 'trustee of a free personality which he accepted at his own peril.' This freedom is at once most dangerous and most valuable. 'Freedom to choose good involves also the freedom to choose what is opposite of good. That God has taken this risk shows His immense faith in man; it is for man now to justify this faith.'[27]

Free-will is as the salt to piety, otherwise heaven itself were matter of compulsion.
In its revolutions rewards and punishment were needless, for 'tis free-will that has merit at the great reckoning.
If the whole world were framed to praise God, there would be no merit in praising God.

Rumi does not believe in the theory of predetermination which absolves men of their responsibilities

[25] *Mathnawi*, Nicholson's translation, III, 1639–40.
[26] Ibid., IV, 2034–35.
[27] Iqbal, op. cit., p. 81.

and tends to work for the decay and degeneration of nations and individuals. He, however, believes that the universal laws of Nature are unalterable. It is predetermined, for example, that if you take a few steps, you will be walking, but the direction in which you walk is certainly a question of your choice; it is entirely left to your discretion and judgment. It is predetermined, for instance, that if you aim a pistol at somebody that person will be mortally wounded. It is now your free choice to select the object – he can be your dear brother, he can be your most deadly enemy.

It is to this extent that Rumi believes in predetermination. He goes thus far and no further. Man is the paragon of existence only because he and he alone has the freedom of choice. For animals lower than man, good and evil do not exist. Therefore the question of their choice does not arise. It is man alone who is confronted by both good and evil. 'Here a world and there a world,' says Rumi, 'I am seated on the threshold.'[28]

Man is potentially lower than the brutes and higher than angels.

> Angel and brute man's wondrous leaven compose
> To these including, less than these he grows,
> But if he means the angel, more than those.

Evil indeed plays an important role in the development of man's personality; without it, realisation of values would become impossible. Things are known through their opposites, and had evil remained uncreated Divine omnipotence would have been incomplete.

> He is the source of evil, as thou sayest,
> Yet evil hurts Him not. To make the evil
> Denotes in Him perfection. Hear from me
> A parable. The heavenly artist paints

[28] For further elucidation, see *Mathnawi*, IV, pp. 355, 357 and 358.

Beautiful shapes and ugly: in one picture
The loveliest women in the land of Egypt
Gazing at youthful Joseph amorously;
And lo, another scene by the same hand,
Hell fire and Iblis with his hideous crew:
Both master-works, created for good ends,
To show His perfect wisdom as confound
The sceptics who deny His mastery,
Could He not evil make, He would lack still;
Therefore he fashions infidel alike
And Muslim me, that both may witness bear,
To Him, and worship One Almighty Lord.

But why, it may be asked, has God created that to which man has given the name of evil? And since He is the only real Agent, who are we to blame for the actions that we are caused to commit? It is characteristic of Rumi that he finds the answer to this old riddle not in thought but in feeling, not in theological speculation but in religious experience. We can feel as one what we must think as two. Everything has an opposite by means of which it is manifested; God alone, Whose being includes all things, has no opposite, and therefore He remains hidden. Evil is the inevitable condition of Good: out of darkness was created light. From this standpoint it possesses a positive value: it serves the purpose of God, it is relatively good.[29]

Rumi, therefore, welcomes evil as being helpful for the development of man's personality. In fact, the conflict of good and evil is inherent in man and his greatness depends on the extent to which he resolves this conflict.

While Rumi certainly concedes that everything is not good in this world,[30] he refuses steadfastly to adopt an attitude of quietude and renunciation but urges, on the contrary, a relentless war against all

[29] Nicholson, *Idea of Personality in Sufism*, p. 55.
[30] Vol. II, lines 2939–42.

آنک گوید جمله حقند احمقیست وانک گوید جمله باطل او شقیست

forces of evil, which, he believes, man by his very nature is capable of overcoming. Indeed, he would be betraying the very ingredients of his nature by refusing to recognise in evil a golden opportunity to carry his personality a step further on the path of development.[31] The existence of evil has, therefore, a positive contribution to make and the development of a man's personality is reflected proportionately to his success in this struggle. Man is, therefore, not left with any justification to complain on this score, for how could he hope to be the paragon of creation without the presence of evil?[32]

Where there is no enemy, there is no Holy War and the question of success does not arise; where there is no lust, there can be no obedience to the Divine Command.[33] And has not the Holy Qur'an made this position abundantly clear with the declaration: 'And for trial will We test you with evil and with good?'[34] Good and evil, therefore, though opposite, must fall within the same whole.[35]

'Moses and Pharaoh are in thy being: thou must seek these two adversaries in thyself. The (process of) generation for Moses is (continuing) till the Resurrection: the Light is not different, (though) the lamp has become different.'[36]

[31] Vol. II, lines 2963–64.

حق تعالی گرم و سرد و رنج و درد   بر تن ما می نهد ای شیر مرد
خوف و جوع و نقص اموال و بدن   جمله بهر نقد جان ظاهر شدن

[32] Vol. IV, lines. 94, 97–100.

در حقیقت هر عدو داروی تست   کیمیای و نافع و دلجوی تست
زین سبب بر انبیا رنج و شکست   از همه خلق جهان افزون ترست

[33] Vol. V, lines 575–76.

چون عدو نبود جهاد آمد محال   شهوت از نبود نباشد امتثال

[34] The Qur'an, xxi. 36.

[35] Iqbal, op. cit., p. 118.

[36] *Mathnawi*, Nicholson's translation, III, 1253–54

Nothing, however, is absolutely evil: what is bad for me may be good for you. And what is more important, evil itself can be turned to good for the righteous. But the soul of goodness in evil can be discerned by love alone.

The freedom of choice, however, is not an end in itself; the end of all freedom is to freely determine to live according to your higher self. So the end of all freedom is self-determination on a higher plane. At the end freedom and determination are identified. Life starts with determination at the lower plane, develops to the capacity of Free Choice in man, in order to rise to a Higher Determinism again, where man makes a free offer of his freedom.[37] Kant perhaps is the first thinker of the West who believed that it is the innermost self of man that expresses itself in the moral law: the moral law is *his* command, *he* imposes the law upon himself, this is *his* autonomy.

While Satan considers it a servitude of the worst order to serve somebody other than his own self, the loyal angel recognises quite clearly that servitude comes when you serve your own baser self and not when you bow to God's command. Milton has beautifully brought out this point in *Paradise Lost*.[38]

This is servitude
To serve th' unwise, or him who hath rebelled
Against his worshipper, as thine now serve thee,
Thyself not free, but to thyself enthrall'd.

Man's love of God is God's love of man, and in loving God, man realises his own personality:

The word 'compulsion' makes me impatient for Love's sake.
'Tis only he who loves not that is fettered by 'compulsion'.
The shining of the moon, not a cloud
Or if it be 'compulsion' exerted by self-will inciting us to sin.[39]

[37] Khalifa Abdul Hakim, *Metaphysics of Rumi*.
[38] *Paradise Lost*, VI, 178–81. [39] *Mathnawi* (Bulaq ed.), I, 59.

And again:

When the predestination of God becomes the pleasure of His servant, he (the servant) becomes a willing slave to His decree,

Not (because of) tasking himself, and not on account of the (future) reward and recompense; nay, his nature has become so goodly.

He does not desire his life for himself nor to the end that he may enjoy the life that is found sweet (by others).

Wheresoever the Eternal Command takes its course, living and dying are one to him.

He lives for God's sake, not for riches: he dies for God's sake, not from fear and pain.

His faith is (held) for the sake of (doing) His will, not for the sake of Paradise and its trees and streams.

His abandonment of infidelity is also for God's sake, not for fear lest he goes into the Fire.

That disposition of his is like this originally: it is not (acquired by) discipline or by his effort and endeavour.

He laughs at the moment when he sees the Divine pleasure: to him Destiny is even as a sugared sweetmeat.[40]

And if such a state be called compulsion, it is not 'common compulsion,' as Rumi puts it:

They possess free will and compulsion besides,
As in oyster-shells raindrops become pearls.
Outside the shells they are raindrops, great and small;
Inside they are precious pearls, big and little.
These men also resemble the musk deer's bag;
Outside it is blood, but inside pure musk.[41]

To be united with the world-soul is, therefore, the most exhilarating bliss for man.

And mind you, man does not attain this union with perfection by contemplation but by a consistent effort at creating in himself all the attributes of Perfection.

Whether one be slow or speedy (in movement), he that is a seeker will be a finder.

Always apply yourself with both hands (with all your might) to seeking, for search is an excellent guide on the way.

[40] *Mathnawi*, Nicholson's translation, III, 1906–14.
[41] Whinfield, op. cit., p. 27.

(Though you be) lame and limping and bent in figure and unmannerly, ever creep towards Him and be in quest of Him.[42]

Greatness or smallness are meaningless in themselves. We are great or small because of the greatness or smallness of our ideals and because of the varying strength of faith and determination with which we seek to achieve them. Given love, faith, determination and an effort at consistent search, our frailty and infirmity can move mountains.

Do not regard the fact that thou art despicable or infirm; look upon thy aspiration, O noble one.
In whatsoever state thou be, keep searching; . . .
For this seeking is a blessed motion; this search is a killer of obstacles on the Way to God.[43]

Farabi offers an interesting contrast to this attitude. About three centuries before Rumi he declared in vigorously accentuated terms that if a man knew everything that stands in the writings of Aristotle, but did not act in accordance with his knowledge, while another man shaped his conduct in accordance with Aristotle's teachings without being acquainted with it, preference would have to be assigned to the former. Rumi completely reverses the emphasis. For him development does not consist in idle metaphysical speculation. He completely rejects the pseudo-mystic quietism which produces a class of irresponsive dervishes who 'remain unmoved in the midst of sorrow, meet praise and blame with equal effect, and accept insults, blows, torture and death as mere incidents.'[44]

When Aristotle drew up his table of Categories which to him represented the grammar of existence. he was really projecting the grammar of the Greek

[42] *Mathnawi*, Nicholson's translation, III, 978–80.
[43] Ibid., III, 1438–42.
[44] Nicholson, *Mystics of Islam*, pp. 44–46.

language on the cosmos. The grammar has kept us to this day ensnared in its paradoxes: free-will and determination, mind and body, ends and means – this categorical structure acts as a screen between the mind and the reality. Arabian and Persian metaphysics is so permeated by Greek philosophy that even Rumi who consciously sets out to repudiate it calls love his Plato and Galen.

Rumi rejects the idea of a closed, predetermined universe which is subject to Nietzsche's gloomy law of 'Eternal Recurrence'. 'There is nothing more alien to the Qur'anic world than the idea that the Universe is a temporal working out of a preconceived plan – an already completed product which left the hand of its Maker ages ago and is now lying stretched in space as a dead mass of matter to which time does nothing and consequently is nothing.'[45]

He is emphatically opposed to those pseudo-mystics, other-worldly idealists, and self-centred aesthetes who would cheerfully ignore the evil, injustice and imperfection of this world, and abandon all active effort on behalf of its reconstruction and seek a cowardly compensation in pursuing their own selfish interests – intellectual, artistic and spiritual – in seclusion. It is only by flinging ourselves into the struggle that we can fulfil the purpose of our life – not by shunning the struggle on earth because our head is in the clouds.

The motive force behind creative evolution is love. It is love which compels matter to become life, and life to become mind. 'This striving for the ideal is love's movement towards beauty which . . . is identical with perfection. Beneath the visible evolution of forms is the force of love which actualises all striving, movement, progress. . . . The indeterminate matter, dead in itself, assumes . . . by the inner force of love, various forms, and rises higher and higher in the scale of

[45] Iqbal, op. cit., p. 48.

beauty. . . . All things are moving towards the first Beloved – the Eternal Beauty. The worth of a thing is decided by its nearness to, or distance from, this ultimate principle.'[46]

Life is a journeying back to God; it proceeds according to a process of evolution. The minerals develop into plants, and plants into animals, animals into man and man into superhuman beings ultimately to reach back to the starting point – a glorious interpretation of the Qur'anic verses 'God is the beginning and God is the end' and 'To Him do we return.'[47]

Rumi compares the soul to a moaning dove that has lost his mate; to a reed torn from its bed and made into a flute whose plaintive music fills the eye with tears; to a falcon summoned by the fowler's whistle to perch upon his wrist; to snow melting in the sun and mounting as vapour to the sky; to a frenzied camel swiftly plunging in the desert by night; to a caged parrot, and fish on dry land; a pawn that seeks to become a king.[48] It is because of love that everything travels towards its origin.

How can a man know God? 'Not by senses, for He is immaterial, nor by intellect, for He is unthinkable. Logic never gets beyond the finite; philosophy sees double; book learning fosters self-conceit and obscures the idea of the truth with clouds of empty words.' Rumi addressing the sceptics asks:

Do you know a name without a thing answering to it?
Have you ever plucked a rose from R, O, S, E?
You name His name; go seek the reality named by it;
Look for the moon in the sky, not in the water!
If you desire to rise above mere names and letters,
Make yourself free from self at one stroke,
Become pure from all attributes of self,

[46] Iqbal, *Development of Metaphysics in Persia*, pp. 33–34.
[47] Khalifa Abdul Hakim, *Metaphysics of Rumi*, p. 25.
[48] Nicholson, *Mysticism in Islam*, p. 117.

That you may see your own bright essence.
Yea, see in your own heart knowledge of the Prophet,
Without book, without tutor, without perception.

This knowledge comes by illumination, revelation, inspiration and inward co-operation. Those who have reached the highest degree of perfection – Muhammad topping the list – have not reached it through logical calculation or laborious cogitation. They have discovered the truth and reality by means of an inward and Divine illumination.

For Rumi, revelation is not a historical fact of the past; it is a living reality and it is open to everyone. To those who are sceptical about the possibility of revelation, Rumi puts a pertinent question. Wherefrom, asks he, did the first man learn to dispose of the dead body of his brother? Was it through revelation and intuition?

کندن گوری که کمتر پیشه بود کی ز فکر و حیله و اندیشه بود

When was grave-digging, which was the meanest trade (of all), acquired from thought and cunning and meditation?

Reason, in fact, is blind and unimaginative, and argument at best is a weak support. Sense-perception does not carry us far and is certainly no equipment for probing the deep realities of Nature. And revelation is nothing but the eternal spirit of man himself.[49] The characteristic of all that is spiritual is its knowledge of its own essential nature. We cannot treat life and consciousness mathematically, scientifically and logically, for how can we depend upon our senses which do not carry us very far? Knowledge is and must remain a vision of reality, a *Weltanschauung*, an intuition.

Love alone takes us to the Reality. For love, ceaseless effort is necessary. Peace comes only when you identify yourself with the one that stands outside this

[49] *Mathnawi*, Nicholson's translation, Vol. IV, 4, p. 344.

struggle. An impetus is given to this love by intense, zealous desire; a compelling urge and a wish devoutful. Decadent Sufism had created useless drones and hypocrites. Such passive life is of no use to Rumi. In his world there is no scope for parasites. Rumi's lover cannot afford to be static and ascetic. He is constantly at war – at war with his own baser self, at war with those elements in the world which hinder or prevent his ascent. It is the very fate of man to struggle.

[50] با قضا پنجه زدن نبود جهاد　　زانکه این را هم قضا بر ما نهاد

We have seen that life emanates from matter and mind emanates from life. It seems, however, that even matter is really spiritual, yet the trend of evolution is only unconsciously felt by it. It is only in man that a full awareness of the trend of evolution is present. We have seen that Rumi explains Evolution by referring to the concept of Assimilation. Man has assimilated into himself all the attributes which belong to the lower species. Thus we may divide man into two parts, viz. one which he has assimilated from the lower species and the other which constitutes its essence – the Divine spark in man. This division of man's nature into two parts corresponds exactly to the bifurcation of human nature effected by Kant and now completely discredited by modern psychology. Man is animated by two naturally hostile principles – animality and divinity. It is on the basis of this distinction that Rumi builds up his moral system. A person who obeys his animal self lives the life of a slave determined for him by forces alien to his essential nature. A person on the contrary who complies with the demands of his higher self lives the life of a free man – determined from within. The higher self is the Divine spark in man and its realisation makes one the source of infinite power and knowledge.

[50] Ibid., I, 976.

Realisation of the ideal self rids one of fears and hopes. 'I am the ruling power in both the worlds here and hereafter; in both the worlds I saw nobody whom I could fear or from whom I could hope to get any favour; I saw only myself.'

One also transcends discursive knowledge and attains to Divine knowledge – which is not sensuous in origin and character. Knowledge is itself a great power – and the ideal man of Rumi, purged of fear and anxiety, enriched by Divine knowledge, holds complete sway over the spiritual and material world.

بلکه والی گشت موجودات را　　بی گمان و بی نفاق و بی ریا
بی مثال و بی نشان و بی مکان　　بی زمان و بی چنین و بی چنان
بی شکال و بی سوال و بی جواب　　دم مزن واللّه اعلم بالصواب

Such a man moves the world according to his desire:

. . . According to whose desire the torrents and rivers flow, and the stars move in such wise as he wills;
And Life and Death are his officers, going to and fro according to his desire.[51]

Such is the 'Man of God,' the perfect man, who assimilates God himself but does not lose his own individuality. Such a man eludes all description.

مرد خدا مست بود بی شراب　　مرد خدا سیر بود بی کباب
مرد خدا واله و حیران بود　　مرد خدا را نبود خورد و خواب
مرد خدا شاه بود زیر دلق　　مرد خدا گنج بود در خراب
مرد خدا نیست ز باد و ز خاك　　مرد خدا نیست ز نار و ز آب
مرد خدا بحر بود بی کران　　مرد خدا بارد در بی سحاب
مرد خدا دارد صد ماه و چرخ　　مرد خدا دارد صد آفتاب
مرد خدا عالم از حق بود　　مرد خدا نیست فقیه از کتاب
مرد خدا زان سوی کفرست و دین　　مرد خدا را چه خطا و صواب

[51] Ibid., III, 1886–87.

مرد خدا گشت سوار از عدم   مرد خدا آمد عالی رکاب
مرد خدا هست نهان شمس دین   مرد خدا را تو بجوی و بیاب

The man of God is drunken without wine,
The man of God is full without meat.
The man of God is distraught and bewildered,
The man of God has no food or sleep.
The man of God is a king 'neath dervish-cloak,
The man of God is a treasure in a ruin.
The man of God is not of air and earth,
The man of God is not of fire and water.
The man of God is a boundless sea,
The man of God rains pearls without a cloud.
The man of God hath hundred moons and skies,
The man of God hath hundred suns.
The man of God is made wise by the Truth,
The man of God is not learned from book.
The man of God is beyond infidelity and religion,
To the man of God right and wrong are alike.
The man of God has ridden away from Not-being,
The man of God is gloriously attended.
The man of God is concealed, Shamsi Din,
The man of God do thou seek and find![52]

[52] Nicholson, Tr., *Divani Shamsi Tabriz*, pp. 30–31.

Chapter 7

Latin Translation of the *Mathnawi*

We have the greatest respect and admiration for Professor Nicholson who devoted a lifetime to the translation of the *Mathnawi* into English. He has chosen, however, to render some 133 out of 25,700 couplets into Latin. His reason he explains in his Introduction to Volume II of the *Mathnawi* (translation of Books I and II). Rumi, he thinks, 'is too outspoken for our taste' on certain topics 'and many pages' of the *Mathnawi* 'are disfigured by anecdotes worthy of an Apuleius or Petronius but scarcely fit to be translated.'[1]

This opinion is paradoxically expressed in introducing the first Book which Nicholson has fully translated into English.

Rumi has been compared to Apuleius and Petronius. The comparison is far-fetched; it is an insult to the memory of a man who is revered as the greatest mystic poet the Muslim world has ever produced.

Apuleius, a Platonic philosopher and rhetorician, is chiefly known for his work *Metamorphoses*, a collection of stories to which his contemporary, Lucian, gave a comic and satiric turn. In his stories the dignified, the ludicrous, the voluptuous, the horrible, succeed each other with bewildering rapidity. Don Quixote's adventure with the wine-skins is borrowed from Apuleius and several of the humorous episodes in his stories reappear in *Boccaccio*.

Petronius is a Roman satirist. He was one-time

[1] P. xvii.

favourite of Nero. His days were passed in sleep, his nights in the pleasures of life. In his last days when he fell from Nero's favour he wrote frivolous verse. He wrote a full account of the Emperor's excesses and of every novel debauchery. This he sealed and sent to Nero.

Does one compare Rumi with such writers?

The *Mathnawi* has been read in the original by millions of people for some seven centuries. We are not aware of an expurgated edition nor are we aware of a demand for one. Nicholson, in assuming the role of a censor, has sought merely to project his own inhibitions. He has passed an unwarranted moral judgment on a man he recognises as the greatest mystic poet of any age. In his Introduction to Volume VI of the *Mathnawi* (translation of Books V and VI), Nicholson pertinently points out:

> Where else shall we find such a panorama of universal existence unrolling itself through Time into Eternity? And, apart from the supreme mystical quality of the poem, what a wealth of satire, humour and pathos! What masterly pictures drawn by a hand that touches nothing without revealing its essential character![2]

And yet he has chosen to divorce from their context a little over one hundred lines from a long poem of nearly 26,000 couplets creating, perhaps unwittingly, an impression that Rumi is, on occasions, a conscious sensualist.

A serious charge has been made and the reader has been denied an opportunity to judge for himself. We propose to analyse the alleged purple patches so that the reader is able to arrive at his own conclusions. In doing so it is relevant to reiterate that we are dealing with the greatest mystic poet of any age, a poet whose range is indeed staggering, who talks in metaphors and comes out with parables and subtle recondite allusions. Rumi was conscious of the possibility of

[2] P. xiii.

casual superficial readers stopping short at his words without making an effort to penetrate their meaning. A parable has a purpose. Rumi reminds his reader:

بیتِ من بیت نیست اقلیمست   هزلِ من هزل نیست تعلیمست

My tent (verse) is not a tent, it is a continent;
my jest is not a jest, it is a lesson.

And he follows up this warning with a quotation from the Qur'an which indeed he seeks to interpret so beautifully in the *Mathnawi*:

ان الله لا يستحى ان يضرب مثلاً ما بعوضة فما فوقها ... واما الذين كفروا
فيقولون ماذا اراد الله بهذا مثلاً يضل به كثيرا و يهدى به كثيرا[3]

Verily, God is not ashamed to set forth as a parable a gnat or what exceeds it. . . . The infidels ask: What is it that Allah means by using this as a parable? The answer is: He lets many be led astray thereby and He lets many be guided aright thereby.

Every temptation, says Rumi, is like a pair of scales; many come off with honour and many with disgrace.

In Book I, nothing seems to have offended the Catholic taste of the translator for all the four thousand verses have been translated into English. In Book II, only eight out of 3810 verses have been rendered into Latin. What are they and what is their context?

The first offending verse is:

داروی مردی کن و عنین مپوی   تا برون آیند صد گون خوب روی[4]

The first line has been obscured by Latin though the second has been mercifully rendered into English. In this part of the poem Rumi exhorts his reader:

Bring the sky under thy feet, O brave one! Hear from above the firmament the noise of the (celestial) music!

Put out of thine ear the cotton of evil suggestion, that the cries from heaven may come into thine ear.[5]

[3] ii. 26. [4] II, 1947. [5] II, 1942–43.

He goes on, in the course of this exhortation, to suggest to the meek and the imbecile:

Remedy your virility and do not be impotent, that a hundred kinds of fair ones may come forth.

Instead of taking the simple line in the sense it has been used, 'the cotton of evil suggestion' seems to have prevented the translator from appreciating the proper perspective.

The next verse, in fact half of it, occurs in a poem entitled 'The Lovers of God'. Rumi is trying to chide man for his childish tendency to deceive himself into believing that this world is the be-all and end-all of life. In order to achieve something worthwhile one must rise higher than the material state. Rumi says:

Thou hast learned a trade to earn a livelihood for the body: (now) set thy hand to a (spiritual) trade.

In this world thou hast become clothed and rich: when thou comest forth from here, how wilt thou do? . . .

The high God hath said that beside those (the next world's) earnings these earnings in the (present) world are (but) children's play —

Don't behave as a child that embraces another child and adopts the position of coitus, merely touching the body (and being under the illusion that he has in fact discovered the thrill and joy of love)[6]

همچو آن طفلی که بر طفلی تند   شکل صحبت کن مساسی میکند[7]

(Or as) children at play set up a shop, (but) it is of no use to them except as a pastime.

Night falls, and he (the child who acted as a shopkeeper) comes home hungry: the (other) children are gone, and he is left alone.[8]

The next lapse into Latin exposes even more forcefully the enormity of the motive attributed to the poet. Here Rumi, in condemning sensuality and pleading for higher goals in life, says:

[6] II, 2592–96. [7] II, 2597. [8] II, 2597–98.

مرد را ذوقِ غزا و کـر و فر   مر مخنث را بود ذوق از ذکر
جز ذَکر نه دینِ اُو و ذِکرِ او   سوی اسفل برد اُو را فِکرِ اُو

A man's delight is in campaigns (for Islam) and in the glory and pomp (of war); *but a eunuch's delight is in man's member.*

His religion and his supplication is nothing but the member (*which he lacks*): his thought (obsession) has borne him down to the lowest depth.[9]

And then Rumi proceeds to warn that even though such a man were to rise to heights of eminence, one need not be afraid of him for he has achieved little:

Though he rise to the sky, be not afraid of him, for (it is only) in love of lowness he has studied.

He gallops his horse towards lowness, albeit he rings the bell (proclaims that he is going) aloft.

What is there to fear from the flags of beggars? – for those flags are (but) a means for (getting) a mouthful of bread.[10]

The conclusion of this episode is followed by a sub-heading in prose which is translated into Latin:

ترسیدن کودك از آن شخص صاحب جثه و گفتن آن شخص که ای کودك مترس
که من نامردم ـ

It merely refers to a boy's fear of a well-fed hefty-looking man who tells him not to be afraid for he is impotent and is not, therefore, likely to assault him. On the contrary, the man is a catamite. While the practice of sodomy may be heinous, the fact of its existence cannot be denied and the mention of the word cannot be tabooed. The fake Sufis and mendicants indulged in this practice and Rumi exposes them mercilessly on more than one occasion in his poem. Does an artist who exposes filth in society become dirty and filthy? And yet this is precisely the insinuation, for why else would a translator seek to black out this portion:

9 II, 3150–51.   10 II, 3152–54.

A well-built man found a boy alone, the boy became pale with fear of the man's intent.
He said, 'Be at ease, my handsome! for you are going to stay upon me.
Even though I am huge consider me a eunuch; sit on me like you would sit on a camel and ride me.'

کنگ زفتی کودکی را یافت فرد   زرد شد کودك ز بیم قصدِ مرد
گفت ایمن بــاش ای زیبـای من   که تو خواهی بود بر بالای من
من اکــر هـولم مخنث دان مــرا   همچو اشتر بر نشین می ران مرا[11]

This is so obviously a commentary on the deceptive appearance of men, and their inner reality – an enormous man is seen in reality to be impotent and a young boy who looks so frail and helpless is in fact virile and vigorous.

In Book III there are no Latin lines. The *Mathnawi* reaches its climax in Book IV which has been universally acclaimed as the most powerful of the long poem. Here Rumi attains heights which have yet to be surpassed. He calls the book, 'the grandest of gifts and the most precious of prizes; . . . It is a light to our friends and a treasure for our (spiritual) descendants.'[12]

From a total of about 4000 verses (3855 to be exact) the translator takes exception to nine odd couplets which in his view are not fit to be translated into English.

The first Latin line appears in the story of the Sufi who caught his wife with a stranger. The story begins:

A Sufi came (back) to his house in the daytime: the house had (only) one door, and his wife was with a cobbler.

The next line is Latinised:

جفت گشته با رهیء خـویش زن   اندر آن یك حجره از وسواسِ تن[13]

[11] II, 3155–57.
[12] Vol. IV (translation of Books III and IV), p. 271.
[13] IV, 159.

Pandering to physical temptation the woman slept with her paramour in that room.

In the next example, the context is completely ignored and curiosity is unnecessarily roused by lapsing into Latin.

At the beginning of his Caliphate, 'Uthman, the third Caliph of Islam, mounted the pulpit of the Prophet. The pulpit had three steps. The Prophet used to preach the sermon from the top of the pulpit. Abu Bakr, the first Caliph, seated himself on the second step. 'Umar, in his reign, sat on the third step. When the reign of 'Uthman arrived, he went on top of the pulpit and sat there. An idle meddling fool pointed out that the first two Caliphs did not sit in the Prophet's place. 'Uthman replied: 'If I tread on the third step, it will be imagined that I resemble 'Umar. And if I seek a seat on the second step, you will say this is the seat of Abu Bakr and that I am trying to be like him. The top is the place of the Prophet, no one will ever imagine that I am like him.' The explanation was convincing. Silence fell on the audience. 'Uthman sat on the pulpit until the afternoon prayer and did not utter a word. An awe had settled on all and there was a silent and eloquent communication between the Caliph and his audience. From that glow of silence came to the heart a joyous sense of freedom and expansion. Rumi makes the point that the vision of the Light is something which is outside the province or the capacity of an Avicenna or a philosopher to describe with some effect. The tongue cannot give expression to the sensation of mystical clairvoyance. The poet says:

> I have said this to you, speaking hypothetically.[14]

And what is said hypothetically is certainly not the

[14] IV, 510.

truth. And then comes the crucial line which has been censored:

خاله را خایه بدی خالو شدی   این بتقدیر آمدست ار أو بدی[15]

Any reader with an elementary acquaintance with Persian would know that the poet is merely taking advantage of the textual similarity between the words to expose the actual dissimilarity between what is meant by them.

If the *Khala* (aunt) had *Khaya* (testicles) she would have been a *Khalu* (uncle), but this is hypothetical – 'if there were.'

And the moral is that there is no point or profit in dealing with hypothetical situations.

The story of Solomon and the Queen of Sheba is well known. In Rumi's version Solomon bids the envoys of Bilqis to return with their gifts. One does not take coal to Newcastle. Solomon gave them loads of gold. 'Lay this gold of mine on top of that gold of yours,' said Solomon and then the layer of Latin is laid on one line:

کوریٔ تن فرجِ استر را دهید[16]

Solomon was not interested in material gifts. He was looking for something more solemn and subtle. Gold is useless. It does not produce anything. It is like a mule. She cannot produce anything either. Gold, he suggests, is better put in the mule's vulva, for Solomon is simply not interested in the lifeless metal. He was aiming at the heart of the Queen of Sheba who is finally brought to him in total submission. While it may be conceded that Solomon does not use an altogether royal idiom in conveying his disapproval to the envoys it is by no means lascivious and there is no point in lodging it in Latin with a view to hiding it from the reader.

[15] IV. 511. [16] IV, 615.

Nicholson's moral conscience revolts even against such an innocent act as the escaping of wind. A sweet flute-player was playing the flute and then, lo and behold, the scene is blacked out because the poet says:

نا گهان از مقعدش بادی بجست[17]

This is carrying conservatism to a limit.

And now we come to what Professor Nicholson would certainly dub a ribald story. But is it?

A woman desired to embrace her paramour in the presence of her foolish husband. She hit upon a clever device. She told her husband that she would climb the pear tree by the house to gather fruit. As soon as she climbed the tree, the woman burst into tears. She rebuked her husband and accused him of homosexuality. She said to her husband:

O despicable catamite, who is the rascal that has fallen upon you? You swoon under him like a woman. Are you, then, but a mere eunuch?

گفت شوهر را که ای مابونِ رد کیست آن لوطی که بر تو می فتد
تــو بـزیــرِ اُو چـو زن بغنــوده‌ ای فـلانِ تو خـود مخنث بـوده‌[18]

The husband told the woman that her head had turned. Perhaps it was the top of that pear-tree which caused the illusion of the husband submitting himself to another man in the presence of his wife. 'Come down from the top of the pear-tree,' he said, 'so that the illusion might vanish.' But the wife repeated that she could see the act with her own eyes. The woman repeatedly asked him who was sleeping upon him:

زن مکرر کرد کآن با برطله کیست بر پشتت فرو خفته هله[19]

'Hark, wife!' replied the husband, 'come down from the tree, for thy head is turned and thou hast become very dotish.' When the woman came down, the husband

[17] IV, 769. [18] IV, 3547–48. [19] IV, 3549.

went up the tree. The woman then drew her paramour into her arms. The husband protested and demanded who was receiving her favours. The husband said: 'O harlot, who is riding you?':

گفت شوهر کیست آن ای روسپی   که ببالای تو آمد چون کپی[20]

'Nay,' said the wife, 'there is no one here but me. Hark, thy head is turned, for you talk errant nonsense.' He repeated the charge against his wife. 'This illusion,' she said, 'springs from the pear-tree. From the top of the pear-tree I was seeing just as falsely as you.'

This story is no mere frivolity. Rumi pertinently points out:

To jesters every earnest matter is a jest; to the wise (all) jests are earnest.[21]

He drives home the point that the pear-tree is the primal egoism where the eye is awry and squinting. When you come down from this pear-tree your thoughts and eyes and words will no more be awry. The crooked tree will become straight and God-revealing only when you show humility, shed egoism, and forgo your greed and chicanery.

Afterwards go up the pear-tree which has been transformed and made verdant by the (Divine) command. 'Be'.[22]

In his Introduction to Vol. VI (translation of Books V and VI) commenting on the signs of the failing powers of the poet, in contrast to the immense power and beauty of Book IV, Professor Nicholson suggests that the last two Books of the *Mathnawi* were 'composed when the author was approaching his seventieth year.'[23] This statement about his age, coming from a scholar of Nicholson's stature, is somewhat surprising. Rumi died at the age of 66 years. Both the

[20] IV, 3553. [21] IV, 3559. [22] IV, 3569. [23] P. xi.

year of his birth (A.D. 1207) and the year of his death (A.D. 1273) are established beyond doubt. He was born the son of a renowned scholar and he died a great divine. Neither his birth nor his death is shrouded in mystery. However, here we are concerned with another aspect of Nicholson's treatment of Rumi. Book V seems to offer the greatest provocation to the translator who has chosen to consign no less than 80 verses to the limbo of Latin.

The first target is the story of the greedy infidel. It goes like this:

Some infidels came to the Prophet's mosque in the evening and asked for hospitality. The Prophet distributed them among his Companions who took them home as their honoured guests. Among the infidels was a stout man with a huge body. No one took him along. Since he was left behind by all, the Prophet took him away. In the Prophet's herd there were seven goats that gave milk. The infidel guest devoured all the food in the house and drank all the milk of the seven goats. At bed-time the maid shut the door of his room, fastened the door-chain from the outside, for she was resentful and angry. At midnight or dawn the infidel had stomach-ache and felt the need to relieve himself. He found the door shut. The urgency increased. In his slumber he dreamed that he was in a desolate place, a lavatory and then on waking up he found:

گشت بیدار و بدید آن جامهٔ خواب   پُر حدث دیوانه شد از اضطراب
ز اندرونِ اُو بر آمد صد خروش   زین چنین رسوایئ بی خاك پوش
گفت خوابم بتر از بیداریم   که خُورم این سُو و آن سُومی ریم[24]

These verses, freely translated simply mean: 'He woke up to find his clothes soiled. He was simply mad and indignant at his disgrace. He said to himself: "My sleep is worse than my wakefulness for on one side I

[24] V, 90–92.

eat and on the other I excrete."'

Having lifted the lid of Latin from this perfectly harmless patch we proceed to finish the story for the context makes it abundantly clear that, by no stretch of imagination, can this episode be called either lascivious, lustful or lewd.

The door opens. And who opens the door? It is the Prophet himself who became hidden in order that the afflicted man might walk boldly away and not see the back or face of the door-opener. A meddlesome fellow purposely brought the dirty bed-clothes to the Prophet saying: 'Look! your guest has done such a thing!' He smiled and said: 'Bring the pail here, that I may wash all with my own hand.'

This incident, explains Rumi, was the occasion of the tradition of the Prophet that the infidel takes his food in seven bowls, while the true believer takes his food in one bowl.

The Maidservant and the Ass is by far the most provocative story in the *Mathnawi*, were one to accept the yard-stick applied so far by the translator. He uses the blue pencil even in the prose heading of the story which begins with the following verses rendered into Latin:[25]

یك کنیزك یك خری برخود فگند   از وفورِ شهوت و فرطِ گزند
آن خرِ نر را بگن خُو کرده بُود   خر جماع آدمی پی بُرده بُود
یك کدویی بُود حیلت سازه را   در نرش کردی پی اندازه را
در ذَکر کردی کدو را آن عجوز   تا رود نیم ذَکر وقت سپوز
گر همه کیرِ خر اندر وی رود   آن رَحم و آن رُودها ویران شود[26]

A passionate, pleasure-loving maidservant had trained an ass to perform the sexual functions of a man. The crafty woman had a gourd which answered the measurement of the male, so that at the time of intercourse only half of it could penetrate. Had the whole member gone into her, her womb and intestines would have been in utter ruin.

[25] Vol. VI, p. 82. [26] V, 1333–37.

The story is allowed to proceed. The ass was becoming lean, and his mistress was worried, but no ailment could be discerned in him. She began to investigate in earnest until one day, through a crack in the door, 'she saw the little narcissus sleeping under the ass':[27]

دید خفته زیر خر آن نرگسک

The ass was treating the maidservant exactly in the same manner as a man takes a woman.[28]

خر همی گایـد کنیزک را چنـان   که بعقل و رسم مردان با زنان

The mistress became envious and said: 'Since this is possible, then I have the best right, for the ass is my property.' The ass had been perfectly trained and instructed and the mistress decided to take advantage of him. Feigning to have seen nothing, she knocked at the door. The maid with a broom in her hand opened the door. The mistress treated her like an innocent person. Later one day she sent her away on an errand. The crafty maid, whilst she went on her errand, knew exactly why she was being sent away. She was saying to herself: 'Ah, mistress, you have sent away the expert. You will set to work without the expert and will foolishly hazard your life. You have stolen from me an imperfect knowledge and you are ashamed to ask about the trap.'

After the maid is gone the narrative lapses into Latin:

بُـود از مستیِ شهـوت شـادمـان   دَر فرو بَست و همی گفت آن زمان
یـافتم خلوت زَنم از شکـر بـانـگ   رَسته ام از چار دانگ و از دو دانگ
از طـرب گشتـه بُـز آن زن هـزار   در شـرارِ شهـوتِ خـر بی قـرار
چه بُز آن کآن شهوتَ اُو را بُز گرفت   بُـز گرفتن گیـج را نبـود شگفت[29]

She was happy at the (anticipation) of the pleasurable passion. She closed the door behind her and said (to herself): 'Now I can shout my

[27] V, 1343. [28] V, 1345. [29] V, 1361–64.

thanks! Now I am free from all worries: (I have perfect uninterrupted privacy).' Out of pleasure her vagina (was singing like) a nightingale. She was impatient for the flame of passion. Having reached the height of excitement it was no wonder she was already feeling dizzy.

Lustful desire, goes on Rumi, makes the heart deaf and blind, so that an ass seems like Joseph, fire like light. Cupidity causes foul things to appear fair. Sensuality has disgraced a hundred thousand good names. Its spell made dung seem honey to you, it caused an ass appear like Joseph. And then we are allowed a peep into the room where the mistress is now closeted with the ass, and of course it is Latin again:

دَر فرو بست آن زن و خر را کشید   شادمانه لا جرم کیفر چشید
در میانِ خانه آوردش کشان   خفت اندر زیر آن نر خر ستان
هم بر آن کرسی که دید اُو از کنیز   تا رسد در کامِ خود آن قحبه نیز
پا بر آورد و خر اندر وی سپوخت   آتشی از کیر خَر در وی فروخت
خر مودب گشته در خاتون فشرد   تا بخایه دَرِ زمان خاتون بمرد
بر درید از زخم کیر خر جگر   رودها بسکسته شد از همدگر
دم نزد در حال آن زنَ جان بداد   کرسی از یك سُو زن از یك سُوفتاد
صحن خانه پر ز خون شد زن نگون   مُرد اُو و بُرد جان ریب المنون
مرگ بَد با صد فضیحت ای پدر   تو شهیدی دیدهٔ از کیر خر[30]

That woman closed the door and dragged the ass and undoubtedly she enjoyed herself. Slowly she pulled him into the house and slept below the big ass. In order to achieve her end she stood on the same chair as she had seen the maidservant use. She raised her legs and the ass penetrated her. From his member he set her on fire. The ass politely pressed the lady up to his testicles until she was dead. The member of the ass burst her liver and tore apart the intestines. She did not utter a word and laid down her life. The chair fell on one side and the woman on the other. The courtyard of the house was smeared with blood, the woman lay prostrate. Without doubt the calamity had come. Such a bad end, O reader; have you ever seen a martyr to the member of an ass!

[30] V, 1382–90.

Immediately after this scene the moral follows:

Hear from the *Qur'an* (what is) *the torment of disgrace*:[31] do not sacrifice your life in such a shameful cause.

Know that the male ass is this bestial soul: to be under it is more shameful than that (woman's behaviour).

If you die in egoism in the way of the fleshly soul, know for certain that you are like that woman.[32]

When the maid returned she found that her worst fears had come true. Addressing the dead mistress she says:

کیر دیدی همچو شهد و چون خبیص   آن کدو را چون ندیدی ای حریص
یا چو مستغرق شدی در عشق خر   آن کدو پنهان بماندت از نظر[33]

You only saw the member which appeared so tempting and sweet to you, but in your greed you omitted to see the gourd. Or else you were so absorbed in your love for the ass that the gourd remained hidden from your sight.

The following verses which bring out the moral of the story have been rendered into Latin:

صاحب دام ابلهانرا سَر بُرید   و آن ظریفان را به مجلسها کشید
که از آنها گوشت می آید بکار   وز ظریفان بانگ و نالهٔ زیر و زار
پس کنیزکْ آمد از اشکافِ در   دید خاتون را بمرده زیرِ خر
گفت ای خاتونِ احمق این چه بُود   گر ترا اُستاد خود نقشی نمود
ظاهرش دیدی سِرش از تو نهان   اُوستا ناگشته بگشادی دکان[34]

The Master of domesticated animals cut off the head of the fools and invited the wise ones to his assembly to eat them. Their flesh alone is useful while the wise ones (have many uses such as) humble prayer and sincere supplication. The maidservant then came in from the little creek of the door and saw the lady dead below the ass. 'O stupid lady!' she said, 'what is this? Did your teacher ever provide you with the proper picture? You saw only the appearance and the secret remained hidden from you. You simply opened a shop without mastering the tricks of the trade!'

[31] عذاب الخزی   [32] V, 1391–93.   [33] V, 1420–21.   [34] V, 1415–19.

A story which may seem saucy and scintillating in parts has to be read in its entirety and judgment suspended until after the author has concluded it. Any court of critics would concede that Rumi is by no means a pedlar in pornography and yet parts of the story being singled out, irrespective of the context, for translation into Latin tend to create an effect which is perhaps entirely opposite to the one intended by the translator. The censored part, like all forbidden fruit, becomes more delicious and one is apt to exaggerate rather than digest it within the general framework of the narrative. Keeping this essential requisite in mind we make bold to relate another story which the translator seeks to obscure by his peculiar technique. If the very mention of sex can cause a flutter in some petticoats, the remedy does not lie in cloaking words which merely reflect a fundamental fact of life. The Sufi, Rumi has stated time and again, is like a highly polished mirror. He only reflects your own reality. If you see an ugly face it is you; and if you see a beauteous visage, it is you. The reader, who makes a powerful, penetrating breach into the island of the *Mathnawi*, will see nothing but light and spiritual fervour. There is a point, therefore, in seeking to liquidate the mystery created by the lavish use of Latin in Book V.

Explaining the case of a person who makes a statement when his own behaviour is not consistent with his statement and profession, Rumi narrates the story of a certain hypocritical ascetic. He had a very jealous wife, and he also had a very beautiful maid-servant. For a long time the wife watched them both until one day she went to the public bath forgetting the silver basin at home. Suddenly she remembered the washbasin and sent the maid home to fetch it. The maid came to life for she knew this was the opportunity she had sought so long. The master was at home and alone. Desire took possession of both the lovers so mightily that they had no thought of bolting the door. At this stage of the story Nicholson bolts the door at the face of the reader for he cannot stand this verse of Rumi:

هر دو باهم در خزیدند از نشاط   جان بجان پیوست آن دم ز اختلاط

Both were besides themselves with joy. Both were locked at that time in an embrace of union.

Then it occurred to the wife that she should not have sent the maid alone to the house. 'I have set the cotton on fire with my own hand, I have put the lusty ram to the ewe.' When the wife arrived home, she opened the door. The maid jumped up in consternation and disorder, the man jumped up and began to say his prayers! The wife saw that the maid was dishevelled, confused and excited; she was witless and unmanageable. She saw her husband standing up in the ritual prayer. And what follows is translated into Latin:

شوی را بر داشت دامن بی خطر   دیده آلوده منی ، خُصیه ، ذَکر
از ذَکر باقیِ نُطفه می چکید   ران و زانو ، گشته آلوده ، پلید
بر سرش زد سیلی و گفت ای مهین   خُصیهٔ مردِ نمازی باشد این
لایقِ ذِکر و نمازست این ذَکر   وین چنین ران و زهار پُر قَذر[36]

Without any fear she lifted up the skirt of the husband and saw his member and testicles wet with semen. From the member were dripping sperm-drops, his thighs and knees were soiled and impure. She hit him on the head and said: 'This, then, is the testicle of a man who says his prayer – this, then, is the member which is worthy of supplication – and this filthy and impure body is engaged in an act of devotion!'

The action of the ascetic gave the lie to his words. We cannot hide our actions from God. On the Day of Resurrection every hidden thing will be made manifest, every sinner will be ignominiously exposed by himself. His hands and feet will give evidence and

[35] V, 2175. [36] V, 2201–04.

declare his iniquity. His eye will say: 'I have cast amorous glances at things forbidden.' His pudendum will say: 'I have committed fornication.' So that the whole body, limb by limb, will testify and words which are not matched by deeds will carry little weight.

Rumi is relentless in exposing the cant and hypocrisy of those who pretend to be saints. The fake Sufis are mercilessly attacked as unrepentant homosexuals. In a brief reference[37] he talks of one such pretender asking a eunuch, with whom he is engaged in an act of sodomy, why he was carrying a dagger. 'To rip open the belly of one who should think of committing evil against me,' answered the eunuch. 'God be praised,' says the fake Sufi, 'that I have no thought of plotting evil against you!' The following two verses are Latinised in this story:

کندهٔ را لُوطی در خانه بُـرد   سرنگون افگندش و در وی قُشُرد[38]
ای مُخنث پیش رفتـه از سپـاه   بر دروغِ ریشِ تو کیـرت گواه[39]

Juhi is a familiar though fictional character in Persian literature. He is a classical jester and, like all fools, his words are full of wit and wisdom. He is always playing pranks, and Rumi narrates a practical joke which is pregnant with meaning.

There was a preacher, very fine in his exposition, under whose pulpit a great number of men and women were assembled. Juhi went to hear him. He got a *chadar* and veil and entered amongst the women without his sex being recognised. Someone asked the preacher secretly – and the question is put in Latin:

مُویِ عانـه هست نقصانِ نمـاز؟[40]

Does the pubic hair hinder prayer?

The preacher replied, again in Latin:

[37] Vol. VI, pp. 150–51. [38] V, 2497.
[39] V, 2510. [40] V, 3327.

گفت واعظ چون شود عانه دراز پس کراهت باشد از وی در نماز[41]

The preacher said that an element of revulsion creeps in the prayer if the pubic hair is too long.

یــا بـآهــك یـا سُتــره بستــرش تا نمازت کامل آید خوب و خوش[42]

It should, therefore, be removed either with lime or shaved with razor so that your prayer is perfectly pleasant and happy.

The questioner then asked at what length it was mandatory to remove the hair so that there was no interference in prayer:

گفت سایل آن درازی تا چه حد شرط بـاشـد تـا نمـازم کم بـود[43]

The preacher replied – and all this in Latin, for it is a secret dialogue – that after the hair was the length of barley seed it was mandatory to shave it off.

گفت چون قدرِ جوی گردد بُطول پس ستردن فرض باشد ای سئول[44]

At this stage Juhi said to the woman beside him: 'O sister, see if my hair has become so long. Advance your hand for the sake of verity and see if it has reached the unpleasant length.' The woman put her hand in the man's trousers and his member hurt her hand! Thereupon the woman gave a loud scream. The preacher said: 'My discourse has smitten her heart.' Juhi answered: 'Nay, it has not smitten her heart but her hand! Would to God it had smitten her heart!'

گفت جُوحی زود ای خواهـر ببین عـانهٔ من گشتـه بـاشـد این چنین
بهر خوشنودیِ حق پیش آر دست کـآن بمقـدارِ کـراهت آمـدست
دستِ زن در کرد در شلوارِ مرد کـیرِ او بـر دستِ زن آسیب کـرد
نعـرهٔ زد سخت انـدر حـالِ زن گفتَ واعظ بـر دلش زد گفتِ من
گفت نه بر دل نـزد بر دست زد وای اگر بر دل زدی ای پُر خِرد[45]

Immediately at the conclusion of this episode Rumi launches into the moral of the story:

[41] V, 3328. [42] V, 3329. [43] V, 3330.
[44] V, 3331. [45] V, 3332–36.

(When) it (Divine Love) struck a little upon the hearts of the magicians (of Pharaoh), staff and hand became one to them.

If you take away the staff from an old man, he will be more grieved than that party (the magicians) were (grieved) by (the amputation of) their hands and feet.[46]

A couplet occurring in the moral of the story is also rendered into Latin: 'Blest is he that has recognised (his) real essence. . . .'[47] '*Spiritual manhood does not lie in hair and genitals, for were it so,* every he-goat has a beard and plenty of hair'[48]:

گر بریش و خایه مردستی کسی   هر بُزی را ریش و مُو باشد بسی

From Juhi's screaming sister we pass on to the story of a father who enjoined his daughter to take care lest she should become with child by her husband.

Once upon a time there was a Khwajah (Master) who had a daughter with cheeks like Venus, a face like the Moon, and a breast white as silver. When she reached maturity, he gave his daughter in marriage to a man who was not a match for her in social rank. He said to his daughter: 'Guard yourself from this bridegroom, do not become with child, for your marriage to this beggar is dictated by necessity. Of a sudden one day he will jump off and leave all behind, and his child will remain a liability.' Every two or three days the father would enjoin his daughter to take precautions. Nevertheless, she suddenly became with child by him but she kept it hidden from her father till the child was five or six months old. 'What is this?' demanded the father; 'did I not tell you to practise withdrawal from him?' 'Father,' said she, 'how should I guard myself? Man and wife are as fire and cotton. What means has the cotton of guarding itself from fire?' He replied – and here we lapse into Latin:

در زمانِ حال و انزال و خوشی   خویشتن باید که از وی در کشی[49]

[46] V, 3437–38. [47] V, 3341. [48] V, 3345. [49] V, 3732.

I told you not to go near him and not to accept his seed. I told you that at the time of climax you should withdraw from him.

She said:

گفت کی دانم که انزالش کیست این نهانست و بغایت دُور دست[50]

How would I know the time of climax? It is hidden and so difficult to anticipate.

He said:

گفت چشمش چون کلابیسه شود فهم کن کآن وقتِ انزالش بود[51]

When his eyes look daggers you should know that it is time for ejaculation.

She said:

گفت تا چشمش کلابیسه شُدن کور گشتست این دو چشمِ کورِ من[52]

Until his eyes begin to look daggers my own eyes are blind and closed (with passion)!

'Not every despicable understanding remains steadfast in the hour of desire and anger and combat,' concludes Rumi.[53]

One more story and we have done with Book V which is loaded with Latin translations.

An informer said to the Caliph of Egypt that the King of Mosul was wedded to a houri. She does not admit of description but he produced her portrait. When the Caliph saw the portrait he became distraught. Immediately he despatched to Mosul an Amir with a mighty army with instructions to bring the beauty to him. The King of Mosul at last surrendered her after a terrible combat. When the envoy brought her to the Amir he straightaway fell in love with her beauty. This, then, is the dilemma. The Amir has been charged to convey the woman safely to the Caliph. But he is now having second thoughts for he is

[50] V, 3733. [51] V, 3734. [52] V, 3735. [53] V, 3736.

himself madly in love with her. The Amir slept over this struggle in his mind. In a dream he slept with the beauty but on waking up he found that he had merely cast his seed on sterile soil:

چون خیالی دید آن خفته بخواب   جُفت شد با آن و از وی رفت آب
چون برفت آن خواب و شد بیدار زود   دید کآن لُعبت به بیداری نبود
گفت بر هیچ آب خود بُردم دریغ   عشوهٔ آن عشوه ده خوردم دریغ
پهلوانِ تن بُد آن مردی نداشت   تُخم مردی در چنان ریگی بکاشت[54]

The steed of his love tore up a hundred bridles. 'What should I care about the Caliph?' he said; 'I am in love, my life and death are the same to me.' With these thoughts the captain turned back from Mosul and went on his way till he encamped in a wooded meadowland. The fire of his love was blazing. His reason and the dread of the Caliph had disappeared. Lust had got the better of reason. He sought to embrace the beauty in her tent. A hundred Caliphs at that moment seemed less than a goat to him. The embrace led him on to sweeter depths and here inevitably Latin comes in:

چون برون انداخت شلوار و نشست   در میانِ پایِ زن آن زن پرست
چون ذَکر سوی مَقر می رفت راست   رستخیز و غُلغل از لشکر بخاست
بر جهید و کون برهنه سوی صف   ذوالفقارِ همچو آتش اُو بکف[55]

He threw away the trousers and sat between the woman's legs; when his member was going straight towards her, a hue and cry arose in the camp. He jumped off and went nude, with a sword like fire in his hand, towards the camp.

He saw that a fierce black lion from the jungle had suddenly rushed upon the centre of the army. The horses were excited and the camp was in confusion. The intrepid captain advanced to meet the lion, smote it with his sword and clove its head; and calmly

[54] V, 3861–64.   [55] V, 3880–82.

returned to his love in the tent. When he appeared before the beauty his virility was still intact; the woman was simply amazed at the sight and surrendered herself with great passion to him.

چونك خود را او بدآن حوری نمود   مردیٔ او همچنان بر پای بود
با چنان شیری بچالش گشت جفت   مردیٔ او مانده بر پای و نخفت
آن بت شیرین لقای ماه رو   در عجب در ماند از مردیٔ او
جفت شد با او بشهوت آن زمان   متحد گشتند حالی آن دو جان[56]

For a while the captain was absorbed in that love affair but soon he repented and adjured her and entreated her not to give the Caliph any hint of what had passed between them. When the Caliph saw her he found her a hundred times more beautiful than the portrait. In the bed chamber he prepared himself to take her. His will was strong but the flesh was weak. As he was about to commence the act he heard the murmur of a mouse. He thought a snake was sneaking somewhere in the mud. The thought disturbed him. The distraction wrought havoc on his nerves. He suddenly felt frigid, frozen and impotent. The woman on seeing this state burst into laughter. She recalled the conduct of the captain who had pierced the lion with a sword and had then pierced her with such passion. The thought tickled her and she could not control her laughter. Her laughter gave the game away to the Caliph. A suspicion came to his heart and he demanded to know the truth. The woman described to the Caliph, point by point, the action in the bridal chamber that was prepared for her on the route. The monarch, on being acquainted with the act of treachery, resolved to conceal and pardon it and gave the slave-girl to the captain. He recognised that his tribulation was a punishment inflicted on him and was the result of his attempt to obtain the girl by

[56] V, 3888–91.

doing a wrong to the ruler of Mosul. He feared that if he should avenge himself, the vengeance would recoil on his own head, as his injustice and greed had already recoiled upon him.

Parts of the story which have been rendered into Latin are given below in original Persian:

آن خلیفه کرد رایِ اجتماع　سوی آن زن رفت از بهر جماع
ذکر اُو کرد و ذَکر بر پای کرد　قصدِ خفت و خیز مهر افزای کرد
چون میانِ پایِ آن خاتون نشست　پس قضا آمد رَهِ عیشش ببست
خَشت و خُشتِ مُوش در گوشش رسید　خفت کیرش شهوتش کلی رمید
وهمِ آن کز مار باشد این صریر　که هَمی جُنبد بتندی از حصیر
زن بدید آن سُستیٔ اُو از شگفت　آمد اندر قهقهه خندش گرفت
یادش آمد مردیٔ آن پهلوان　که بکشت اُو شیر و اندامش چنان[57]
شیر کشتن سوی خیمه آمدن　و آن ذَکر قایم چو شاخِ کر گدن[58]

Book VI comprises 4915 verses, out of which 33 have been singled out for translation into Latin. The first target is the story of the Hindu slave who had secretly fallen in love with his master's daughter. On learning that the girl was betrothed to the son of a nobleman, the slave fell sick and began to waste away. No physician could diagnose his disease and he did not dare disclose it. One night the girl's father told his wife that she was in the place of a mother to the slave, and that she should try to gain his confidence and find out his trouble. The lady was kind to him and soothed him until he divulged the secret. She was horrified to learn that the whoreson of a Hindu should desire her daughter, but she restrained herself and told the story to her husband. The master pleaded patience. He told his wife to convey to Faraj, the slave, that they would break off the match and marry the girl to him. The mistress did not at first approve of the vile disgrace but agreed at the husband's insist-

[57] V, 3942–48.　[58] V, 3967.

ence to act the role assigned to her. The result was the remarkable recovery of the slave. The master gave a feast and announced that he was arranging a match for Faraj. The slave felt doubly assured at this public announcement. Later, on the wedding night, the master artfully dyed the hands and feet of a youth with *henna*, he decorated his forearms like a bride and dressed a sturdy youth in the veil and robes of a beautiful bride.

The scene in the bed chamber has been blacked out, for the master, having displayed to Faraj a hen, had actually given him a cock:

شمع را هنگامِ خلوت زود کُشت   ماند هندو با چنان کگ درشت
هندوك فریاد می کرد و فغان   از برون نشنید کس از دف زنان
ضربِ دف و کف و نعرهٔ مرد و زن   کرد پنهان نعرهٔ آن نعره زن
تا بروز آن هندوك را می فشارد   چون بود در پیش سگ انبانِ آرد
روز آوردند طاس و بوغِ زفت   رسم دامادان فرج حمام رفت
رفت در حمام او رنجور جان   کُون دریده همچو داق تونیان[59]

At the time of retiring he quickly put out the light. The Hindu was left alone with the stout man. The Hindu yelled and shrieked, he begged and entreated him, but owing to the sound of music outside, nobody heard his cries. The noise of drums, the clapping of hands, and the clamour of men and women drowned his cries so that the Hindu fell a prey to the strong man until dawn. The sturdy scoundrel fell on the slave like a hungry dog falls on food.

In the morning were brought forth the ceremonial copper bowl and the bells and Faraj, according to the traditional marriage customs, was led to the bath. The miserable wretch repaired to the bath with his back shredded into pieces like a tattered cloak.

From the bath the slave returned to the bridal chamber, a laughing stock to all. Beside him sat the master's daughter dressed like a bride. Her mother too was sitting there to keep watch, lest he should make any attempt in the daytime. He eyed her sullenly for a while, then he burst forth: 'May no one,'

[59] VI, 305–10.

he exclaimed, 'live in wedlock with a nasty bride like you. By day your face is the face of fresh young ladies and by night your member is worse than an ass's.'

روز رویت رویِ خاتونانِ تر   کیر زشتت شب بتر از کیر خر[60]

Even so, the poet concludes, all the pleasures of this world are very delightful when viewed from a distance before the actual test. Seen from a distance they appear like fresh water, but when you approach them they are a mirage. The world is a stinking hag though by reason of her great blandishments she displays herself like a young bride.

Hark! Do not be deceived by her rouge, do not taste her sherbet which is mixed with poison!
Have patience, for patience is the key to joy, lest like Faraj you fall into a hundred straits.[61]

Here is another story.

A beggar came to a house and asked for a piece of bread. The owner of the house said: 'Where is bread in this place? Are you crazy? How is this house a baker's shop?' 'At least,' he begged, 'get me a little bit of fat.' 'Why,' said he, 'it isn't a butcher's shop.' He said: 'O master of the house, give me a pittance of flour.' 'Do you think this is a mill?' he replied. 'Well, then,' said he, 'give me some water from the reservoir.' 'Why,' he replied, 'it isn't a river or a watering place.' Whatever he asked for, from bread to bran, the house-holder was mocking and deriding him. The beggar went at last into the house and drew up his skirt.

اندر آن خانه بجست و خواست رید[62]

He jumped into the house, and wanted to ease himself

تا درین ویرانه خود فارغ کنم[63]

Since this is a ruin, I had better answer the call of nature.

[60] VI, 315. [61] VI, 319–20. [62] VI, 1256. [63] VI, 1257.

The two lines given in Persian have been translated into Latin.

Arguing that masculinity does not come from every male and warning the wise against listening to the fair-spoken ignorant man, the poet brings in the dilemma of a eunuch who has the attributes of both sexes and yet does not belong to either:

او دو آلت دارد و خنثی بود　　فعلِ هر دو بی گمان پیدا شود
او ذَکر را از زنان پنهان کند　　تاکه خود را خواهر ایشان کند
شله از مردان بکف پنهان کند　　تاکه خود را جنس آن مردان کند
گفت یزدان زآن کُس مکتوم او　　شلهٔ سازیم بر خرطوم او
تاکه بینایانِ ما زآن ذو دلال　　در نیآیند از فنِ او در جوال[64]

He has two tools and he is a eunuch. The function of both (tools) is undoubtedly clear.

He hides his member from women so that he can appear as one of them.

He hides his concealed vagina from men so that he can claim to belong to their sex.

God saw that from his hidden organ we would make a snout so that the wise ones do not discover what the dual personality has in store (for them).

The translator has censored the remark of a woman to a man that, notwithstanding the multitude of women on earth, men find them insufficient for enjoyment and turn to men:

در لواطه می فتید از قحطِ زن　　فاعل و مفعول رسوای زمن[65]

The subject recurs and has again been Latinised:

چونك اندر مرد خویِ زن نهد　　اُو مخنث گردد و گان می دهد
چون نهد در زن خدا خویِ نری　　طالب زن گردد آن زن سعتری[66]

When God implants in a man the nature of a woman, he becomes a eunuch and a catamite: when He implants in a woman the masculine nature she becomes a lesbian.

[64] VI, 1425–29.　[65] VI, 1732.　[66] VI, 2995–96.

Towards the end of Book VI is a story of two brothers, one of whom had a few hairs on his chin while the other was beardless. Even portions of the prose heading of the story have been translated into Latin. The story is as follows.

A beardless boy and a youth with a few hairs on his chin came to a festive gathering in an assembly place in the town. The party remained busy enjoying themselves till the day was gone and a third of the night had passed. The two boys went to sleep in a house for celibates. The youth who had four hairs on his chin was handsome while the beardless boy was ugly in appearance. The ugly boy, for fear of an assault on him by a sodomist, placed twenty mud bricks on his backside:

هم نهاد انـدر پسِ کُون بیست خشت[67]

A ruffian who was homosexual and was sleeping in the same house for celibates waited for his opportunity and slowly and tactfully removed the bricks. When at last he began to make advances he startled the boy from his sleep. The boy woke up.

لـوطی دَب بُـرد شب در انبهی خشتهـا را نقـل کـرد آن مشتهی
دست چون بروی زد او از جا بجست گفت هی تو کیستی ای سگ پرست[68]

The boy, asked why after all he had placed bricks on his back, replied that he was sick and had taken precautions because of his weakness. The man said: 'If you are ill, why don't you go to a hospital or to a doctor?' 'Why,' said the boy, 'where can I go? Wherever I go, I am persecuted. Some foul ungodly miscreant like you springs up before me like a wild beast. Not even in the dervish-convent do I find safety for a moment. A handful of greedy pottage-eaters direct their looks at me, their eyes bursting with carnal desire:

[67] VI, 3847. [68] VI, 3848–49.

چشمها پُر نطفه کف خایه فشار[69]

Since the convent is like this, what must the public market be like? A herd of asses and boorish devils!' After making the complaint the boy looked at the youth who had four hairs on his chin and said: 'He is quit of trouble by reason of the two or three hairs. He is independent of the bricks and of quarrelling over the bricks with a wicked young ruffian like you. Three or four hairs on the chin as a notice are better than thirty bricks around my anus':

بر زنخ سه چار مو بهرِ نمون   بهتر از سی خشت گردا گردِ کُون[70]

The story of the drunken king and the jurist is interesting. A king brought a learned doctor into his banquet-hall by force and made him sit down. When the cup-bearer offered him wine the doctor averted his face and began to look sour and behave rudely. The king said to the cup-bearer: 'Come, put him in a good humour.' The cup-bearer beat him on the head several times and made him drink the wine. The tormented man drained it in dread of receiving further blows. He became tipsy and merry and began to make jokes and tell ridiculous stories. He became pot-valiant and jolly and snapped his fingers. The rest is in Latin:

شیر گیر و خوش شد انگشتك بزد   سوی مبرز رفت تا میزك کند
يك كنيزك بود در مبرز چو ماه   سخت زیبا و ز قِرناقانِ شاه

★ ★ ★

عمرها بوده عزب مشتاق و مست   بر کنیزك در زمان دَر زد دو دست
بس طپید آن دُختر و نعره فراشت   بر نیامد با وی و سودی نداشت
زن بدستِ مرد در وقت لقا   چون خمیر آمد بدستِ نانبا[71]

He became jolly, snapped his fingers and went to the toilet. There he came across an extremely beautiful slave-girl from the royal staff. . . . For years the eager bachelor had been full of frustrated desire. He

[69] VI, 3857. [70] VI, 3868. [71] VI, 3941–46.

now immediately pounced upon the slave-girl. The girl resisted and raised a hue and cry, but it was of no avail. A woman in the hands of a man at the time of such an encounter is like dough in the hands of a baker.

The baker kneads it now gently, now roughly, and makes it groan under his fist. Now he draws it out flat on a board, now for a bit he rolls it up. Now he pours water on it and now salt. He puts it to the ordeal of oven and fire. Thus are the sought and the seeker intertwined: the conquered and the conqueror are engaged in this sport. The jurist was so beside himself that neither continence nor asceticism remained in him. The jurist threw himself on the nymph: his fire caught hold of the cotton. And now a line in Latin:

جان بجان پیوست و قالب ها چخید   چون دو مُرغ سر بریده می طپید[72]

The jurist returned to the banquet hall, and seeing that his absence was protracted hastily seized the wine-cup. The king was in a temper. The jurist shouted to his cup-bearer: 'Why do you sit dumbfounded? Give him wine and put him in good humour!' The king laughed and said: 'I am restored to my good humour: the girl is thine!'

Towards the end of Book VI the poet argues that one cannot achieve much without necessary training and equipment and in doing so he cites a few examples, such as: If you go into a mine without having the necessary capability, you will not gain possession of a grain of gold. The incapable man, he argues, is like a lamp without oil or a wick that gets neither much nor little from the flaming taper. If one who cannot smell enters a garden, how should his brain be delighted by the fragrant herbs? But Latin comes in when he points out that were an impotent man to secure the most beautiful virgin, she would be of no use to him. One sees little point in leaving out these two verses from the English translation:

[72] VI, 3959.

همچو عنینی که بکری را خرد گرچه سیمین بر بود کی بر خورد

* * *

همچو خوبی دلبری مهانِ غر بانگِ چنگ و بربطی در پیش کر[73]

The hundred odd lines which have been singled out for a translation into Latin are part of a long poem of some 26,000 couplets spread over six volumes which could certainly not be read in a sitting or two. We have collected them in a single section and the impact, therefore, on the reader is wholly out of proportion for we have telescoped in a short space the material which is spread over thousands of pages in the original work. So far as we know, the English reader has had no opportunity yet to assess for himself the one hundred odd lines which were not available to him in any single volume in translation. The original in Persian has also been made available to the serious student of Rumi who will now judge for himself. All that we wish to say in concluding this study is to repeat a line from the Qur'an, for this indeed sums up the spirit of the *Mathnawi*:

و تلك الامثال نضربها للناس لعلهم يتفكرون[74]

And these are similitudes that We set forth for mankind that they may reflect.

[73] VI, 4426–29. [74] lix. 21.

Select Bibliography

I. Works in Oriental Languages

Aflaki, *Manaqib-ul-'Arifin*. Trubner Series.

Ahmad, Yusuf b., *Al-Manhaj-ul-Qavi li-Tullab-ul-Mathnavi*. Egypt, 1289 A.H.

Ali Genjeli, *Konya*. Istanbul.

Astrabadi, *Thamrat-ul-Akhbar*. Ed. Osman Turan. Ankara, 1946.

Attar, Farid-ud-Din, *Asrar Namah*. Tehran, 1298 A.H.

— —, *Divan*.

— —, *Mantiqu't-Tair*. Ed. and tr. Garci de Tassy. Paris, 1963–64.

— —, *Tadhkirat-ul-Auliya'*. Ed. R. A. Nicholson. London/Leyden, 1905–07.

Baha-ud-Din, *Kitab-ul-Ma'arif*.

Baha Walad, *Walad Namah*.

Barq, Ghulam Jilani, *Danish-i-Rumi-o-Sa'di*. Lahore, 1963.

Basiri, Ali Akbar, *Dastanha-yi Mathnavi*. Shiraz, 1964.

Chelebi, Auliya, *Siyahat Namah*. Istanbul.

Darvish, M., *Shakkah-ha-yi Gul*. Tehran, 1962.

Daryabadi, Abdul Majid, Ed., *Fihi-ma-Fihi* (*Malfuzat-i-Jalal-ud-Din Rumi*), Azamgarh, 1929.

Dashti, Ali, *Sayri Dar Divan-i-Shams*. Tehran, 1964.

Daulat Shah, *Tadhkirah-i-Daulat Shah*.

Farozan Far, Badi'uz-Zaman, *Ahadith-i-Mathnavi*. Tehran, 1969.

— —, *Khulasah-i-Mathnavi*. Tehran, 1942.

— —, *Kitab Fihi ma Fihi*. Tehran, 1951.

— —, *Kulliyat-i-Mathnavi*. Tehran, 1963.

— —, *Ma'akhiz-i-Qisas va Tamthilat-i-Mathnavi*. Tehran, 1969.

— —, *Risalah dar Tahqiq-i-Akval va Zindigani Maulana Jalal-ud-Din*. Tehran.

al-Ghazali, *Ihya 'Ulum-ud-Din*. Bulaq, 1289 A.H.

— —, *Maqasid-ul-Falasifah*.

— —, *Mishkat-ul-Anwar*. Tr. W. H. T. Gairdner. London, 1924.

— —, *Al-Munqidh min al-Dalal*. Cairo, 1309 A.H.

— —, *Tahafut al-Falasifah*. Tr. Sabih Ahmad Kamali. Lahore, 1958.

al-Hamavi, Yaqut, *Mu'jam-ul-Buldan*.

al-Hujwiri, *Kashf-ul-Mahjub*. Leningrad, 1926. Abridged trans. R. A. Nicholson. London, 1936.
Humai, Jalal al-Din, *Tafsir-i-Mathnavi-i-Mawlavi*. Tehran, 1970.
Ibn 'Arabi, *Fusus-ul-Hikam*.
— —, *Tafsir*.
Ibn Battutah, *Tuhfat-ul-Nuzzar*. Ed. and trans. C. Defremery and B. R. Sanguinetti. Paris, 1853–58.
Ibn-ul-Athir, *Kitab-ul-Kamil fi'l-Tarikh*. Leyden, 1851–76.
Intizam, Farah, *Ishq-i-Mawlana*. Tehran, 1966.
Iqbal, 'Abbas, *Tarikh Mufassil-i-Iran*. Tehran.
Ja'fari, Muhammad Taqi, *Tafsir va Naqd va Tahlil-i Mathnavi Jalal al-Din Muhammad Balkhi*. Tehran, 1970.
Jalal al-Din Rumi, Mawlana, *Barguzidah-i-Divan-i-Shams Tabriz*. Tehran, 1957.
— —, *Maktubat*. Tehran, 1956.
Jamalzadah, Muhammad Ali, *Bang-i-Nai*. Tehran, 1950.
Jami, *Nafhat-ul-Uns*. Ed. Nassan Lees. Calcutta, 1859.
Jurjani, Sayyid Isma'il, *Dhakhirah-i-Khwarizmshahi*.
al-Juwaini, *Tarikh-i-Jahan Gusha*. Ed. Mirza Muhammad b. Abdul Wahhab Kazvini. Gibb Memorial Series, Leyden/London, 1912.
Kafafi, Muhammad Abd al-Salam, *Jalal al-Din al-Rumi Fi Hayatihi va Shirih*. Beirut, 1971.
— —, *Mathnavi, Translation and Commentary*. Tehran, 1965.
al-Kalabadhi, Abu Bakr Muhammad, *Kitab-ul-Ta'arruf li Madhhab-i-Ahl-il-Tasawwuf*. Ed. A. J. Arberry. Cairo, 1934.
Kamil b. Husain, *Tarikh-i-Halb*.
Khalil Mukriman, *Seljuk Devri*. Istanbul.
Kazimzadah Iranshahr, Husain, *Tafsir-i-Ma'navi bar Dibachah-i-Mathnavi*. Tehran, 1955.
al-Makki, Abu Talib, *Qut-ul Qulub*. Cairo, 1301 A.H.
Mustawfi, Hamdullah, *Nuzhat-ul-Qulub*. Tr. Le Strange.
Nizami Ganjavi, *Makhzan-ul-Asrar*.
Nizami 'Urudi, *Chahar Maqalah*. Tr. E. G. Browne. Gibb Memorial Series XI. London, 1921.
al-Qushayri, Abu'l-Qasim, *Al-Risalat-ul-Qushayriyah*. Cairo, 1318 A.H.
— —, *Raudat-ul-Jannat*.
Sadiqi, Parviz, *Sad Ruba'i*. Tehran, 1971.
Sahib Javahir, 'Abd al-'Aziz, *Javahir al-Athar Fi Tarjuma Mathnavi Mawlana*. Tehran, 1957.
Sakir, Ziya, *Hazreti Mevlana*. Istanbul: Anadolu Turk Kitap Deposu, 1943.
Sami', Shams-ud-Din, *Qamus-ul-'Alam*. Konya.
Sana'i, *Divan*. Tehran, 1274 A.H.
— —, *Hadiqah*. Ed. and trans. J. Stephenson. Calcutta, 1910.

al-Sarraj, Abu Nasr, *Kitab-ul-Luma'*.
Shibli Nu'mani, *Swanih Maulana Rum*. Azamgarh.
Sipahsalar, Faridun, *Risalah Faridun Sipahsalar*.
Wassaf, *Tarikh*.
Yazdani, Ghulam, 1885–1962, *The Mathnavi of Jalal-ud-Din Rumi*, reproduced from a MS dated 1103 A.H., written by 'Abd-ul-Karim, son of Mir Maliki, son of Mirza Ibrahim, son of Imad al-Husaini. Intro. in English and Urdu, Munich, 1933.
Zia, M. Konya, *Siyahat Hatiralari*. Istanbul.

II. Works in European Languages

Ameer Ali, S., *The Spirit of Islam*. Christophers, London, 1923.
Arasteh, A. Reza, *Rumi the Persian: Rebirth in Creativity and Love*. Lahore, 1965.
Boyle, J. A., *The History of the World Conqueror*.
Bretschneider, Dr E., *Medieval Researches from Western Asiatic Sources*.
Browne, E. G., *A Literary History of Persia*. London and Cambridge, 1902–24.
— —, *Arabian Medicine*. Cambridge, 1921.
Bukhari, Professor S. A. W., *History of Islam*. Bangalore, 1942.
Chittick, William C., *The Sufi Doctrine of Rumi: An Introduction*, with a Foreword by Seyyed Hossein Nasr. Tehran Aryamehr University, 1974.
Coleridge, *Biographia Literaria*.
Conde, J. D., *History of the Dominions of Arabs in Spain*. 3 Vols. 1854.
Davis, Hadland, *Rumi: the Persian Mystic*. Lahore, M. Ashraf.
de Boer, T. J., *The History of Philosophy in Islam*. Tr. E. R. Jones. London, 1903.
d'Ohsson, C., *Histoire des Mongols*.
Fisher, H. A. L., *History of Europe*.
Grant, *History of Europe*. London, 1917.
Gulawanta Singha, *Maulana Jalala-uda-Din Muhammad Rumi* (Punjabi). 1971.
Hakim, Khalifa Abdul, *Metaphysics of Rumi*. Lahore, 1959.
Harry, Myriam, *Djelaleddine Roumi, Poète et Danseur Mystique*, Paris, 1947.
Hitti, P. K., *History of the Arabs*.
Howorth, *History of the Mongols*.
Huart, C., *Les Saints des Derwiches*. Paris, 1918.
Hudson, W. H., *An Introduction to the Study of Literature*. London, 1913.
Iqbal, Mohammad, *The Development of Metaphysics in Persia*.

Iqbal, Mohammad, *The Reconstruction of Religious Thought in Islam*.
Jalal al-Din Rumi, Mawlana, *Discourses of Rumi*. Tr. with a commentary by A. J. Arberry. London, J. Murray, 1961.
——, *Masnavi i Ma'navi: the Spiritual Couplets of Maulana Jalal-ud-Din Muhammed Rumi*. Tr. and abridged by E. H. Whinfield. London, Octagon Press, 1973.
——, *More Tales from the Masnavi* by A. J. Arberry. London, Allen and Unwin, 1963.
——, *Selected Poems from the Divani Shamsi Tabriz*. Ed. and tr. by Reynold A. Nicholson, Cambridge, University Press, 1898, 1952.
——, *The Masnavi by Jalal-ud-Din Rumi*, Book II, tr. for the first time from the Persian into prose, with a commentary by C. E. Wilson. London, Probsthain & Co., 1920.
——, *The Mesnevi (usually known as the Mexneviti sherif, or holy Mesnevi) of Maulana (our Lord) Jelalu'd Din, Muhammad, er-Rumi*. Book the First. Together with some account of the life and acts of the author, of his ancestors, and of his descendants; illustrated by a selection of characteristic anecdotes, as collected by their historian, Mevlana Shemsu'd-Din Ahmed, el Eflaki, el Arifi. Tr. and the poetry versified by James W. Redhouse. London, Trubner & Co., 1881.
——, *Tales of Mystic Meaning, being Selections from the Mathnawi of Jalal-ud-Din Rumi*. Tr. with an intro. by R. A. Nicholson. London, 1931.
——, *The Ruba'iyat of Jalal al-Din Rumi*. Select translations into English verse by A. J. Arberry, London, E. Walker, 1949.
Jarret, B., *The English Dominicans*. London, 1931.
Kennedy, *History of the Great Moghals*.
Lane-Poole, Stanley, *Medieval India under Mohammadan Rule*.
——, *The Mohammadan Dynasties*. London, 1894.
——, *The Moors in Spain*. London, 1912.
McCabe, *Splendour of Moorish Spain*. London, 1935.
Macdonald, D. B., *Aspects of Islam*. New York, 1911.
——, *Development of Muslim Theology, Jurisprudence and Constitutional Theory*. London, 1903.
Mandonnet, P., *St Dominic and His Work*. 1944.
Massignon, Louis, *La Passion d' al-Hallaj*. 2 Vols. Paris, 1922.
Mayer, L. A., *Saracenic Heraldry*. Oxford, 1933.
Milton, *Paradise Lost*.
Nasr, Seyyed Hossein, *Science and Civilization in Islam*. Cambridge, Harvard Univ. Press, 1966.
Nicholson, R. A., *Eastern Poetry and Prose*. Cambridge, 1933.
——, *The Idea of Personality in Sufism*. Cambridge, 1923.
——, *Mathnawi of Jalaluddin Rumi*. Text, translation and commen-

tary. E. J. W. Gibb Memorial New Series:
Books I and II — text. Vol. IV, 1, 1925.
Books I and II — translation. Vol. IV, 2, 1926.
Books III and IV — text. Vol. IV, 3, 1929.
Books III and IV — translation, Vol. IV, 4, 1930.
Books V and VI — text. Vol. IV, 5, 1933.
Books V and VI — translation. Vol. IV, 6, 1934.
Books I and II — commentary. Vol. IV, 7, 1937.
Books III to VI — commentary. Vol. IV, 8, 1940.

— —, *Rumi, Poet and Mystic.*

— —, *Selected Poems from the Divani Shamsi Tabriz.* Cambridge, 1898, 1952.

Pickthall, Marmaduke, *Lectures on Islam.* Hoe and Co., Madras, 1932.

— —, *The Meaning of the Glorious Koran.* G. Allen & Unwin, London.

Prawdin, Michael, *The Mongol Empire: Its Rise and Legacy.*

Redhouse, *Mesnevi.*

Saiyidain, K. G., *Iqbal's Educational Philosophy.*

Sharif, M. M., Ed., *A History of Muslim Philosophy.* 2 Vols. Vol. I, 1963; Vol. II, 1966. Otto Harrassowitz, Wiesbaden, 1966.

Walz, A., *Compendium Historiae Ordinis,* Praedicatorum, Rome, 1930.

Wells, H. G., *A Short History of the World.* Thinkers Library, London, 1945.

Wensinck, A. J., *Muslim Creed.* Cambridge, 1932.

Whinfield, E. H., *Rumi.* Trubner's Oriental Series, London, 1887.

Yacoub Aetin Pasha, *Contribution à l'Étude de blason en Orient.* London, 1902.

Zwemmer, S., *A Moslem Seeker after God.* London, 1920.

III. Miscellaneous

Ahmed Ibn Kemal Pasha, *Nigaristan.* MS. in the library of Istanbul University.

Catholic Encyclopaedia. 15 Vols. 1907–14.

Encyclopaedia Britannica. 1952 Edition. Vols. XIV, XVI, XVIII.

Encyclopaedia of Islam. Luzac & Co., London.

Guide to the Konya Museum.

Shirwani, Zain-ul-'Abidin, *Busṭan-ul-Siyahah.* MS. with Professor Ali Genjeli of Istanbul University.

Shorter Encyclopaedia of Islam, 1961.

Index

'Abbas Iqbal, 23 n.
'Abdul Hakim, Dr Khalifah, 266, 270
'Abdul Majid Daryabadi, 71 n.
Abel, 199
Abish, 10
Abraham, 199, 206; *see also* Khalil
Abruzzi, 1
Abu 'Ali Sina, *see* Avicenna, Ibn Sina
Abu Bakr, 49, 179, 298
Abu Bakr al-Shibli, *see* Shibli
Abu Jahl, 199, 224; *see also* Bu'l-Hakam
Abu'l-Fida, 25
Abu Nasr al-Farabi, *see* al-Farabi
Abu Nasr al-Sarraj, *see* al-Sarraj
Abu Nuwas, 205
Abu Talib al-Makki, 98, 99
Acre, 16
Adam, 163, 181, 187, 189, 190, 196, 197, 201, 212, 214, 231, 232, 238, 241, 245, 264, 265; fall of, 189, 240
Adharbayjan, 27
Afghanistan, 26
Aflaki, 50, 54, 59, 60, 67, 89, 105, 109, 111, 117, 120
agens, 103
Ahmad, 179, 185, 206; *see also* Muhammad, Mustafa, Prophet
Ahmad ibn Kemal Pasha, 39 n.
'Aims of Philosophers,' 80; *see also* *Maqasid-ul-Falasifah*
'Ala-ud-Din Kaikubad, 44, 45, 47, 60, 86 n.
'Ala-ud-Din Muhammad (Khwarizm Shah), 21, 22, 23, 26, 50
'Ala-ud-Din Muhammad (son of Maulana Rumi), 120
'Ala-ud-Din, Sultan, 61
Alchemy of Happiness, 79
Aleppo, 18, 43; *see also* Halab
Alexandria, 80
'Ali, 204
Ali Genjeli, 39 n.
Alp Arslan, 42
Alps, 26
Altamsh, Shams-ud-Din, 9
Amalric, 8
Ameer Ali, 36 n.
Amin Ahmad Razi, 50, 112 n.
Amir Khusrau, 10
A Moslem Seeker after God, 36 n.
Amu Darya, 29
ana'l-'abd, 97
Ana'l-Haqq, 96, 97
Anatolia, 48 n., 99
anthropomorphists, 243
Antichrist, 231; *see also* Dajjal
Antioch, 16, 43
ape-spirit, 186
appearances, external scenic, 139
Apuleius, 284
Arabian Medicine, 93 n.
Arabs, 213
Aragon, 14
Aral, sea of, 27
Arberry, A. J., 159 n.
Archbishop of Bourdeaux, 31 n.
'arif, 239
Aristotle, 20, 83, 99, 204, 262, 277
Armenia, 42
Art for art's sake, 145
Arzinjan, 60
asceticism, 176, 313, 320
'ashiq, 239
Ashraf, brother of Kamil (q.v.), 17
Asia, 11, 16, 42, 68 n.; Central, 22, 35; Minor, 19, 43; Western, 35
Asiatics, 48 n.
Asrar Namah, 88, 89 n., 91
Assassins, 19
Assissi, 8
Astrabadi, 39 n.

'Attar, Farid-ud-Din, 35, 56, 57, 59, 88, 89, 90, 91, 94, 168
Augustine, St, 19
Augustus, Philip, 14, 20
Auliya Chelebi, 39 n.
Averroes, 7, 99; *see also* Ibn Rushd
Avicenna, 25; *see also* Abu Ali Sina, Ibn Sina
Ayyubids, 16, 18

Badi '-uz-Zaman Farozan Far, *see* Farozan Far
Badr, battle of, 232
Baghdad, 28, 29, 30, 34, 35, 42, 52, 59, 60, 80, 85, 94, 96
Baha-ud-Din, Muhammad ibn al-Husain al-Khatibi al-Baqri, 51, 52, 53, 54, 55, 56, 57, 59, 60, 61, 62, 63, 64, 70, 71
Baha-ud-Din Tusi, the poet, 86
Bahram Shah, Fakhr-ud-Din, 60
al-Baihaqi, 36
Balban, 10
Balkh, 25, 49, 53, 54, 55, 56, 57, 58, 59, 88, 91, 96, 108
Baluchistan, 26
baqa', 154, 205, 255
Basil II, 41
Bavaria, 43
Bayazid al-Bistami, 94, 95, 99, 108, 113
Baybars, 18, 19
Beatrice, 131
becoming, 194, 197
Being, 101, 195, 250, 255
Bena, 8
Bergson, 150, 270
Bethlehem, 17
Bhakti movement, 9
Biographia Literaria, 144 n.
Bilqis, 291
Black Sea, 44
Boccaccio, 284
Brahma, 9
Bretschneider, Dr E., 48 n.
Brienne, 17
Brindisi, 17
Browne, E. G., 11 n., 26 n., 27 n., 32 n., 35 n., 55 n., 93, 107 n., 131
Browning, 139
Bughra, 23
Bukhara, 25, 45
Bukhari, S. A. W., 7 n.
Bulgaria, 136
Bu'l-Hakam (Abu Jahl, q.v.), 224
Burhan-ud-Din Muhaqqiq Tirmidhi, 64, 86, 167
Bustan al-Siyahah, 39 n.
Byazi, 48 n.
Byzantine, 41, 42, 43, 44; Empire, 12, 48 n.,
Byzantium, 41

Cain, 199
Cairo, 30, 99
Caliphate, 28, 29, 290
Caliphs, 28, 290, 305
Campagna, 1
Caracorum, 33
Catalonia, 9
Categories, 277
Celestial Wisdom,
certainty, knowledge of, 236; vision of, 226; intuitive actuality of, 226
Chahar Maqalah, 93, 94
Charles XII of Sweden, 27
China, 27, 34, 136
Chinese, 76, 191
Chingiz Khan (Zingis, Temuchin, Tehimkis, Jenghis, Tchinkis, Chungaze [zin+gis]), 11, 17, 22, 23, 25, 26, 27, 30, 33, 36, 46, 55
Christ, 16, 242; *see also* Jesus
Christendom, 35
Christianity, 8, 11, 16, 19, 38
Christians, 4, 5, 6, 12, 100, 136
clairvoyance, mystical, 290
Coleridge, 144 n.
Commedia, 262
Comnenus, Alexius, 43
Companions (of the Prophet), 294
Conde, Dr J. D., 7 n.
Constantinople, 5, 13, 15, 43, 44
continence, 313
Cordova, 37, 99, 262
corporealists, 243
Cosmic Ego, 185
Cosmic Self, 177
Crusades, 4, 5, 6, 11, 13, 14, 15, 18, 19
cupidity, 297

Dajjal, 231; *see also* Antichrist
Damascus, 17, 18, 43, 67, 68, 80, 85, 99, 117, 118, 121, 126
Damietta, 9, 16, 18
Damimah Mathnavi Maulana, 117 n.
Dante, 13, 130, 261, 262
Danube, 11
Darwin, 269, 270
Darwinians, Darwinists, 269
Daulat Shah, 105, 110, 120
David, 218
De Boer, 262
Deccan, 131
Delhi, 27
'Deliverance from Error,' 81; *see also al-Munqidh min al-Dalal*
Democritus, 269
de Narbonne, Yvo, 31 n.
dervishes, 277
Destiny, 226, 276, 281
determinism, 231, 235, 237, 275
Development of Metaphysics in Persia, 152 n.
Dhakhirah-i-Khwarizmshahi, 93
dhat, 103; *see also* Essence
Dhu'l-Nun, 94, 95, 96; *see also* Thawban ibn Ibrahim
Diogenese, Romanus, 42
Divan-i-Shams-i-Tabriz, 107 n., 128, 130, 131, 134, 141, 146, 151 n., 153, 154 n., 159, 161, 162, 164, 175, 240
Divan (of 'Attar), 89
Divan (Sana'i), 89
Divan (tr. A. J. Arberry), 159 n.
Divine Beauty, 102
Divine Blessing, 98
Divine Command, 274
Divine Energy, 231
Divine Glory, 240
Divine Illumination, 231, 280
Divine Immanence, 196
Divine Knowledge, 282
Divine Love, 108
Divine Message, 188
Divine Names, 104
Divine Omnipotence, 100
Divine Pleasure, 276
Divine Purpose, 260
Divine Reason, 183
Divine Realm, 150
Divine Secrets, 69
Divine Spark, 281
Divine Transcendence, 196
Divine Unity, 250
Divine Wisdom, 193
Dominic, St, 7
Don Quixote, 284
dualists, 251
Duality, 136, 231

East, 4, 11, 42, 51, 99, 136, 262
Eastern Empire, 5, 41, 44
Eckhart, Meister, 8
Edessa, 43
egoism, primal, 293
Egypt, 5, 8, 16, 18, 19, 30, 43, 304
Egyptians, 30
emanation, 204, 252
Encyclopaedia Britannica, 175 n.
Encyclopaedia of Islam, 131
England, 13, 14
Englishmen, 13
epistemology, 171
Essence, 101, 103, 193, 253, 266; *see also dhat*
eternal beauty, 279
eternal bliss, 169
Eternal Recurrence, 278
eternity, 134, 136, 285
Euphrates, 22
Europe, 1, 2, 4, 6, 7, 11, 12, 14, 15, 38
European civilisation, 4, 12, 15
European States, 15
Eve, 102
Everlasting Abode, 245
evolution, 171, 186, 267, 281; creative, 267, 270; dynamic process of, 267; religious, 259, 261, 271; struggle for, 270; subjective, 125

Fak-i-Izafat (elision), 137
fa'il, 104
fa'iliyyah, 103
Fakhr-ud-Din Razi, *see* Razi
fana', 205, 253, 255
Farab, 24 n.
al-Farabi, Abu Nasr, 83, 92, 93, 262, 277

Farozan Far, 50 n., 51 n., 54 n., 57 n., 58 n., 64 n., 69 n., 70 n., 79, 87 n., 117, 126, 167 n., 173 n.
fatwas, 72
Fihi-ma-Fihi, 50 n., 57, 58 n., 70 n., 71 n., 79, 88, 97, 126 n., 145 n., 167 n., 173 n.
Fiqh, 63
First Mover, 73
Fisher, H. A. L., 11 n., 14 n.
Flanders, 14
Form, 73, 125, 193, 208
France, 5, 13, 15
Francis, St, 7, 8
Franciscan Order, 8
Frederick II, 16, 17
free will, 185, 231, 232, 235
French feudalism, 5
Friars, 7
Fusus (al-Hikam), 99 n.

Gabr, 136
Gabriel, 196, 198, 201, 204, 205, 263
Gairdner, 78 n.
Galen, 184, 219, 243, 278
Gaykhatu Khan, 34
Georgia, 27
Germans, 14, 27
Germany, 6, 8, 16, 43
Ghayath-ud-Din Kaikhusru, 86 n.
Ghazali, 37, 38, 51, 52, 53, 62, 71, 72, 73, 75, 76, 77, 78, 79, 80, 81, 82, 83, 86, 93, 99, 262, 263
Ghazan Khan, 11
Ghaznah, 21, 22, 89
Ghouls, 260
Ghulam Dastgir, 131
Gibraltar, 1
Gnosis, sufi, 256
God, attributes of, 73; City of, 19; calls Himself 'Hearing,' 'Knowing,' 'Seeing,' 37; man of, 125, 285; real Agent, 273; realm of, 63; transcendent, 262
Goethe, 264
Gohar Khatun, 60
Golden Horde, 30
Granada, 6
Grant, 7n.
Great Feast, 63
Greece, 5, 62; evasive philosophy of, 169
Greeks, 14, 41, 43, 45, 76, 192; churches, 10; Empire, 43; *see also* Rumis
Gregory IX, 17
Guelf, 14
Guide to the Konya Museum, 39 n.
Gurgan, 94

Hadiqah, 79, 88, 89
Hafiz, 158
Haft Iqlim, 61 n., 66 n., 110 n.
Halab, 67, 68; *see also* Aleppo
Halivia, 67
Hallaj, Mansur, 91, 96, 97, 99, 208, 243, 244, 245, 264
Hamdullah Mustawfi, 39 n.
Hanafites, 36
al-Haqq, 101
haqq al-yaqin, 220
harmony, 75, 123, 134; musical, 73
al-Harrani, 36
Hasan b. Sabbah, 35, 107
hawa, 223
Hejaz, 56, 85
Hell, 197
Henry of Flanders, 14
Herat, 25, 45
Hind, 211; *see also* Hindustan, India
Hindoos, 211
Hindustan, 25; *see also* Hind, India
Hisam-ud-Din Chalapi, 167, 168, 240
Hisn al-Akrad, 18
Histoire des Mongols, 55 n.
History of Europe, 7 n., 11n.
History of Philosophy,
History of Philosophy in Islam, 262 n.
History of the Arabs, 28 n.
History of the Domination of the Arabs in Spain, 7 n.
History of the Great Moghuls, 33 n.
History of the Mongols, 30 n.
Hitler, 23
Hitti, 28 n.
Holy See, 14
Howorth, 30 n., 31 n., 34 n.
Huart, C., 39 n.
Hudson, 134 n.
Hujjat-ul-Islam, 52

Hujwiri, 97, 98
Hulagu Khan, 27, 29
huma, 244
Hungary, 43
Husain ibn Ahmad Khatibi, 49
Husami Namah, 175
Husam-ud-Din, 175, 205
Hyderabad, 131

Iblis, 102, 232, 240, 273
Ibn al-Mu'tazz, 85
Ibn 'Arabi, 99, 100, 101, 102, 103, 104, 195
Ibn Battutah, 110–11
Ibn Hamdin, Qadi of Cordova, 37
Ibn Rushd, 93, 262; *see also* Averroes
Ibn Sina, 83; *see also* Abu Ali Sina, Avicenna
Ibn-ul-Athir, 25, 32, 57
Ibrahim ibn Adham, 91, 94, 95
Iconium, 41, 43, 44
Idea of Personality in Sufism, 51 n.
Ihya' Ulum (al-Din), 71–72, 75, 76, 79; *see also Revival of Religious Sciences*
Ilahi Namah, 89, 168
Il Khans, 28, 34, 35
'ilm al-yaqin, 220
Imams, Shi'ite, 204
'Incoherence of Philosophers,' 80; *see also Tahafut al-Falasifah*
India, 9, 22, 25, 136; *see also* Hind, Hindustan
Indus, 22
Innocent III, Pope, 11, 13
Intellect, 86, 128, 150, 187, 190, 192, 194, 210, 214, 238, 261, 263, 279; higher kind of, 150; of intellects, 179, 265 n.; Universal, 192
Introduction to the Study of Literature, 134 n.
intuition, 82, 150, 190, 261, 263, 264, 280
Iqbal, 264 n., 270 n., 278 n., 279 n.
Iran, 44, 80; *see also* Persia
Iranians, 145; *see also* Persians
Iraq, 19, 136
'Iraqi, 131
'irfan, 223
Isabelle, 17
'ishq (love), 75, 101, 122, 129, 130, 134, 137, 138, 147, 156, 157, 173, 177, 187, 211, 216, 232, 237, 239, 241, 242, 243, 244, 245, 246, 247, 253, 259, 260, 261, 278, 280, 281; sublime, 132
Islam, 1, 2, 3, 4, 5, 7, 8, 11, 12, 13, 14, 15, 16, 29, 35, 37, 38, 81, 105, 106, 122, 166, 229
Isma'il Jurjani, Sayyid, 93
Israfil (Seraphiel), 228
Istanbul, 87
istighraq, 97
'Izz-ud-Din Kaikaus, 44, 68

jabr, 79, 234
Jaffa, 17
jalal, 253
jamal, 222, 253
Jaml, 51 n., 59, 102 n., 109, 110, 120, 175
Jerusalem, 16, 17, 43, 85
Jesus, 163, 184, 201, 202, 229; *see also* Christ
Jihad, Holy War, 63, 274
John, King, 14
John the Baptist (Yahya), 206
Joseph, 216, 248, 260, 273, 297
Judgment, Day of, 87
Juhi, 301, 302, 303
Junaid, 96
al-Juvaini, 22 n., 30, 57

Ka'bah, 149, 250
Kalabadhi, 97
Kaikaus, *see* 'Izz-ud-Din
Kaikhusru, *see* Ghayath-ud-Din
Kamal-ud-Din Ibn-ul-'Adim, 67
Kamil b. Husain, 67 n.
Kamil, Sultan, 17
Kant, 266, 275, 281
kasb, 79
kashf, 100, 263
Kashf al-Mahjub, 94, 97, 98
Kawakib al-Muziyyah, 109 n.
Khadir, 183, 214
Khalil, 250; *see also* Abraham
al-Khalq, 101
Khudawandgar, 48
Khulasah-i-Plathnavi, 89
Khurasan, 26, 42, 49, 52, 94, 136, 169

khwajah-i-lawlak, 241
Khwarizm, 24, 26, 50, 57
Khwarizm Shah, 23, 24, 25, 50, 57
al-Kindi, 92, 93, 262
Kitab al-Luma', 97
Kitab al-Ma'arif, 50, 70
Kitab al-Ta'arruf, 97
Kitab al-Tawasin, 96 n.
Kitab al-Tawbah, 79 n.
Konya, 39, 40, 41, 42, 43, 44, 45, 46, 47, 55, 60, 61, 64, 65, 68, 80, 99, 108, 110, 116, 121, 124, 127, 128, 153
Kurdistan, 27
Kutabkhanah Salim Agha, 87
Kutula Khan, 30

Lak Van, 42
Lalai Samarqandi, Khwajah, 60
Lands of the Eastern Caliphate, 39 n.
Lane-Poole, S., 5 n., 6 n., 10 n., 22 n.
La passion d'al-Hallaj, 96 n.
Larinda, 60, 61
Lawa'ih, 102 n.
Lawrence, D. H., 135
Lectures on Islam, 12 n.
Leibniz, 269
Les Saints des Derwiches, 39 n.
Le Strange, 39 n.
life, higher goals in, 287
Literary History of Persia, A, 11 n., 55 n., 107 n.
Logos, 241
Lorraine, 43
Louis IX, 4, 18
love, *see* *'ishq*
Lubb-ul-Albab, 49 n.
Lucian, 284
Lull, Ramon, 8
lyricism, 129, 130

al-Ma'arif, 54
Ma'arif-i-Burhan Muhaqqiq, 64 n., 87
Macdonald, D. B., 38 n.
macrocosm, 178
maddah, 103
Madrasah Mustansariya, 59, 60
Magdeburg, 8
Magna Carta, 14
Mahdi, 204
Majd-ud-Din Baghdadi, 54
majesty, supreme, 142
Majma'-ul-Fuqaha', 49 n.
Makhzan-ul-Asrar, 92
al-Makki, *see* Abu Talib
Malikah-i-Jahan, 50
Malikshah, 21
Mamluk Sultans of Egypt, 16, 30
man, city of, 19; development of, 267; fallen, 19; ideal, 282; immortal, 136, 137, 158; perfect, 163, 165, 197, 204, 205, 230, 240
al-Manahij-ul. Qavi li Tullab-ul-Mathnavi, 48 n.
Manaqib-i-Aflaki, 51 n., 66 n.
Manaqib-ul-'Arifin, 48 n., 52 n., 59 n., 89 n., 108 n.
Mansur Hallaj, *see* Hallaj
Mantiqu'ttair, 88, 168
Manzikert, 42
Maqalat-i-Shams-ud-Din, 108 n.
Maqalat-i-Walad Chalpi, 108 n.
Maqasid-ul-Falasifah, 80; *see also* 'Aims of Philosophers'
al-Marrakush, 99
Mary, 163, 202, 242
Massignon, 96 n.
Mas'ud, Sultan, 36
materialists, 83
Mathnavis, 89
Mathnavi Waladi, 61
mazhar, 104
Mecca, 1, 59, 60, 99, 257
Mechtild, 8
Medieval Researches from Western Asiatic Sources, 48 n.
Merv, 26, 45
Mesopotamia, 27
Metamorphoses, 284
metaphors, 285
Metaphysics of Rumi, 270 n., 275 n.
Mevlevi Order, 130
microcosm, 178
Middle East, 21
Milton, 275
Miramar, 9
Mishkat-ul-Anwar, 77, 78
Moaning Pillar, 206
Mohammad, Mirza, 22 n.
Mongol Empire, 11
Mongolia, 27
Mongols, 3, 9, 16, 17, 19, 21ff., 59

Moon, 303
Moors in Spain, 5 n.
Moses, 7, 168, 183, 197, 202, 206, 208, 210, 214, 216, 222, 224, 264, 274
Mosul, 43, 304, 305, 307
Mu'aviyah, 264
Mu'azzam, 17
Muhammad (the Prophet), 12, 29, 38, 51, 108, 204, 228, 241, 264, 280; *see also* Ahmad, Mustafa, Prophet
Muhammad Ghauri, 9
Muhammad Kazvini, Mirza, 102 n.
muhaqqiq, 98
al-Muhasibi, 94
Muhyid-Din 'Abdul Qadir, 109
mujahadah, 98
Mu'jam-ul-Buldan, 39 n.
Mukrimin Khalil, 39 n.
munfa'il, 104
munfa'iliyyah, 103
al-Munqidh min al-Dalal, 78, 82, 263 n.; *see also* 'Deliverance from Error'
muqallid, 98
Murcia, 99
mushahadah, 98
music, celestial, 286
'music of the spheres' (Pythagorean conception), 73
Muslim Creed, 101 n.
Muslims, 2, 6, 7, 8, 9, 10, 11, 17, 21, 37, 38, 39, 41, 80, 87, 243
Muslim Spain, 20
Muslim States, 29
Muslim Theology, Jurisprudence and Constitutional Theory, 38 n.
Muslim world, 21, 80
Mustafa, 199; *see also* Ahmad, Muhammad, Prophet
Mustansir Billah, 60
Musta'sim, 29
al-Mutanabbi, 70
Mu'tazilites, 71, 150, 197, 208, 210, 217
mysticism, 76, 95, 96, 256
Mysticism in Islam, 279 n.
Mystics of Islam, 277 n.

Nafhat-ul-Uns, 51 n., 66 n., 109 n.
Nafs, 100, 103, 222, 223
nafs-i-ammarah, 223
nafs-i-mutma'innah, 223
Najm-ud-Din Kubra, 46
Names (*Asma'*), 190
al-Naqd, 82 n.
Naturalism, 265, 269
naturalists, 83
Nazareth, 17
Nazis, 23
Necessitarianism, 235
necessarians, 185
Neoplatonism, 262
Nero, 285
Nicaea, 11, 14, 42, 43
Nicholson, 38 n., 41 n., 76, 77 n., 78 n., 87 n., 91 n., 92, 93 n., 94 n., 96 n., 97 n., 98 n., 99 n., 104 n., 107 n., 115 n., 117 n., 122 n., 130 n., 131 n., 132 n., 134 n., 146 n., 149 n., 150 n., 151 n., 154 n., 175 n., 263 n., 276 n., 277 n., 279 n., 280 n., 283 n., 284, 285, 292, 293, 300
Nietzsche, 278
Nigaristan, 39 n.
Nile, 43
Niron Caiat, 30
Nishapur, 25, 45, 56, 59, 88, 93
Night of Power, 212
Nimrod, 199
Nizam College, 131
Nizami, 72
Noah, 164
non-space, 178
Normans, 17
Northern Africa, 1
not-being, 101, 237
Noureddin, 43
Nubia, 19
Nuri, 96
Nur-i-dil (light of the heart), 77
Nur-ud-Din Muhammad, 107
Nuzhat-ul-Qulub, 39 n., 44 n.

Ogotoi, 33
Omar Khayyam, 59, 88, 92
Order of Friar Preachers, 7
Orientalists, Western, 284
Osman Turan, 39 n.

Paganism, 153

Paleologus, Michael, 19
Palestine, 15
Papacy, 15
Paradise, 178, 189, 196, 197, 223
Paradise Lost, 275
Paris, University of, 20
patiens, 103
Paul, St, 7
Persia, 21, 23, 25, 27, 29, 33, 34, 35, 42; *see also* Iran
Persian Empire, 21, 45
Persian Gulf, 22
personality, development of, 272; free, 271
Petronius, 284
Pharaoh, 97, 183, 208, 222, 223, 224, 244, 245, 262, 274
Pharisees, 37
Philip the Fair, King, 15
Pickthall, 12 n.
Plato, 7, 83, 93, 262, 278
Plotinus, 204
polytheism, 196
Pope, 4, 6, 14, 15
pornography, 299
Portugal, 14
pottage-eaters, 311
predestination, 236
predeterminism, 235
Prophet (of Islam), 2, 69, 82, 104, 149, 176, 179, 181, 186, 187, 188, 198, 199, 204, 205, 210, 212, 214, 226, 231, 232, 241, 251, 280, 290, 294, 295; *see also* Ahmad, Muhammad, Mustafa
Provence, 1
Pythagoras, 73

Qabus ibn Washmgir, 94
Qaisar-i-Rum, 48 n.
Qamus-ul-'Alam, 39 n.
Qanun, 93
Qarun (Korah), 189, 206, 224
Qasim Anwar Shah, 48
Qilij Arslan, 44
quietism, 186, 224, 277
Qur'an, 2, 3, 12, 13, 24, 36, 37, 40, 62, 63, 69, 72, 83, 104, 106, 148, 176, 177, 186, 222, 232 n., 233, 235, 271, 274, 284, 286, 298, 314; 'Qur'an in Pehlevi,', 40, 69, 83, 89, 175
Quraysh, 232
Qushayri, 98, 99
Qut al-Qulub; 98, 99
Qutb, 204

Radi-ud-Din Nishapuri, 49
Ramanuja, 9
ratiocination, 172
Raudat-ul-Jannat, 54, 57
Rayy, 36
Razi, Fakhr-ud-Din, 53, 54, 55, 57, 93, 107
Raziya, Sultana, 9
Reality, 111, 150, 171, 179, 183, 187, 193, 195, 208, 209, 210, 214, 224, 230, 248, 249, 280; eternal and temporal aspects of, 176; life of, 270; Supreme, 148; ultimate, 266
Reason, 77, 179, 184, 188, 190, 209, 230, 262, 263, 280; Pure, 78; Universal, 187
Reckoning, Day of, 234
Reconstruction of Religious Thought in Islam, 150 n., 264 n.
Redhouse, 107 n.
Renaissance, 2
Resurrection, 100, 193, 228, 274, 300
Revelation, 82, 85, 86, 113, 182, 264, 280
Revival of Religious Sciences, 37, 81, 82; *see also Ihya 'Ulum*
Richard I, 14
Risalah Faridun Sipahsalar, 51 n., 126 n.
Risalat al-Qushayriyah, 98, 99
Roman Church, 6, 10
Roman Empire, 12, 13, 20, 21
Roman justice, 13
Roman Republic, 21
Romans, 13
Rome, 13
Ruh, 222
Rukn-ud-Din Sanjabi, 39
Rum, 65, 78, 136, 173
Rumi, Poet and Mystic, 38 n.
Rumis, 76
Rustam, son of Zal, 152

Sa'd b. Abu Bakr Zangi, 54

Sa'di, 10, 29, 35, 92, 131, 141
Sadr-ud-Din Qonawi, 47, 99
Saidi (Sidon), 17
Saints, Visionary, 113
Saladin the Kurd, 10, 17, 43
Salah-ud-Din Zarkob, *see* Zarkob
Saljuqs, 11, 21, 41, 42, 43, 44, 45, 46, 47, 48 n., 60; of Iconium, 17
Sama', 73, 74, 160
Samarqand, 25, 45, 57, 58
Samiri, 224
Sana'i, 57, 79, 86, 87, 88, 89, 90, 91, 92, 168
Sanjar, 26
Saqsin, 136
Saracenic Heraldry, 18 n.
Saracens, 7
al-Sarraj, Abu Nasr, 97
Satan, 212, 264
scepticism, 52, 135
sceptics, 273
Scholasticism, 3
Selected Poems from the Diwani Shamsi Tabriz, 87 n., 92, 107 n., 130, 131 n., 134 n., 146, 151, 154, 171
self, animal, 281; ideal, 282; immortal, 135, 136
sensuality, 287, 297
separation, 250
Seville, 99
Shafi'ites, 36
Shahnamah, 48 n.
Shajar ad-Durr, 10
Shams-i-Tabriz, 40, 68, 70, 80, 107, 108, 109, 110, 111, 112, 113, 114, 115, 130, 162, 163, 164, 167, 169, 170, 171, 172, 175, 240
Shams-ud-Din (ruler of Shiraz), 141
Shams-ud-Din Altamsh, *see* Altamsh
Shams-ud-Din Isfahani, 68
Shams-ud-Din Sami, 39 n.
Sharh-i-Hal-i-Maulavi, 54 n., 126 n.
Sharh-i-Mathnavi, 104
Sharif-ud-Din, 48 n.
Sheba, Queen, 291; *see also* Bilqis
Shibli (Nu'mani), 50 n., 59 n., 88, 117 n.
Shibli, Abu Bakr, 94, 96
Shihab-ud-Din Suhrawardy, Shaikh, 59
Shiraz, 141
Shuhud-i-Haqq, 103
Sicily, 1, 17
Siger of Brabant, 20
Sind, 210
Sindians, 210
Siyahatnamah, 39 n.
Siyahat Hatiralari, 39 n.
Socrates, 83
Solomon, 7, 154, 206, 209, 215, 291
Sophisticism, 235
Soul, Divine origin of, 262; Infinite, 195
spacelessness, 161
Spain, 1, 4, 6, 7, 8, 20, 99
Spinoza, 265, 266
Spirit of Islam, 39 n.
Spirit, Universal, 205
Splendour of Moorish Spain, 5n.
Stephenson, 79 n., 90 n.
Sufis, 3, 52, 54, 78, 111, 130, 154, 192, 195, 208, 225, 226, 227, 228, 229; fake, 288, 301
Sufism, 52, 88, 91, 94, 95, 96, 98, 99, 229
Sultans of Rume, 22
Sultan Walad, 55, 61 n., 109, 116, 119, 130, 167
Sunnah, 2, 230
Swanih Maulana Rumi, 50 n.
Sweden, 27
Sykes, Percy, 27
Syria, 1, 16, 18, 29, 44, 60, 68, 117

ta'at (obedience), 98
Tabriz, 34, 92, 108, 117
Tadhkirah Atish-Kadah, 110 n.
Tadhkirah-i-Daulat Shah, 60, 108 n., 110 n.
Tadhkirat-ul-Auliya', 94
Tahafut-ul-Falasifah, 80; *see also* 'Incoherence of Philosophers'
tajalli, 103, 240
taqlid, 261
Taqudar (Ahmad Khan), 11
Tarikh-i-Halab, 67 n.
Tarikh-i-Jahan-Gusha, 22 n., 57 n., 108 n.
Tarikh Mufassil Iran, 23 n.
Tarikh-i-Wassaf, 54 n.
Tariq, 5
Tartary, 25

Tawasin, 97 n.
tawfiq, 98
Templars, 19
Temuchin, 22, 23, 55; *see also* Chingiz Khan
Thamarat-ul-Akhbar, 39 n.
Thawban ibn Ibrahim (Dhu'l-Nun, q.v.), 94
Thilly, 262 n.
Thomas, St, 7
Thrace, European, 43
Tigris, 43, 95
Time, 285; a category of understanding, 266; and space, 141, unreality of, 267
timelessness, 207
Traditions, 37, 57, 63, 72
Transoxiana, 34
Tripoli, 16
Tunis, 5
Turanshah, 18
Turkistan, 90
Tus, 52

'Umar, 290
'Union,' 251
Unity, 149; higher, 265; sun of, 251
Ural mountain, 22
'Uthman, 290
Utrar, 24

Vaughan, Henry, 269 n.
Venus, 303
Vishnu, 9

Walad Namah, 48, 60, 61 n., 64 n.
wali, 222
Wali Muhammad, 104 n.
Wassaf, 54
Wensinck, A. J., 101 n.
West, 2, 4, 11, 14, 19, 92, 136, 275
Western Church, 13
Whinfield, 87 n., 102 n., 115 n., 168 n., 256 n., 260 n., 268 n., 276 n.
World-Idea, 241

Yaqut Hamavi, 39 n.
Yahya, 206

Zafar-Namah, 48 n.
Zain-ul-'Abidin Shirwani, 39 n.
Zal, 152
Zangi, 43
Zarkob, Salah-ud-Din, 125, 128, 130, 163, 167, 170, 171, 240
Zia, M., 39 n.
Zin, 43 n.
Zuhur-i-zan as mard, 103
Zwemmer, S., 36 n.